From
Seatwork
to
Feetwork

Second Edition

This book is dedicated to Mrs. Douville, Miss Tanner, and Mrs. Roggenbaum—teachers who took the time to find out what made me tick.

From Seatwork to Feetwork

Engaging Students in Their Own Learning

Second Edition

RON NASH

Foreword by Marcia L. Tate

CORWIN
A SAGE Company

A SAGE Company

FOR INFORMATION:

Corwin

A SAGE Company

2455 Teller Road

Thousand Oaks, California 91320

www.corwin.com

SAGE Ltd.

1 Oliver's Yard

55 City Road

London, EC1Y 1SP

United Kingdom

SAGE Pvt. Ltd.

B 1/I 1 Mohan Cooperative Industrial Area

Mathura Road, New Delhi 110 044

India

SAGE Publications Asia-Pacific Pte. Ltd.

3 Church Street

#10–04 Samsung Hub

Singapore 049483

Acquisitions Editor: Jessica Allan
Associate Editor: Kimberly Greenberg
Editorial Assistants: Cesar Reyes and
    Katie Crilley
Project Editor: Veronica Stapleton Hooper
Copy Editor: Gretchen Treadwell
Typesetter: Hurix Systems Pvt. Ltd.
Proofreader: Catherine Forrest
Indexer: Sheila Bodell
Cover Designer: Karine Hovsepian
Marketing Manager: Stephanie Trkay

Printed in the United States of America

Library of Congress Cataloging-in-Publication Data

Nash, Ron, 1949-, author.

From seatwork to feetwork : engaging students in their own learning / Ron Nash ; foreword by Marcia L. Tate. — Second edition.

pages cm
Includes bibliographical references and index.

ISBN 978-1-5063-2378-7 (pbk. : alk. paper)
1. Active learning. 2. Motivation in education. I. Title.

LB1027.23.N374 2015
371.3—dc23   2015028520

This book is printed on acid-free paper.

15 16 17 18 19 10 9 8 7 6 5 4 3 2 1

Contents

Introduction

Going to a professional baseball game provides me with a great deal of fun and relaxation. There are those who think the sport is too slow, but for me the pace of the game is just right. With a seat down the first-base line and access to a gazillion concession stands, I can spend hours enjoying the game. Having met the people near me in the stands, I can talk with them about weighty matters like which pitchers have their stuff and which hitters are in the midst of a hot streak. Those conversations provide me with new information and insights from other fans. That said, I never kid myself into thinking I'm anything other than an attendee. I'm *attending* the game, and never suffer under the illusion that the manager is going to ask me to play second base or left field. That is perfectly okay with me; I paid for the privilege of sitting in the stands and watching the professionals do the work. I'm on the bench, so to speak, with no expectation of shifting from a relatively passive role (unless one of our guys hits a home run, in which case my popcorn and soda are in imminent danger of flight) to one that is more active. I can talk with whom I like, get up when the spirit moves, and even leave the stadium when I want. I'm in charge. I'm there to watch, and the baseball teams are there to win; for me at that time and in that place, *there is great balance in the universe.*

While a case can be made for wanting to field the best sports team to win as many games as possible and draw the line between players and fans, our educational system ought to be geared toward engaging *all* our students in ways that take advantage of the particular talents and interests that become apparent for each of them over time. There is *something* they do well, and as educators we need to help them discover and develop those strengths as partners in the learning process. The alternative, as James, Allison, and McKenzie (2011) affirm, is that "children who are bored in school become disconnected from what happens in the classroom" (p. 6). This is particularly true of boys faced in school with "enforced inactivity," the antidote to which is "any lesson that provides control, choice, challenge, and complexity, together with a teacher who cares" (p. 6). Students, especially those at the secondary level, can mostly be found at their desks, facing the teacher and the screen. They are not normally free to stand at will or leave when they like. Theirs is a passive role that keeps them in their seats most of the time. They may well consider this enforced inactivity something to be endured, not enjoyed, for the most part.

Students today have so many more things competing for their time outside school, all of which put the passive nature of school in stark contrast to the incredible array of extracurricular choices available to them in the twenty-first century—electronic and otherwise. It may not be until they leave school that they come off the bench and into the game at home and with their family and friends in a decidedly more social—and for them more desirable—setting. They want to *do* something, not sit and watch someone else have all the fun.

Teachers and administrators can—and should—create learning experiences that get everyone into the game in meaningful ways; after all, we want everyone to succeed when it comes to their education—boys and girls alike. This means differentiating instruction in ways that incorporate the visual, the auditory, and the kinesthetic. It means allowing and encouraging students to tap into the plethora of information available to them outside the traditional sources (textbooks and lecture). It means getting students to cooperate and collaborate in ways that improve the finished product or project, as well as their own comprehension and communication skills. It means incorporating instructional techniques that will make students at times independent and interdependent learners in an age where teamwork and collaboration are much valued. Graduates of our K–12 system need to be able to stand, perform, and succeed on their own two feet as we help them become confident lifelong learners capable of solving problems and making quality decisions in life and on behalf of their employers in the workplace.

To the extent that students can feel disengaged and disconnected while sitting at their desks day in and day out, we must begin to present them with learning experiences that get them up, moving, sharing, processing and analyzing information, making inferences, defending their choices and conclusions, and—to a much greater extent—receiving opportunities to display the kind of creativity and innovative impulses that drive the world today. This will involve an increasingly hybrid educational system that decreases the amount of face-to-face direct instruction even as it taps into modern technological advances that harness the power of things virtual. In the end, it is about balance.

For teachers close to retirement, like the fictional high school social studies teacher we'll meet in Chapter 1, it may be enough to simply increase the amount of student engagement and accept a world less dependent on lecture, worksheets, and the still-ubiquitous half-hour educational videos. Every teacher can commit to reducing the amount of seat time and replacing seatwork with feetwork—shifting students at every level from passive observers to active participants in their own learning. All teachers can replace the teacher-to-student information flow with a much more multidirectional system where student-to-student discourse and processing becomes the norm.

The purpose of this book is not to predict exactly what the brave new world of education will look like in a decade or two, although we will touch on that occasionally; it is intended rather to help teachers begin to make the transition from an essentially passive environment to a much more active one along a change continuum. It is meant to help teachers make that shift to a lesser or greater extent, even as our educational system shifts in fits and starts toward what I believe will be a much more customized and individualized environment over time. Teachers a few years from retirement may never take part in this *ultimate* transition, but they can serve their students well by getting them off the bench and into the game on a regular basis. Teachers at the beginning of their professional careers will no doubt see an incredible—and inevitable—makeover of the entire educational system.

Foreword

Imet Ron Nash more than fifteen years ago when I facilitated professional learning for the teachers in the Virginia Beach City Public Schools. I was immediately impressed with Ron's professionalism, knowledge, enthusiasm, and respect from his colleagues. Ron and I became friends and I soon learned that he and I had a great deal in common. At the forefront was our determination to provide professional development for educators and to write books dedicated to ensuring that students are active participants in their own learning. To this end, I wrote the best-selling *Worksheets Don't Grow Dendrites* series of books and Ron wrote the best-selling *Active Classroom* series devoted to this same purpose. You see, we both understand that the person in the classroom doing the most work is growing the most brain cells or dendrites. In many classrooms today, that person is still the teacher. However, with the digital natives residing in our classrooms, that person needs to be the student.

Ron's original book, *From Seatwork to Feetwork*: *Engaging Students in Their Own Learning,* enables teachers to change this paradigm. Ron uses the effective brain-compatible strategy of storytelling as he consistently refers to the classroom of a high school history teacher named Ed. By incorporating another brain strategy—metaphor, analogy, and simile—Ron compares active student engagement with *getting into the game*. In this way, he draws his readers into the text.

Ron's chapter where he delineates the positive correlation between the learning process and physical exercise is certainly my favorite. In the name of increased academic achievement, school systems are removing physical education and any other form of activity from the curriculum while the brain research is relating that we ought to be doing just the opposite since anything learned while the brain and body are moving is long remembered. This is the reason that people never forget how to drive a car, ride a bike, or play the piano.

Another chapter in this book reiterates the fact that *less is more*. Rather than simply covering content, teachers should slow the instruction down long enough to allow students to reflect and talk about what they are learning. Another chapter is devoted to the brain-compatible instructional strategy of cooperative learning and collaboration, which provides a vehicle for the purpose of student engagement. Ron relates the importance of developing student–teacher relationships while ensuring that the established routines and procedures make active engagement easy to accomplish.

The second edition of *From Seatwork to Feetwork* promises to provide the reader with two completely new chapters, as well as revised chapters from the original work with the addition of completely new and updated material. There are two new appendices.

As soon as Ron's books are published, I immediately add them to my professional library. The second edition of *From Seatwork to Feetwork* will be no exception. You would be very wise to do the same!

Marcia L. Tate
Author, *Worksheets Don't Grow Dendrites* Series

Preface

When observing K–12 classrooms around the country, I continually ask myself one basic and overriding question: Who is doing the work? By that I mean, who is most fully engaged in the learning process? In many cases, it is the teacher who is doing the moving (active), explaining (active), describing (active), summarizing (active), and inferring (active); it is often the teacher who is asking—and who may wind up answering—the questions. In too many cases, students are in passive mode as they sit (often for an entire class period), listen (or appear to listen), complete worksheets (alone), watch (or at least stare at) videos, and take summative quizzes or tests. The amount of *seatwork* (students working individually at their desks) far surpasses the amount of *feetwork* (students working collaboratively, processing information regularly, reflecting in journals or verbally in pairs, blogging as part of a book study, transitioning from their desks to standing activities that take place at charts or designated stations in the classroom, and adding the skills for interdependent learning to that of the independent learning prevalent in traditional classrooms). The nation has become obsessed with "seat time," assuming that more of this "hunkering down" at desks and tables will result in higher standardized test scores.

Goodlad (2004), after he and his team of researchers visited more than 1,000 classrooms, said that the data they gathered supported "the popular image of a teacher standing or sitting in front of a class imparting knowledge to a group of students" (p. 105). My own observations over the years support Goodlad's conclusion that "explaining and lecturing" are the preferred modes of delivery, and "relatively rarely are students actively engaged in learning directly from one another or in initiating processes of interaction with teachers" (p. 124). Student interaction and collaboration, which may be more commonplace in primary grades, decreases as the students get older and high-stakes testing enters the picture.

The role of teachers must change if we want to engage students in their own learning and prepare them for their own futures. Marc Prensky (2010) says that teachers must do less talking and instead become real partners in the learning process. My observations over the years support Prensky's assertions that when teachers talk, students often go to a better place in their minds. Acknowledging this phenomenon, Prensky says, "I often liken this to Federal Express: you can have the best delivery system in the world, but if no one is home to receive the package, it doesn't much matter" (p. 10). Zwiers (2014) speaks to the role teachers must assume if we are to get kids meaningfully engaged in their own learning: "We can't be simply right-answer hunters; rather we must be supportive coaches in the learning process, advocates who listen to all answers, questions, and issues and then provide tools and skills to enable students to reach their goals" (p. 271). By contrast, a teacher once told me his job was to give the kids the information. If they didn't get it, that wasn't his problem. He was, perhaps, the ultimate classroom CIO (chief information officer).

Students put up with this until they can literally remove themselves from an educational system addicted to a one-way street of instructional delivery. Wolk (2011) laments that even with higher standards in place, "Of every 100 students who start the 9th grade, about 30 drop out, and, according to recent studies, another 35 or so graduate without being adequately prepared either for college or the modern workplace" (p. 32). The increasingly proper and more effective role for teachers is that of someone who can facilitate and accelerate the learning for students who must be far more engaged and involved than they currently are.

The teacher who explains, illustrates, describes, and summarizes is working at the second level (comprehension) of the cognitive ladder. As I think back to my first year as a teacher, I no doubt learned more about U.S. history during those nine months in the classroom than in college. In truth, I gave myself quite a workout at that comprehension level; I also worked my way up the cognitive ladder to analysis and inference as I combined what I already knew with what I was uncovering in the way of new information, *and by so doing increased my level of understanding of my subject area.* The good news is that I learned much during my first year of teaching—my students, not so much. Looking back, I see now that I got the workout and they got the worksheets.

In many classrooms, I see teachers who are doing up to 80 percent of the actual work during the class period. Students are too often in passive mode, carrying perhaps 20 percent of the workload. To the extent that common wisdom still says that talking is teaching, too many teachers continue to lecture. But if one *learns* by talking, discussing, explaining, illustrating, describing, summarizing, and asking questions, then we need to shift the percentages. Teachers need to give the 80 percent to their students, while keeping the 20 percent for themselves in their critical role as facilitators of process in the classroom. I would say to teachers at every grade level, *keep the 20, and give students their 80.*

In the book's first and ninth chapters, we'll meet a veteran—and totally fictitious—social studies teacher, Ed, who finally comes to the realization that something is decidedly wrong in his high school class-room. While observing a history teacher in another high school, Ed has his eyes opened. The classroom he visits could not be more different from his own, and his reflections on that experience force him to look closely in the mirror to see what changes might benefit him and his students.

Chapter 1: Mirror, Mirror

Ed's realization that his digital-native students are wired differently, the changing nature of the global economy and the increasingly important collaborative skill set employers require, the increased importance of an informed citizenry, the passive nature of his classroom system, and the brief yet eye-opening visit to another classroom all provided the context for Ed's willingness to change the how of what he did. In this first chap-ter, we'll visit Ed's classroom and state the case for shifting students from passive to active mode.

Chapter 2: Their World and Welcome to It

In this chapter, we'll explore the ways things have changed in education over the years, particularly as it relates to technology. Teachers who were once the primary source of information in the classroom simply cannot compete with what is available to digital natives at the click of a mouse. More than ever, teachers need to think of themselves as facilitators of process, accelerating their students' continuous-improvement journeys by letting them do the explaining, paraphrasing, clarifying, analyzing, inferring, and evaluating. If these are the skills that will serve them down the road, then these are the skills our educational system needs to work into the curriculum.

Chapter 3: Exercise and Learning

State testing has everyone scrambling to provide more seat time; the word goes out to get the kids to "hunker down" and spend more time "covering the material." What gets squeezed out is often anything related to physical exercise, from recess to physical education classes. Exercise reduces stress and, says Jensen (2008), "It enhances circulation so that individual neurons can get more oxygen and nutrients" (p. 38). This chapter explores the relationship between exercise and the learning process. We'll visit some classrooms where teachers are using strategies that combine movement and exercise with content.

Chapter 4: Reflection and Discourse

History teachers see themselves as having a unique problem: Every year adds another section or chapter to textbooks already overstuffed with everything imaginable related to their subject matter. The book itself, along with ubiquitous pacing guides, almost guarantees that while much may get covered, little may be learned. If we really want students to understand anything related to our content, we must take the time to slow down and give them opportunities to reflect and process information. In this chapter, we'll see why less may be more, and highlight ways to get students engaged in meaningful ways.

Chapter 5: Perspective and Empathy

Put two or more students together and ask them to discuss something . . . anything . . . and they will run headlong into the perspectives of their peers, even as they become more aware of their own. Students should learn it is perfectly acceptable to disagree with someone else, but good listeners make an effort to understand what others are saying. This also applies to teachers who want to become more student-centered. As the center of influence in the classroom, one good question is this: "Can the teacher," asks Hattie (2012), "stand in the shoes of the student and see his or her perspective of the learning" (p. 158)? An unwillingness on the part of students to seek the perspectives of others and empathize with partners can place impenetrable barriers in the way of communication and collaboration.

Chapter 6: Competition and Collaboration

Competition is at the heart of sports, and the race is always on to be number one. Those who come in at number two are often thought to be losers. In education, however, teachers ought to be working with students to surpass their personal best in whatever it is they are doing in the classroom. Also, collaboration among students can harness the power of the group when it comes to problem solving or indeed anything that involves brainstorming, decision making, creativity, and innovation. Students who can cooperate with others and collaborate constructively will be in a much better position to succeed in a workplace that values such skills. In this chapter, we'll explore the benefits of collaboration.

Chapter 7: Frontloading and Facilitating

Getting students more involved in their own learning—giving them their 80—takes a good deal of frontloading on the part of teachers and students alike. Efficient classroom processes must be established and rehearsed, the classroom climate must be one that is safe for learning, the arrangement of furniture must be conducive to increased student interaction, and teachers must consider how to make the transition from chief information officer to facilitator of process. In this chapter, we'll discover ways to provide a solid foundation that combines relationship building and process development.

Chapter 8: Feedback and Praise

As any coach knows, feedback is the lifeblood of the continuous-improvement process. Basketball players need the kind of external feedback an experienced coach understands how to provide. Students at any level need the kind of feedback teachers know how to make available every step of the way. Students need to know how to close the gap between where they are today and where they want to be tomorrow or down the road. Praise is not feedback in that it generally does nothing to help close the gap. We'll look at the difference between the two in this chapter.

Chapter 9: Give Them Their 80

In this chapter, we'll revisit our veteran high school history teacher, Ed, as he considers what changes he might make during his last few years before retirement. We'll also lay out some practical suggestions for teachers who want to shift the workload to the students, including taking the time to observe other teachers who are a bit further along the change continuum and who may have much to share. It was as a result of one such classroom observation that Ed decided to make some changes of his own.

Chapter 10: Show the Status Quo the Door

The ubiquitous and deliberate distractions that inhabit any online text today make it almost impossible to concentrate or focus when trying to read something on the screen; this is rewiring the brains of our students in ways that may make it more challenging for teachers who want those students to pause, take a couple of deep breaths, and thoughtfully consider what they have read, heard, or seen. Lecture, worksheets, and those thirty-minute educational videos are going to have to give way to classroom time devoted to helping students think critically, ask questions, question answers, cooperate and collaborate with peers, analyze information, make inferences, draw conclusions, and defend those conclusions.

If we want students to be involved in their own learning, then we as educators—at every level—must commit to changing the how of what we do. We must get students into the game on a regular basis, and the game itself is changing as students have access to literally everything in the way of information at any time of the day or night. In the past, it was teachers who used the available technology (movie projectors, film-strip projectors, and overhead projectors) while students sat passively and observed, or simply punched out mentally. Today's students are the ones who ought to be using the technology (laptops, desktops, hand-held electronic devices, and the software for presentations) as they move off the sidelines and onto their own continuous-improvement highways. As they do this, says Prensky (2010), "The common thread is that students learn on their own, alone or in groups, by answering questions and solving problems with their teacher's help, coaching, and guidance" (p. 15). This will take time, however, as an increasing number of teachers decide either to retire in the face of change or to change the way they teach.

The good news is that change is happening in many schools and districts around the country, as lecture and other forms of direct instruction give way to far more active learning processes that engage and excite students. I have seen teachers who literally reinvent themselves in an effort to make major shifts from seatwork to feetwork for the students in their care. In such cases, the energy level of teachers increases as they tap into the considerable energy of students who suddenly find themselves at the center of the action rather than on the sideline. Because they are no longer trying to simply inform or entertain, teachers who commit to a much more active classroom environment often tell me they are much happier at the end of the day. The way a teacher feels at the end of the day is critical when we face the fact that we are losing new teachers at a prodigious rate around the country. The way a teacher feels and approaches her job, I have found, has a direct effect on the way students behave. Students who truly believe that the teacher not only loves what she is doing but also has their best interests in mind are much more likely to get into the game on a voluntary basis.

Classrooms can be vibrant and happy places if the teachers in charge of those classrooms commit themselves to creating a climate conducive to learning. Having observed hundreds of classrooms at all levels over the years, I can feel the excitement and energy in a classroom—and I can feel the lack of it just as clearly. Digital natives need to be involved; they need to be in the game, and they are impatient with a pedagogy that encourages them to be passive observers in an educational system that is becoming increasingly discordant for young people who have complete control of everything they learn in a digital world—until they move to a student desk, face forward, and are told to "pay attention." The price of simply "paying attention" is too high, and great teachers have been the ones who have paid attention to who their students are, how their students learn, and how important the role of teachers as coaches and partners can be in today's world.

Acknowledgments

I would like to acknowledge the hundreds of teachers who have invited me into their classrooms over the years. Their energy and enthusiasm is a constant source of inspiration, and I have learned much from them and from their students. Much of what I have observed on those occasions has made its way into the pages of my books, and I am indebted to those who have made it possible for me to share specific lessons, strategies, and activities.

The great folks at Corwin, beginning with my acquisitions editor, Jessica Allan, are just incredible people. Veronica Stapleton Hooper, my production editor, along with my copy editor, Gretchen Treadwell, and proofreader Catherine Forrest, have proven themselves incredibly talented and efficient partners in the production process. The cover designs for all my Corwin books have been created by Karine Hovsepian, who never fails to capture in color and design exactly what I might have done, had I her artistic talent.

Finally, and as is always the case, I thank my wife, Candy, for her continued love and support.

About the Author

Ron Nash is the author of seven books from Corwin, including two bestsellers, *The Active Classroom* (2008/2014, 2nd ed.) and the first edition of *From Seatwork to Feetwork* (2012). Ron's professional career in education has included teaching social studies at the middle and high school levels. He also served as an instructional coordinator and organizational development specialist for the Virginia Beach City Public Schools for thirteen years. In that capacity, Ron trained thousands of teachers and other school-division employees in such varied topics as classroom management, instructional strategies, presentation techniques, relationship building, customer service, and process management. After Ron's retirement from the Virginia Beach City Public Schools in 2007, he founded Ron Nash and Associates, Inc., a company dedicated to working with teachers in the area of brain-compatible learning. Originally from Pennsylvania, Ron and his wife Candy, a French teacher, have lived in Virginia Beach for the past thirty years. Ron can be reached through his website at www.ronnashandassociates.com.

1

Mirror, Mirror

Ed stood at his classroom window with his hands on the high sill, watching the autumn leaves swirl in the courtyard two floors below. It was late October, and homecoming was scheduled for Friday night. Ed had been at this high school for twenty-seven homecoming games, and he had taught ninth-grade U.S. history in the classroom in which he now stood for eighteen of those years. The building was new eighteen years ago, and former students who had been with him when he had helped plant the courtyard trees occasionally came to visit; he had for many years been teaching the children of his former students in this small town, the town where he had grown up. Ed had been "Eddie" then, and he was still Eddie to relatives and the friends of relatives who knew him in his youth. His students knew him as Mr. B.

The old high school Ed had attended as a student, and in which he had begun his teaching career, had become a home for senior citizens. His parents were gone now, but they had been proud of his position as a teacher in his hometown. Ed was a late Boomer, born in 1959; he had graduated from college in 1984, having stayed right through the completion of a master's degree. The high school principal for whom "Eddie" had caused many a stressful afternoon hired him to teach tenth-grade geography right out of college. The year the new building opened, Ed moved to this classroom and began teaching the U.S. history course he had long sought. Now, standing at his classroom window with the familiar courtyard view, his mind sifted at random through the memories of homecoming games and dances of almost three decades—and the swirling leaves of other late autumn afternoons.

"Mr. B.?"

Ed turned to find one of his ninth graders, a cross-country runner, standing in the open doorway. "Hello, Curt," said Ed, smiling as he turned from the row of windows. "How was practice?"

"Great," said Curt, "and my ankle is pretty well healed, I think. It felt good today, and I'll be ready for the county meet in a couple of weeks. Mr. B, do you have a copy of that worksheet you gave us on Monday? I've managed to lose mine."

"Sure," said Ed, and he moved to his desk to retrieve a fresh copy of the Chapter 5 worksheet. Handing the paper to Curt, he said, "There you go. I'll see you tomorrow."

"Okay, Mr. B. Thanks. This is due Monday?"

"Yes," said Ed, and he stood in the doorway while Curt walked down the hallway, stuffing the worksheet into his pack as he walked.

Ed had been married but was now divorced, and he had no children. He had always enjoyed the relationships he had built with his students, but in his quiet and reflective moments, Ed was beginning to experience some doubt about his own ability to really *connect* with them. His once rock-solid confidence in his teaching abilities was beginning to crumble a bit. As a ninth-grade teacher, he had long since realized that it was at this grade level that many of his students quit school, or at least struggled with school's relevance to their lives. He had heard enough and read enough to realize that the entire nationwide school system was often unable to connect with a new generation of students who perhaps needed more than the system was willing or able to deliver.

Over the years, Ed had participated in the blame game in the faculty lounge, as he and his colleagues had pointed the finger at the administration (too unsupportive), the textbooks (too difficult), the parents (too lax), and even the students (too lazy) as the sources of problems related to student apathy, stagnant or declining student achievement, the rising number of discipline referrals, and an increase in the dropout rate. Teachers lamented that students "no longer wanted to learn" in the way that "we did when we were young!" Ed had spent many years listening to those tired arguments; teachers came and went, but the patter was the same. The blame game was predictable and seemingly eternal, *but Ed was beginning to think playing it was an excuse for not searching for and subsequently finding solutions to those same problems.* Making excuses helped Ed and his colleagues avoid looking in the mirror and getting introspective about root causes that might just include their own deficiencies.

Ed sat at his desk and graded a few essays. One of the night custodians appeared in the doorway, and said, "Hi, Mr. B. Do you mind if I clean your room?"

Ed looked up and smiled. "Go ahead, Nate. I'm just doing my homework."

Looking at his watch, Ed realized that it was almost 5:30. He normally did not eat until 7:00, so he continued to grade papers, glancing up now and then to see the custodian as he straightened the desks and continued to clean the classroom. Ed noticed that the dust mop Nate was using was the exact width of the narrow aisle between each row of desks, and something occurred to him that he had not considered in all his years of teaching—*his classroom was set up for cleaning.* The distance between rows had not been determined by Ed; it had been set by the building custodians decades ago. A recent visit to another history classroom helped him see this and many other things related to the what, how, when, and why of his own teaching methodology.

At the request of one of the assistant principals in his building, Ed had gone to another high school in a nearby district to observe a history teacher whose standardized test scores were exceptionally high, and he had come back with his eyes—and perhaps his mind—opened. That visit was two days ago, and he could not get what he had seen out of his mind. There had been an assembly during the morning in the school he was visiting, and this resulted in shorter class periods. His assistant principal had informed Ed about the time change for his visit and provided a cover for Ed's classes beginning at 10:30. Ed drove to the school, signed in and received a visitor's badge, then headed for Room 112. A student met him at the door and took him to an empty student desk in a back corner of the room. The student took a couple of minutes to show Ed his journal, including the pages at the back where he tracked his own test progress using a run chart. The teacher was making the rounds, pausing occasionally at a desk to have a whispered conversation. She had obviously left the whole matter of greeting Ed entirely up to the student, who was, Ed thought, doing a wonderful job of making him feel right at home.

The teacher announced to her ninth graders that they had thirty seconds to finish, then she walked up front and had them put their journals away in a large plastic pocket at the side of each student desk. The student who had greeted Ed excused himself and went back to his desk. Ed noticed that in this classroom the desks were in rows fairly close to the walls, and they were angled inward. There was a single row along the back wall; there was no traditional teacher's desk. There was a small cabinet in the corner that the teacher later explained held everything her desk used to hold.

This unique placement of furniture had the effect of opening the center of the classroom, creating a large area that puzzled Ed until the teacher had her ninth graders stand and move to that open space. They raised their right hands and, when instructed, proceeded to pair up, shaking hands as they found partners. The teacher stood on a short stool and had them turn toward her. When they were all facing in her direction, she gave them instructions to discuss the short story on the Underground

Railroad they had just finished. There were some prompts on the Smart Board that helped her students get started. While they talked in pairs, she walked around the room and listened to various conversations. She stopped a few times, long enough to ask some of her students if they would share with the class what they had just shared with partners. When the students agreed to share, the teacher thanked each in turn and moved on. These paired conversations went on for a little more than three minutes, and the teacher, standing on her stool once more, raised her hand and asked them to finish their thoughts and turn toward her.

The teacher then had several students share with the entire class what they had discussed, and she recorded four main points on the whiteboard. After this, she had them thank their partners and take their seats, at which point they added the four points, along with anything else they wanted to record, in their journals. While they wrote, she walked around the room and placed a piece of light yellow paper in the shape of a circle on each desk. With two minutes to go in the class period, she asked them to write on the circle any questions related to the Underground Railroad that "were still going around" in their minds. As they left the classroom, the teacher collected the circles and added them to the pile she had from the other classes. As she walked by the desk at which Ed was seated, she leaned over and whispered, "My homework!" The questions were feedback for the teacher, and they let her know what she still had to cover as it related to the pre–Civil War abolitionist movement and the Underground Railroad in particular.

Ed was in his twenty-eighth year of teaching, yet he had seen nothing like this. In fact, Ed could not remember observing in more than one or two other classrooms in all that time. He had pretty much been on his own, and this was a new experience—one that had caused him to stand staring into the courtyard outside his room on a cool and breezy autumn afternoon, pondering some important things: In the classroom he had observed, the students seemed to be doing the work while the teacher facilitated process. In his own classroom, by contrast, Ed did most of the work, and his students did . . . *what*, exactly? They looked at him, for the most part. They smiled and even laughed on occasion, especially when Ed displayed what everyone agreed was an excellent sense of humor, and they seemed to be taking notes when they needed to. If things *seemed* fine in his classroom, why was it that the test scores in that other teacher's classroom were so much higher? Why was it that the essays she showed him were so much better? How was it that her students seemed so much more engaged and . . . well, happier and more confident?

The truth was that this observation had, over the past two days, caused him to begin to question his own teaching methodology. The teacher he had observed, Peggy Sandillos, spent her entire lunch and prep period with him, discussing how she had created what was obviously a very different—and amazingly dynamic—learning environment in a classroom that was otherwise a physical carbon copy of his own. Peggy told Ed she had come to the conclusion at the end of her fifth year of teaching that she was doing too much work, while her students did too little. They both agreed that students may look at the teacher while going to a better place in their minds. Peggy had a discussion with her students about this very phenomenon, and they opened up, revealing their tricks of the trade, so to speak. They were, it seems, quite good at pretending to "pay attention" while contemplating something completely removed from the *content du jour*. It was then, she said, that she realized she had to shake things up in her classroom. This was feedback she could not ignore.

Peggy had made the decision to do everything she could to get them truly engaged and to decrease the amount of in-classroom "on stage" work she did on a daily basis. This decision to engage her students in their own learning in a much more active way had been a good move for her and her students, and she told Ed she had never looked back. She was in continuous-improvement mode now, and she would work to make her classroom an even better and more welcoming place for her students. In her new role as a facilitator of process, she no longer led from the front of the room; Peggy led from *within,* and partnered with her students in a very learner-centered classroom—and she was getting results.

His mission accomplished, the night custodian said goodbye, and Ed straightened his desk, stood, and headed for the parking lot. He pointed his car in the general direction of his favorite restaurant and told himself he would no doubt spend a good deal of time there this evening; he had much to consider. If something was going to change in his own classroom, then he would have to look in the mirror and confront the status quo.

Comfort in the Status Quo

Many teachers move from school year to school year with different faces looking up from the student desks, and cling to the same traditional methods of delivering information. The status quo becomes a comfortable companion. Change is not something people in any organization normally seek on their own or even accept when it comes their way from the powers that be; indeed, people resent mandated change as an outright assault on a status quo that has over the years become a good friend. Members of any organization may resent interference, according to Smith (2008): "There is fear of failure and threats to values and ideals. People are being asked to leave their comfort zones, and naturally they will resist" (p. 16). In four decades in education and educational sales, I have seen this resistance over and over again, and I have been *part* of that resistance on more than one occasion. Just as we feel comfortable and perfectly happy with that old chair in the den, we feel comfortable and personally satisfied with the way things are in our classrooms. The ones who may become increasingly *uncomfortable* and out of touch with our status quo may well be the young people of a new century vastly different from the last. They also may be veteran teachers like Ed who have come to the conclusion that students—and the world they inhabit—are changing.

Even if students had *not* changed over the past several decades, there would be a case for a system of continuous improvement in education. In our own lives, we all want the professionals with whom we work—electricians, doctors, mechanics, roofers, dentists, surgeons, and lawyers, to name a few—to be in constant self-improvement mode. Skills in any of these areas need updating; an example is that of the car mechanic. My first car was a '61 Chevy. This was a simple machine that was, by today's standards, easy to maintain. I could look under the hood and see all the way to the ground past the engine block. Looking under the hood today is, by contrast, a daunting experience for a Baby Boomer used to doing basic maintenance. The power plant of a modern car is a complicated piece of machinery and electronics that requires a highly skilled and trained workforce to keep it operating at peak efficiency. Mechanics today need much more than a small box of tools in the way that teachers need more than what was needed in the 1950s and 60s, when I was growing up.

An assembly-line educational system could be said to have worked reasonably well when it fed an assembly-line manufacturing system that created and sold products all over the world, especially after World War II, when many nations were faced with trying to recover from a scale of death and destruction not previously known. The United States had little foreign competition at that point, the unemployment rate was low, and the educational system fed a growing economy with graduates who, by today's standards, tended to stay with the same employer for long periods of time, if not for their whole careers. A high school student who belonged to her school's Future Teachers of America club could pursue a four-year degree in a teacher-preparation program and, with role models provided by high school teachers and college professors, continue the best traditions of the profession: lecture, frequent summative quizzes and tests, worksheets, filmstrips, educational videos, and a basic routine that had been relatively unchanged for decades.

The status quo hardens and becomes institutionalized over many years, not only for teachers, but for students as well. In fact, students have learned, as Hattie and Yates (2014) so aptly put it, "the art of becoming invisible." Every educator reading this book has probably become invisible in a classroom, night class, or professional-development session. Hattie and Yates remind us this is so:

> We developed skills enabling us to opt out of lesson participation.
> It is possible to appear slightly attentive, while avoiding direct

eye gaze, avoiding excessive movement, shrinking slightly into the seat rather than sitting upright, or using the bluffing tactics such as pretending to be reading or writing. It is possible to sit in a classroom, away from its focal centre, cause little disturbance, and virtually never be noticed. (p. 47)

If you're smiling right now, it may be you remember, as I most certainly do, attempting to become invisible, while watching my teachers work.

In classrooms where teachers do most of the work and students sit too often as passive observers, the students, especially in secondary schools, often rely on the status quo to *keep* themselves passive. Their own status quo may have become comfortable over the years, and they may resist efforts to shift them from passive to active mode. In many conversations with middle and high school teachers, they tell me their students often rebel against standing and getting into pairs for a discussion. This tells me we are not providing opportunities for students to be engaged in verbal collaborative activities in a consistent way from kindergarten through high school. If a sophomore has spent the past several years in passive mode, the teacher who insists on paired and group reflection and conversations is going to encounter resistance. Unfortunately, faced with such opposition from students, many otherwise well-meaning teachers may simply revert to a teacher-to-student communication flow, rather than insisting on the multidirectional discourse that will give students the communication skills they need in the twenty-first century.

Teachers who think today's students have short attention spans need to watch them as they pursue what *interests* them in ways that confirm their ability to concentrate and focus in a very real and effective way. According to Prensky (2010), "What today's kids *do* have a short attention span for are our old ways of learning" (p. 2). Kids who progress from one classroom and grade level to another in passive mode, watching and listening to the teacher, increasingly see the gap between the choices they have in their personal lives and the choices available to them in classrooms. In ways that have become familiar to them in their personal lives, students want to be directly involved in their own learning. The status quo teachers find comfortable is often teacher-centered and decidedly uncomfortable for students, and teachers need to examine the teaching traditions that have seemed to serve *them* well in favor of innovations that serve students better.

This shift from passive to active mode should not be negotiable; students need to be able to think critically, communicate, cooperate, and collaborate to compete in a tough job market that includes millions upon millions of the world's citizens. Districts must reach out to the business community for more than just the occasional assistance provided through business-partner programs. Students need a steady flow of information from all segments of the business community, from service-oriented jobs to health care to high-tech companies like Google and Microsoft. It is one thing for teachers to tell middle school students what is needed to compete in tomorrow's job market; it is another to hear it from companies who are desperate for workers with skills that match the positions available.

Students who are expected to be able to communicate effectively in oral and written form must be required to communicate in pairs, trios, quartets, and on occasion in front of a classroom full of peers. Listening skills must be part of the curricular framework in every subject. Students must write, edit, peer edit, and be held to a high standard that includes grammar, style, and content. Students who are expected to think interdependently must experience collaboration on a daily basis.

There are no shortcuts here; telling is not teaching. It is not enough to *tell* students how to write; students must write frequently, and they should be able to write on topics that interest them. It is not enough to *tell* students what is involved in listening effectively; students must practice the art of listening. It is not enough to *tell* students what makes an effective team; students must work in teams with high expectations and an effective system of self-evaluation (checklists and rubrics) to hone their skills in this regard. Students must do the work while teachers facilitate process.

Much of this work today can be done online, as students compose paragraphs, essays, or papers on their home computers and communicate collaboratively through the use of teacher-mediated blogs and online learning platforms like Edmodo. Project instructions, checklists, rubrics, and much else can be placed on a teacher's website, and this information can help and inform parents eager for knowledge about what has been or will be assigned. Students can communicate with peers and teachers concerning assignments and content in any number of ways in a digital world that is the norm for digital natives. This requires considerable adjustments on the part of teachers like Ed, veteran teachers who have constructed a status quo that may seem under attack from a digital world with which they may have only a passing familiarity. Shifting the workload to students requires that teachers take into account a social and digital environment not of their making.

We Who Did the Work

When I started teaching in the early 1970s, I really had little to consider or worry about other than finding a job in a profession where there were far more applicants than positions. I was fortunate to find a teaching position, and walked into my first classroom to find that the student desks were in six rows of six, and there was an overhead projector facing a pull-down screen in the front of the room. The implication was clear, and I left the furniture where it was. After all, the expectation—*everyone's* expectation, from the administration to the parents to the students—was that things would continue in the room in which I stood that morning in much the same way they had for the past several decades in this traditional and completely standard school. In this journey, the destination, the speed with which my students traveled, the course corrections—indeed, all the decisions of any import—were made by me. At the same time, I felt comfortable with the current, standard set of expectations, and it guided my approach to teaching. I had a good deal of freedom, but what I *knew* was what I *did*. My past was prologue to my students' futures for that first school year.

I accepted that role, and I did so because my narrow perspective on the subject of what needed to be done, and by whom, came from my career as a student. Mine was, as a consequence, a teacher-centered classroom. I provided the feedback, such as it was, and it was not very helpful to my students because it was too general in nature; I dictated the rules and classroom norms; I did most of the talking and questioning; the textbook and I were pretty much *it* as sources of information went. I spent untold hours grading summative quizzes and tests that presaged a move into a new chapter and new material, and I devoted even more hours to grading essays that, in essence, were simply rough drafts when my students completed them as part of my chapter or unit tests. By Wednesday afternoon, I was tired, and by Friday, I was running on empty. I submit that my experience was not unlike those of my peers, for the simple reason that *we were doing most of the work.*

Our students showed up each morning knowing *they would watch us do most of the work.* I talked, and they sat. I moved around the room, and they sat. I wrote on the board, and they sat. I knew nothing of peer editing, checklists, rubrics, reflective journals, formative assessments, or any number of student-directed mechanisms for continuous improvement. The one great thing that resulted from my doing the work was that I learned a good deal about the history of the United States, because I moved up and down the cognitive ladder from knowledge through comprehension to analysis and synthesis on a regular basis. It was a wonderful learning experience for me, come to think of it—but not so much for my students.

Ed, our fictional, veteran high school history teacher whom we met at the beginning of this chapter, had the good fortune to spend some time in the classroom of someone who figured out that if students are to succeed and enjoy that success, then they are the ones who need to do the talking, moving, collaborating, editing, thinking, writing, and many other things that naturally and effectively accelerate their own improvement. For Ed, being able to take the balcony view in another classroom allowed and encouraged him to look in the mirror to see just how what he was doing compared and contrasted with the teacher whom he observed—and Ed chose to reflect on this as someone now open to change.

As a social studies teacher, Ed was beginning to understand the implications of an increasingly interconnected global economy on the educational status quo. For a couple of years, Ed had begun to question his own teaching methods, and with each passing year he found it harder to reach and teach his students. The old ways did not match up with the new kids. It was not until Ed observed a teacher who was younger than he—and closer to the generation of students she was teaching—that he realized that if the students had changed considerably over his twenty-seven years in the classroom, he was going to have to make some changes. He was going to have to meet the kids where they were with teaching methods different from those he had been using since the electric typewriter, overhead projector, and ditto masters passed as state-of-the-art technology.

The truth is that there are still tens of thousands of teachers from the Baby Boomer generation (1946–1962) who continue to teach in our classrooms and who are increasingly frustrated by students who seem not to be interested in learning. Stick around a high school faculty lounge for any length of time and you may hear this being said more than once. This frustration is understandable, because digital natives have been weaned on things they can control: video games, computer programs, access to the Internet, instant and pervasive electronic social connections that may befuddle a Boomer, plus access to hundreds of TV channels and media. These same kids get to the classroom in a school constructed along assembly-line principles (classrooms dedicated to specific subject matter, screens that may not yet be interactive, straight rows of desks, bells that signal the beginning and end of a class in the way that whistles might once have signaled the beginning and end of a factory shift, and teachers who still disseminate information along a two-way highway— teacher to student and student to teacher). There is no pause button that accompanies the teacher who chooses to lecture; there is no instant link to whatever it is that the teacher may have said that may have excited the curiosity of a student; and the student who has complete control of his electronic world at home finds he has no control whatsoever over what happens before and after the class bell rings in school.

The world of the digital native is a decidedly learner-centered world, and he may feel uncomfortable and frustrated with an educational system that has him moving from English (in *this* room with *this* teacher) to social studies (in *that* room with *that* teacher) in a way that denies the interconnectedness and "linkability" to which he has become accustomed when sitting in front of a screen—*and in full control of process mechanisms*. What ensues is what may well be described as a struggle for control of the processes of learning. Put bluntly, a student whose electronic environment is fluid and seemingly limitless in scope comes into conflict with a teacher whose method of delivery is static and inflexible. Something has to give for the simple reason that students today need to be prepared for their future in a world where entirely new jobs are created daily, and where critical thinking, communication, problem solving, and collaboration are increasingly becoming the coin of the realm.

Off the Bench and Into the Game

In my first years of teaching, I put a lot of effort into honing my presentation skills. I wanted to make my lectures entertaining, and I wanted, when possible, to make my students laugh. I uncovered my notes on the overhead transparencies one at a time, so that my ninth graders could write them down and then "pay attention" as I explained the significance of whatever it was they just wrote into their notebooks. I sharpened my storytelling skills, and I worked on my voice modulation, timing, and body language. There is, of course, nothing wrong with any of this, except for the fact that those were pretty much all the tools in my toolbox. Communication was essentially one way unless it involved a conversation between a student and me, most often generated by me and not by the student. I asked most of the questions that got asked, and I have to admit to answering many of my own questions.

As a history teacher and a student of history, I found the subject matter nothing less than fascinating, and I often wondered why my students did not want to immerse themselves in something as important as the *topic du jour* in U.S. history, world cultures, or geography. Theirs was a passive role, and their engagement was limited to say the very least. Gunter, Estes, and Schwab (1999) have it right when they say that the teacher's enthusiasm about what the teacher hopes is an eminently interesting subject is simply not enough. If "teaching has the effect of engaging learners in the process of understanding, of bringing learners into close contact with what the teacher wants them to learn, and of giving learners an opportunity to explain what they understand, then learning is likely to occur" (p. 3). Learning is not a spectator sport.

I once walked into a high school classroom in North Carolina, and it took me a couple of minutes to figure out who the teacher was. She was not, as it turned out, more than a few years older than her high school juniors, and the student who met me at the door took charge of getting me acclimated to what was going on in the classroom. Everyone was in groups, either standing or seated, and they were all on task. This science class was totally engaged to the point where test results were tracked (class average) on a run chart, and students spent time reflecting on why the class average went up or down, or remained the same. These students were into discovering root causes as part of their journey into the land of critical thought and productive collaborative discourse. Having interviewed them for several minutes before the end of the class period, I can say with 100 percent certainty that they loved it, and they hated classes in which they spent their time *watching the teacher work* and in which they freely admitted going to sleep on occasion. The students in this high school science class were participants, not attendees, and they were doing the work. As a result, they were *also doing the learning*—and, as revealed during my ten-minute conversation with them that day, they appreciated a teacher who knew how to engage them in a meaningful way. She had also taken the time to build working relationships with her juniors that paid great dividends throughout the school year. Her students understood and appreciated their role as participants in their own learning, along with her role as a process facilitator. Theirs was an active role in a system of continuous improvement; they were engaged because they saw the benefit for them.

In a Canadian Education Association (CEA) study, only 37 percent of the 32,000 Grade 6–12 students surveyed "reported being intellectually engaged in language arts or mathematics classes," and this lack of engagement was even lower for students in the higher grades (Levin, 2010, p. 89). The CEA report concluded that improving the education of students should include "more engaging teaching practices, more effective assessment practices, and stronger relationships between teachers and students" (p. 90). In a meta-analysis of teacher–student relationships, Marzano (2003) found, "In a study involving 68 high school students, 84 percent said that discipline problems that occurred could have been avoided by better teacher–student relationships" (p. 42). My experience over four decades tells me that teachers who are willing to take the time and put forth the effort to build solid relationships are far more likely to find students who not only behave better but also are far more willing to become involved and engaged in their own learning. I have been in classrooms where the atmosphere is so toxic that very little actual learning takes place.

> Getting students into the game means creating a classroom climate that allows them to take risks and make mistakes.

Getting students into the game means creating a classroom climate that allows them to take risks and make mistakes. It involves a transition from the command-and-control mode of many teachers to a more collaborative norm where students and teachers share responsibility. Students must know that teachers are not going to use or allow the use of sarcasm or bullying on the part of anyone in the classroom—least of all the teacher. Students will not willingly give themselves over to engagement mode if they do not feel safe. It is the responsibility of the teacher who wants to create a more cooperative and collaborative environment to create a level of trust, respect, and safety that inspires students and facilitates learning.

The View From the Balcony

One can learn much by simply observing students and their teachers. After spending a considerable amount of time in hundreds of K–12 classrooms over many years, here are some observations from what I perceive to be some highly successful classroom environments and systems:

1. In classrooms where students are responsive and seem perfectly comfortable with peer collaboration, it is obvious that the teacher–student relationships, as it was in that North Carolina high school science classroom, are solid. In such environments, teachers are far more relaxed, and they spend little or no time at all dealing with discipline problems. Positive teacher–student relationships have a high effect size (.72) and, affirms Hattie (2012), "The essence of positive relationships is the student seeing the warmth, feeling the encouragement and the teacher's high expectations, and knowing that the teacher understands him or her" (p. 158). This does not just happen; those teachers work on developing those relationships. It can also begin before school even starts, with phone calls to parents. Teachers who get to know parents early are putting relationship money in the bank against the day when they have to make a withdrawal. That telephone conversation about Norm's progress—or the lack thereof—with his father is considerably more pleasant and productive if at least a rudimentary teacher–parent relationship is already in place when that call is made.

2. In classrooms where students often process information successfully in pairs or groups, it is obvious that the student-to-student relationships are as well developed and attended to as those between the teacher and her students. Once again, this does not happen by chance. Successful teachers start working on student-to-student relationships on the first day of school.

3. In the most organizationally efficient classrooms, transitions are smooth, and no time is wasted with students wandering around the room or gazing longingly out the window. Students in these classrooms are busy and focused. Transitions must be rehearsed until the standard is met or exceeded; simply *explaining* how transitions should work is not enough. If once-smooth transition processes break down, that cannot be ignored; the processes must be revisited and adjusted.

4. The acquisition of new information in the most successful classrooms is followed by time for students to process that information in pairs, trios, or groups. Exit strategies put student reflections

and questions in the hands of teachers who can spend time in the evening finding out where students are in their understanding of important concepts or topics.

5. In many classrooms, students have permanent learning partners, so that teachers who recognize that students need to process or come up with a set of questions can put everyone in pairs quickly and efficiently. This can be done seated or standing, but having several permanent partners chosen during the first week of school saves time later on.

6. Questions on the part of teachers or students are followed by sufficient wait time (three or four seconds). Even *after* a response is given, teachers wait to give students time to process. Effective teachers understand that everyone processes information at different speeds, and thus they are patient enough to stand still . . . and *wait*. While this is difficult for many teachers who abhor silence in the classroom, it is necessary.

7. Teacher talk is kept to a minimum in learner-centered classrooms; these teachers believe that he who does the talking does the learning, and *structured* student conversations are built into lessons. Teacher talk is replaced by student-to-student communication that harnesses the power of active listening as well as confident speaking.

8. Teachers in powerful classroom environments understand that students need to move; movement and exercise, as we will see in Chapter 3, enhance learning. These teachers make movement and exercise part of their classroom structure.

9. Teachers in highly successful and efficient classrooms understand that *there are no shortcuts to improving the oral and writing skills so important to effective communication.* Students write, receive feedback, make changes, edit their own work and that of their peers, and are connected to the sense of urgency I see in great teachers.

10. Finally, in particularly powerful classrooms, I have observed that effective procedures accelerate progress on the part of teachers and students alike. These procedures are all established during the first five days of school, with a clear explanation and plenty of practice. Procedures become effective when they become routine. Again, explaining classroom processes is not enough; every process that makes up the teacher's classroom system must be explained and then rehearsed until it becomes routine (Wong & Wong, 2009).

Teachers can be effective if the environment is safe, curiosity and discovery are valued, relationships are solid, and students are engaged in the processes that are part of a dynamic and purposeful continuous-improvement effort. There is one more element that can no longer be ignored, for the simple reason that it is where today's students live; it is where they are, and where they are is in a digital world. In the words of Don Tapscott (2009), "Net Geners are not content to sit quietly and listen to a teacher lecture. Kids who have grown up digital expect to talk back, to have a conversation" (p. 126). Not being so involved leads quickly to boredom for today's students, especially when they are so clearly and deeply engaged online when not at school. The disparity between what goes on in their private lives and what goes on in the classroom simply highlights the gap that can exist when teachers are determined to stick to lecture and otherwise create an essentially passive environment for students.

Technology is not a panacea for all that ails what may well be described as a broken educational system, but the idea of more student engagement has to take into account where stu-

> . . . At the click of a mouse, any Net Gen student can tap into most of what is available on anything, anytime and anywhere.

dents are in their technological development. This is going to require a good deal of retooling for digital-immigrant teachers who may feel threatened by the technological skills the kids they are teaching take for granted. Teachers who are willing to experiment and take risks on behalf of kids are in a much better position, regardless of their age, to meet their students where they are, and my experience is that students appreciate the effort.

The fact is that students are used to communicating with one another, but a great deal—perhaps most—of that communication takes place online, and not face-to-face. While online learning platforms like Edmodo can provide the opportunity for online communication when it comes to projects, book clubs, and brainstorming, students need to be skilled at face-to-face communication as well. Standing in front of a classmate—armed with good speaking and active-listening skills—a student can learn to focus in a way that is virtually impossible when reading anything online. It also helps with relationship building, and the job of the teacher today, according to Sprenger (2009), is to provide balance. "If we can help students balance the gifts technology brings with these human gifts, they will have everything they need" (p. 39). Both sides of this balancing act (increased student-to-student conversations and the use of blogs or wikis) will require teachers to confront the status quo in their classrooms. It will also require considerable administrative and technical support for classroom teachers.

Students are also appreciative of teachers who take the time to solicit their input constantly throughout the course of the school year. In my last two years of teaching, I spent the last day of school getting feedback from my seventh graders. I used a two-page feedback mechanism that let me know what I needed to change for *next* year's students. I waited until the last day of school to get any formal feedback, and what I managed to discover had not one morsel of benefit for the kids giving me the feedback. I did make changes the next year, but what could I have done for this year's students had I solicited feedback periodically throughout the school year? What changes might I have made in my instructional practices had I simply taken the time to ask them what they thought on a regular basis?

My students back then helped me work and improve around the edges of a traditional system of delivery. Predictably, they urged me to talk less and give them more choice in assignments. This is still good advice, and particularly important in a world where at the click of a mouse, any Net Gen student can tap into most of what is available on anything, anytime and anywhere. In education today, we need to work into our methodology the virtually limitless sources of information available to the average student. When students are online, their curiosity can be satisfied, and their sense of discovery is just a link away. They can talk with anyone, anytime, and anywhere instantaneously. In a traditional classroom, both time and the pace of life can slow down for students who are used to images that flash by in a nanosecond. This slow pace frustrates today's students, as does the one-way flow of information all too prevalent in classrooms around the country. Teachers may interpret the boredom etched into the faces (and body language) of students as "Today's kids just don't want to learn!" I have heard that over and over again from teachers whose students are simply not responding positively to a system that makes them passive observers.

Our continued tendency to drag students kicking and screaming through a lock-step curriculum stands in sharp contrast to their need to take learning where the links and the information take them. In curriculum documents all over the country, we have pacing guides that tell teachers where they ought to be at a given time in a given school year. Our attempts to teach to the middle leave students who could proceed more quickly bored silly, and those who need to proceed more slowly are left in the dust. What Tapscott (2009) calls "broadcast learning" is not serving Net Geners whose problem is not a lack of information. "Students need to be able to think creatively, critically, and collaboratively; to master the 'basics' and excel in reading, math, science, and information literacy, and respond to opportunities and challenges with speed, agility, and innovation" (p. 127). I would argue that the same is true of educators. We need to be able to think creatively, critically, and collaboratively about the nature of the entire educational system as it exists today, and we will need to respond to opportunities and challenges in a way that is flexible and innovative.

To succeed in the long run, teachers must be willing to do as our history teacher Ed did; he paused long enough to look in the mirror and see whether he was really effective as the teacher he wanted to be. After observing an excellent history teacher in her classroom, and following that with over an hour of great conversation with that teacher, Ed found himself willing to compare and contrast what he saw there with what he did on a daily basis. He realized that after many years in the classroom, there were things he could and should do to improve professionally. Teachers—new or veteran—must be willing to look at how they do what they do, and then work with administrators and colleagues alike to put themselves on a path to continuous improvement.

Final Thoughts

There are two things that can be done nationwide, and the first of these can be done more quickly and more effectively right away. Individual districts, schools, and teachers should commit themselves to moving quickly away from classrooms where teachers are constantly on stage in command-and-control mode. *Feetwork* as defined in this book is not just getting kids up and moving in the classroom, although that is desirable and beneficial; it means that students must be *participants* in their own learning, rather than *attendees* in a passive process. Attendees attend, but participants participate. The second thing we must do as a nation is to stop thinking of education in terms of "when the bell rings we will all move from math to English" to a more personalized system that allows—and indeed dictates—that students proceed at their own rate toward their own goals, using every technological advance and every critical-thinking and communication skill that can be provided to facilitate that progress. This will take time and will need to be a districtwide or at least a schoolwide effort, and it is happening around the country now. District leaders need to identify and visit those sites to see how a more personalized structure is working out for staff and students alike.

Wolk (2010) cites progress in one such school in Minnesota, the New Country School. With no classrooms, students have their own work spaces much as they might in an office. The faculty members at the school work with students one-on-one, and students work individually and in groups as the occasion demands. "Students also evaluate themselves, using a performance rubric to rate their work in three areas: critical thinking, leadership and innovation, and their performance on specific projects" (p. 20). Laptops are standard fare, and books are everywhere, but the one-size-fits-all approach to learning does not apply at the New Country School. The whole bells-driven notion of one discrete subject after another may well disappear in favor of many different kinds of more personal learning with teachers as true facilitators of that learning.

Teachers, administrators, and school counselors need to commit to helping students find areas of interest where their progress can be faster; in all likelihood, this is where they will find gainful employment down the road. I applaud magnet schools that permit students to find out if nursing or legal work or any other potential field is what they really want. I congratulate teachers and counselors who meet together to discuss the relative strengths of students, and how those strengths can be leveraged into real progress and success for them. I had three teachers who recognized my love of reading and my ability to write; they encouraged me at every turn—I have never forgotten that. They instinctively understood that my future was not as a mathematician or a scientist or an accountant, and while they helped me progress in those areas of relative weakness, they helped me soar when it came to reading and writing. In my case, those three teachers understood my strengths, facilitated my progress, and let the eagle fly. I have dedicated this book to them.

In Chapter 2, we take a look at schools and teachers who let the eagles fly by fully embracing the belief that if every child is going to learn, every child is going to have to be engaged in the learning.

2

Their World and Welcome to It

Thinking back from a distance to my high school typing class, I can remember the day I was permitted to use the lone electric typewriter in the classroom. The others were manual machines, and it was a big deal to earn the right (by typing the most words per minute without a mistake) to move to the corner table and use that marvelous piece of state-of-the-art technology. We learned the mechanics of typing in that classroom, and our core-subject teachers all had us writing papers, test essays, and other formal pieces of writing. We diagrammed sentences in all four levels of English. We learned to write by writing frequently. Although word processors, PCs and laptops, and iPads have moved us forward in terms of ever more sophisticated ways of transferring thoughts to files and then to paper, there is still no shortcut to getting students to write well. They have to write frequently and receive timely and meaningful feedback from teachers, peers, checklists, and rubrics.

By the same token, there is no shortcut to helping students learn to communicate orally in an articulate manner, and verbal and written forms of communication are linked. Indeed, according to Keene and Zimmermann (2007),

> Oral language development plays a critical role in learning to read and write well. Children's syntax (oral and written grammar, story structure, and use of conventions) and vocabulary (using more

precise and purposeful words) develop because they spend time talking at home, to their teachers, and with other children. (p. 40)

Students should be made aware of these connections, and communicating frequently in writing and orally should be a regular part of every content area at every grade level. It must be the science teacher's job and the history teacher's job to reinforce the rules of the road when it comes to composition and grammar. Students should be part of structured conversations in health and math classes. Where these students today are is in a world where these twin communication skills are in high demand, and colleges and universities should not have to include remedial courses in writing for up to a third of incoming freshmen. If, as I believe, there is less adult-directed conversation at home when compared with the pre–computer, pre–cell phone, and pre-Internet era, it is critically important that students take part in teacher-facilitated conversations at school—at every grade level. Once again, this is not a one- or two-day process; to communicate effectively, students must practice communicating orally *and* in writing frequently and at all grade levels.

Students are entering a world that values communication, problem solving, and teamwork. Evidence of that comes from a 2010 survey conducted by the American Management Association (AMA) sent to 2,115 managers and company leaders. The results showed that companies increasingly look to hire workers who can demonstrate what they call the four Cs: critical thinking, collaboration, communication, and creativity (AMA, 2010). A whopping 81 percent of the companies surveyed said they looked for evidence of communication skills when hiring. This is not to say that reading and math are not valued; it does say that our educational system in the United States must change to provide students with a set of solid communication skills that will only become more important with time. Again, every teacher in every subject area needs to reinforce those skills; it cannot be left up to the language arts teachers to tackle writing and oral communication.

Educators need to work with students on critical-thinking skills that include questioning what they see on the Internet and hear on radio and television. More than ever, students must be able to distinguish fact from opinion and dig more deeply into the possible motives behind what appears online or in print. Being able to sort through the simply overwhelming amount of information available online without merely accepting it at face value will not only help students in the workplace of today and tomorrow; it is also essential to becoming good citizens in a vibrant democracy. Students who learn to look at what they read, see, and hear in the classroom with a healthy amount of skepticism are much more likely to be skeptical when they hit the Enter key and move into cyberspace. Teachers at every grade level need to encourage students to ask questions and question answers in a way that will help them in life and in the world of work.

To Cover or Uncover the Curriculum

With one exception in the late 1970s, when I taught U.S. history at whatever level, my social studies colleagues and I tried to "cover" the history of the United States in one year—all of it. We did this in chronological fashion, so that wars came and went, along with colonization, immigration, national expansion, presidential elections, recessions, and depressions. The ones who may have been *most* depressed were social studies teachers faced with the fact that each passing year added another chapter to an already burgeoning textbook crammed with every person, place, date, fact, and historical figure imaginable. The sad fact of the matter is that social studies teachers are *still* trying to cover U.S. history in one year in many districts, and attempting to do so in chronological fashion for the most part. Tradition is a hard taskmaster.

To the extent that these teachers can "cover" the material (and this goes for any subject area, not just social studies), the job may get done by adhering to pacing schedules and barreling through chapter after chapter at breakneck speed. But this is done at the expense of the amount of time needed to slow down, pause, reflect, discuss, and let students do the explaining and ask the questions. I flew through the history of our country so quickly the students could not *possibly* have become meaningfully engaged in anything, *and that was almost forty years of history ago.* Imagine what it must be like today, with larger, heavier textbooks and the demands of standardized tests that pull teachers in the wrong direction—away from time that otherwise might be dedicated to deepening understanding in the major strands of history: conflict, freedom and civil rights, the rise of manufacturing and labor, and the role of the judiciary, to name a few. These major themes cry out for sufficient time spent in discovery, discussion, and debate.

The textbook I provided for my students was the major source of information available to them, except on those rare occasions when I added primary sources to the mix. There were, and still are, plenty of history teachers who bring those valuable primary resources into play and courageously buck the continuing trend to race through the curriculum at the speed of an out-of-control freight train. There are issues like the environment, energy, globalism, health, and immigration that demand adequate conversation and debate. The United States is in serious need of a national discussion about the future of transportation in this country, and the perfect place to do that is in the high school classrooms of students whose fortunes may rise and fall on our ability as a nation to deal with and compete in the areas of transportation, clean energy, manufacturing, and increasingly critical ecological issues. Rather than trying to cover absolutely everything in the curriculum, we ought to be helping students *un*cover a curriculum that is smaller—trading breadth of coverage for depth.

The Internet is awash in information of every kind, and the digital natives of today know exactly how to navigate through what is out there; this is their world. As a child and as a teenager, I chose to spend my time outdoors. Today's kids spend several hours a day at some kind of screen, accessing information at a rate and to an extent that is mind boggling to digital immigrants like me. I'm the first one to say that I wish children would spend more time in outdoor activities, and I wish teenagers would use their cell phones while on a treadmill or elliptical machine (and not in a car). The fascination digital natives have with everything electronic can be harnessed for their ultimate benefit, provided we as educators are willing to meet them where they live.

The day will come when textbooks will be replaced by small and inexpensive laptops that students will carry gladly in place of a heavy backpack filled with books and notebooks. But laptops in the hands of students consigned to listening to the teacher lecture for a long period of time can be a double-edged sword. As described in Carr (2010), one pair of Cornell researchers had two groups of students listen to a lecture. One group listened and took notes in the traditional way, while a second group had access to the web while listening. "A log of their activity showed that they looked at sites related to the lecture's content but also visited unrelated sites, checked their e-mail, went shopping, watched videos, and did all the other things that people do online" (p. 130). Predictably, perhaps, a follow-up assessment showed poor results for the group that had Internet access while the lecture unfolded.

Prensky (2010) reports that in college classrooms where students have their own laptops, they use them for purposes other than those related to the subject. Prensky does not blame the students for this. The technology, he says, "does not support lecturing or telling pedagogies at all. Given nothing interesting to do on the powerful machines in front of them, students will use them as they wish" (p. 103). Seeing students and teachers as partners in the learning process, Prensky points out that teachers have an obligation to make certain that whatever current technology exists is incorporated into the classroom structure. New technologies cannot simply be grafted onto the traditional educational infrastructure without a considerable—but necessary—disruption of the status quo.

There are school districts around the country providing laptops or tablets for every student, and I applaud that move as long as ways are found to integrate them into a curriculum that should still require face-to-face interactions. Also, just as college instructors have an obligation to find ways to harness the power of computers and engage students productively in the technology, so too must K–12 teachers faced with laptops in the hands of students change their style of delivery. If lecture and teacher talk continue to predominate, the computer may become nothing other than an expensive spiral-bound notebook, or a diversion for students unwilling or unable to keep up with the one-way flow of information from the front of the classroom.

In Brad Ward's fifth-grade classroom in Virginia Beach, Virginia, his students use laptops every day. Ward has them working on performance tasks frequently, projects that are enhanced by using Edmodo, an online learning platform that allows Ward to check progress frequently in formative mode on the way to a more summative assessment at the end of the task. Using Edmodo, Ward creates folders that permit students and their parents to access if they have content-related questions. There is a backpacking feature that allows students to work on word-processing documents at home. Laptops in Ward's classroom serve not as an escape from teacher talk, but as an indispensable support mechanism in a student-centered classroom. Students are rarely at their desks in his classroom; Ward doesn't much care where they work as long as they are engaged.

When planning for the use of laptops in classrooms, then, it would make sense to find ways to fold their use into an interactive structure where students don't feel the need to go to the website of their choice for the simple reason that *lecture is not the main mode of delivery.* Students who are engaged by design when they are in the classroom will find fewer reasons to find a handy escape route. In more learner-centered classrooms, teacher talk is held to a minimum and, as in Brad Ward's fifth-grade classroom, it is likely to be followed by an activity that allows students to process that information, ask questions, and seek the kind of information online that is directly related to the task at hand. In classrooms where students are deeply engaged in their own learning, teachers are free to observe, ask probing questions, hold the occasional one-on-one conference with students, and generally check progress as students work.

Regardless of the amount of technology available in the classroom, teachers need to change the physical state of students by providing opportunities to stand, move, and process information in standing pairs or groups. Students may be seated and listening to the teacher or students may be seated and working on a laptop; either way, they are sitting—sometimes for long periods of time—when there are other processing options available—a standing pair share or a gallery walk, to name two. My experience is that students appreciate being able to stand, move, and share as a way of varying the classroom routine—no matter the grade level.

> . . . Teachers need to change the physical state of students by providing opportunities to stand, move, and process information in standing pairs or groups.

Death of a Thousand Ruts

In Chapter 1, our veteran high school social studies teacher, Ed, reached a point in his career where he sensed, through observation and reflection, the enormous gap that was widening between his way of teaching and his students' way of learning. He guessed that although his ninth graders liked him and appreciated his sense of humor, they often allowed their minds to wander when he was explaining something related to the core subject—history. After twenty-seven years, there was a sameness in his approach to teaching. Not to put too fine a point on it, Ed was in a rut.

There are thousands and thousands of teachers all over the country just like Ed, teachers who may well be increasingly uncomfortable with their jobs, perhaps in large measure due to the fact that they are misreading the feedback they are getting from students. It is not, as I think many teachers sincerely believe, that kids today don't *want* to learn. Today's generation, as with all generations, learns *constantly,* making connections and thinking at a high level in their daily lives. Learning is a part of life, and learning is a function of our brains.

In fact, our brains and other organs are functioning before birth, says Smilkstein (2003), citing research that has found "a newborn recognizes the mother's voice, showing that the fetus, innately and naturally, without instruction or example, hears and then remembers this particular voice" (p. 52). Children are innately curious. This constant state of wonder and learning continues, and young children often drive adults crazy because they are always asking questions; this is a normal way of trying to understand the world they find themselves in. In doing this, they direct their own learning in a way that is perfectly natural, but as kids grow older, teachers and adults too often seek to replace their questions with the answers we want them to find. "Somewhere on the way to adulthood," affirm Gunter, Estes, and Schwab (1999), "children inevitably get the idea that becoming a grown-up means leaving the world of questioning for the world of knowing" (p. 122). In a multiple-choice test, for example, the answer is already there; the student has only to find it among the false choices we teachers have inserted. The message may be that their questions are not as important as our answers. *We know what you need to know; now find it among the choices we have provided.*

The problem, of course, is that life is not a multiple-choice test. The workplace, especially in an increasingly global and competitive economy, is not like this. No employer sits a group of employees down and says, "Your job today is to find the answer to a great problem that confronts us as a company. We *know* what the answer is, but we want you to find it among these four choices. Do your own work." If employers already know the answer to the challenges with which they are grappling on a daily basis, then they don't need to pay someone to simply find the gem among the semiprecious stones. Solving problems involves asking questions and questioning answers, analyzing data, inferring, evaluating, creating, innovating, and ultimately adjusting processes and systems on the continuous-improvement highway. Multiple-choice tests are cheap and easy to grade, but they normally don't give students much of a workout on the cognitive ladder.

For students not attuned to lecture and other forms of teacher talk, a ninety-minute block with someone who lectures, has students read aloud from the textbook, and shows videos without helping students work out the connections between the video and the subject matter can be both boring and unproductive. To learn, students have to grapple with the material on their own and in collaboration with others. Not all students are auditory learners, and teachers need to vary their teaching methods so that those who are highly visual or kinesthetic have a shot at understanding and remembering course content.

Allen (2008) differentiates between *Red Light teachers* and *Green Light teachers*. A Red Light teacher, as defined by Allen,

> doesn't take into account the needs of the majority of kids in his classroom who find it hard to learn from just listening, reading, and writing. He gives no thought to kinesthetic learners. He doesn't use music or novelty to engage reluctant learners and encode strong memories. He doesn't embed cognition through drama, drawing, or social interaction. (p. 3)

I once heard a teacher say, "Lecture didn't kill me, and it won't kill them!" Red Light teachers like this, according to Allen, would do well to "adjust their strategies to match the fast, exciting, interactive world" inhabited by today's generation of students (p. 3). Professional development at the district and building levels must be geared toward helping teachers make the kind of minor adjustments or major changes that will allow them to connect with and better serve the students in their care. Principals and other instructional leaders must observe teachers frequently, and they must provide the kind of formative support that will improve instruction while increasing the competence and confidence of teachers like Ed who may otherwise feel things slowly slipping away. Building administrators who are in classrooms on a frequent and regular basis will help teachers like Ed. It was an assistant principal who arranged for Ed to visit the classroom of another ninth-grade history teacher in another district. Continuous improvement in the classroom should not be dependent on chance or the occasional epiphany on the part of faculty members; instructional leaders at the building or district level should be in classrooms observing, modeling, and otherwise assisting teachers like Ed confront the status quo in a positive and consistent manner.

Students who are trained to pass quizzes and tests, often by cramming the required material into short-term memory for the purposes of getting the grade and satisfying the teacher, are not necessarily going to be able to handle challenges and problems posed in the workplace and in their adult lives. We have to give their minds a workout in school, one that takes advantage not only of how students' brains learn, but also what they are going to need to survive and thrive in the world of tomorrow. Individual teachers like Ed can begin to make the necessary changes in individual classrooms, but it goes well beyond that. Schools and school districts need to realize that it is not enough to applaud this or that teacher for shifting a few individual classrooms from teacher-centered to learner-centered; there must be an overall effort to make those changes on a massive scale. In developing curricula at every level, educators must "select pedagogical strategies that will most effectively help students learn by using their brain's innate learning process" (Smilkstein, 2003, p. 30). The care, feeding, and exercising of student brains must become of primary concern to every educator in the United States. If we commit to doing this, the kids will be alright, and they will take care of whatever standardized tests come their way.

First Steps Toward the Next Step

The current system of education in this country will, I believe, go through some fundamental changes in structure in the next couple of decades. Life is not neatly divided into subject areas where the same bell that announces it is time to change subjects subsequently informs students they are late. The role of teachers is changing, and will continue to change, at an ever-increasing pace. The teacher as chief information officer will become the teacher as facilitator of process. This means teacher talk as a mode of delivery is—and should be—an endangered species. What teachers are beginning to realize, perhaps, is that the tendency of students today to socialize and explore can be put to good use; it can be harnessed and made to serve students well in a restructured system that helps students understand the forces, concepts, and challenges that will shape their future.

There are, in fact, teachers who are doing just that; they are tapping into the ability of students to identify and access sources of information, and they are channeling this generation's socialization skills in a way that gets them deeper into the material—and *provides the time to allow them to do this.* There are teachers who model for students the whole idea of finding evidence to support conclusions or assumptions that should not be taken at face value or go untested. I work with a colleague who consistently asks questions like, "If we did this, what might happen?" Companies worldwide are looking for workers who know how to ask questions and question answers. Prior to the publication of *The Global Achievement Gap*, Tony Wagner (2008) asked the CEO of a large company what he looked for in new employees. The CEO said he looked "for someone who asks good questions" because while new employees could be brought up to speed with technical skills in the normal course of training, they could not be taught how to ask the right questions (p. 2).

In a highly competitive global economy, the ability to ask questions, question answers, and work collaboratively are all valued commodities, as are creativity and innovation. It takes *time* to help students develop these thinking, communication, and collaboration skills. There is no shortcut here, and time must be found for students at all grade levels to get a mental workout in these critical skill sets.

Today's great teachers realize that literally tearing through a curriculum guide or textbook at breakneck speed to cover everything may mean students wind up learning little along the way. Anyone who wants to improve anything he or she does must stop and reflect frequently; it is part of the continuous-improvement process. This may require curriculum coordinators and teachers alike to sit down and decide if there is too much material to cover in a given curriculum, regardless of the subject area. One teacher told me he was continually frustrated by his students' seeming inability to learn to speak and write with any fluency in his classes. One summer, he simply treated his language arts curriculum as one would flowering bushes and trees in the winter; he got out the pruner and went to work removing what he considered to be relatively unnecessary or superfluous material, making room for new growth. As a result, he could slow down and actually engage his students in a way he had not been able to do before. The grades and attitudes of his students improved, and he told me he never regretted making the changes.

Curriculum developers and teachers have to be able to take risks on behalf of kids, risks that include pruning the curriculum so that students can reflect on and collaboratively process new information. This may mean that students cover less but understand more. It may mean that a social studies teacher can use the several wars our country has found itself in to discuss the whole concept of conflict and renewal in a way that reveals common strands running through our history. It might also allow those same teachers to expand to a more substantive examination of our place in the world, especially today, along with some structured reflecting and brainstorming about what our place in the future might be. Once again, we are back to some powerful questions that beg for a good deal of reflection and dialogue: "What would happen if?" or "Given where we appear to be now, what does the future hold for us as a nation?" or "What evidence can you find this evening that supports or refutes our government's decision related to the new immigration law?" or "Where might you go to find out what companies are looking for in prospective employees?" followed by "See what you can discover this weekend about what the workplace of tomorrow will look like." These are open-ended questions and assignments that challenge students familiar with an electronic world to harness its power to explore and discover. Students today can explore and discover electronically in a way that would have been utterly impossible just a couple of decades ago.

Traditional teaching methodology has at its heart teacher-centered processes like lecture and other forms of teacher talk that are generally aimed at those students who can effectively function in this highly auditory environment. Students who do not process quickly will fall by the wayside, while students who function perfectly well in this type of situation may be three steps ahead of the teacher—and bored silly. This was bad enough prior to the development of computers and video games. It doesn't require a super-human effort in the area of observation for teachers to realize that some among their students are lost, while others long to forge ahead, driven by either a competitive spirit or a desire simply to know and understand more.

The gap between traditional teacher-directed and teacher-assessed instruction stands today in stark contrast to the incredible amount of self-directed learning students can do when they are in total charge of their own forward progress with personal computers and an ever-increasing number of video games. Kids today are used to playing games providing immediate feedback that can be used to make adjustments and facilitate a move to the next level. Players, singly or in pairs or groups, are all the while completely absorbed and focused on solving the myriad problems the game presents, sometimes at breakneck speed. "Games teach kids to choose wisely," says Prensky (2006), "by making the consequences of poor choices meaningfully bad, and allowing them to try again and again until they learn whatever they need to learn to make the right choice." Prensky adds, "This is a lot better for both kids' learning (and for kids' psyches) than the system of the teacher who, at the end of the term, puts down a grade on a final or report card and moves on" (pp. 199–200).

This is an important point, because teachers who are digital immigrants may feel—understandably so—threatened by a system of learning that does not require the intervention of "an expert" and relies on making mistakes, making adjustments, and making progress. One of the things teachers can do immediately to tap into that self-directed impulse so deeply ingrained in students today is to develop checklists and rubrics that students can use to gauge where they are along their own continuous-improvement journeys. Students who are using these two tools do not need to wait for teacher-assisted feedback. If checklists and rubrics are well developed, and adjusted and improved over time, students can self-adjust on the way to writing an excellent essay or giving a top-level presentation in class. I know teachers who have enlisted the help of their students in creating those checklists and rubrics, and I would think teachers can explain the parallels between making progress in a video game and making progress in writing an essay or formal paper as a way of framing the relevance of the process.

Harnessing the Power of the Group

The way a classroom is run does not have to be presented to students as a *fait accompli.* This is traditionally how it is done; teachers create the ground rules and format, and students come along for the ride—sometimes kicking and screaming all the way. It reminds me of kids in the car who look up occasionally and ask their parents, "Are we there yet?" *Someone* is aware of the destination, along with how to get there, and junior will be informed at the appropriate time of the imminent arrival. In many classrooms, the students not only go along for the ride; they help plan the journey. This early involvement helps give students a say in the process and a stake in the outcome.

In Mary Kendrick's English classroom, she began one school year by involving her high school students in a unit called "Creating Our Class." She presented her tenth graders with open-ended questions that dealt with how they would interact in the classroom, as well as what they hoped to accomplish. Small-group discussions in Kendrick's classes were followed by whole-class conversations that allowed students to bring together ideas explored in the smaller group settings. Students also read essays that dealt with school life (e.g., boring lectures, getting picked on, losing a friend), and more discussions and a good deal of journal writing followed. The processes established during this opening unit were put to good use on subsequent student discussions of works of literature for Kendrick's ninth graders (Kendrick, 2010).

Students can also be involved in an exploration of what makes a good speaker or presenter. Students could begin with composing a list of what Wicks, Peregoy, and Wheeler (2001) refer to as *drivers* and *restrainers*. Things that help make an oral presentation *effective* (drivers) might include speaking clearly and making eye contact with the audience; those things that might work *against* an effective presentation (restrainers) might include making distracting gestures or mumbling (p. 105). This comparison provides ample time for reflection and helps students analyze something more deeply than otherwise might be the case. Teachers, of course, could simply tell students what makes a good oral presentation, but students will benefit more if they are part of an analysis that helps them arrive at some conclusions of their own. Having come up with a list of drivers and restrainers, students can discuss how to overcome the items on the latter list; doing this helps students understand what gets in the way of a good presentation, and what makes presentations comparatively more powerful.

As students eliminate the list of restrainers, they may add to the drivers listing. In removing *mumbling* from the restrainer listing, the drivers column can benefit from the addition of *speaking clearly*. If *lack of eye contact* was initially on the restrainer list, *making eye contact* can be moved to the drivers list, and this can serve as the starting point for a discussion about just how much eye contact is necessary (and how much is too much). Once the list of restrainers has been reduced or eliminated, and the drivers listing has been expanded, a natural next step might be letting students help develop a useful rubric for oral presentations that can be used in the classroom.

Teachers can certainly come up with their own list of "what makes a good oral presentation" or "what makes a good listener" as they get the year going in the fall, but it is far more helpful and interesting for students if they have a say in brainstorming, analyzing, and synthesizing in ways that provide a much deeper understanding of the skills they are going to need to develop to be successful—not only during that school year, but also down the road as they enter a twenty-first-century work-force that values that kind of critical thinking. Having these kinds of discussions and getting students used to collaborating early in the school year will pay dividends later on when they are required to ponder, share, analyze, and synthesize information related to specific course content.

Not Their Grandfather's Homework

Early in my teaching career, I gave my students homework assignments almost every night. I did that, as I think back on it now, for the simple reason that it was an important part of the educational status quo. Parents expected it, administrators expected it, and the kids expected it; they didn't necessarily *like* it, but they expected to have assignments in their classes all the same. Do we really need all that homework? If homework is more about compliance than demonstrating understanding, perhaps we need to reexamine our motives in assigning it. "If we can assess learning without all those homework assignments," affirms Vatterott (2009), "and the students have learned what we wanted them to learn, we don't need the homework assignments" (p. 126). I know excellent teachers whose students perform beautifully in class, and those teachers give few overnight homework assignments. Parents used to seeing tons of assignments coming home night after night often question these teachers early in the year—until it hits them that their daughter now loves school and is willing to do more work at home *on her own*.

It does not take students long to understand that a good deal of what they are sent home with by way of homework assignments is busywork. Teachers often make homework a fairly large chunk of the total grade, and students who truly care about the grade will do the work even if they doubt its usefulness or efficacy. Fill-in-the-blank assignments are too open to copying from other students to be of much value, and students who try to do the homework only to come face-to-face with the fact that they don't really understand what they are supposed to understand may feel frustrated. Also, if the assigned homework incorporates the use of a particular skill, according to Marzano, Pickering, and Pollock (2001), students should be familiar enough with the skill so that the assignment can be completed successfully. "Practicing a skill with which a student is unfamiliar is not only inefficient, but might also serve to habituate errors or misconceptions" (p. 63).

Allen and Rickert (2010) suggest that teachers spend time in the first few days of school discussing the whole concept of homework. During the twenty to thirty minutes Allen and Rickert recommend be devoted to this classroom conversation, teachers "might start by asking [students] about their previous experiences with homework. You'll usually hear some good stories and some bad ones" (p. 121). This exercise reveals to students that *this* teacher fully understands that some assignments are busywork, while other assignments may lead to some confusion or anxiety among students. It also gives teachers the perfect opportunity to describe exactly the kinds of things students can expect when it comes to assignments and projects intended to be done, at least in part, at home.

Feedback is the lifeblood of the continuous-improvement journey for students, and I count myself among those who believe that *fewer* homework assignments with *more* feedback will in the end be of more practical use to students. Students themselves can provide each other with valuable feedback as well. "Often," according to Vatterott (2009), "teachers will simply ask students to meet in groups to compare their homework answers, ask each other questions, and then report back to the teacher" (p. 115). They could do this, in fact, with a relevant rubric at their desks, or check it against one the teacher posts on the screen. The teacher can, as students work together and compare their work, circulate around the room; the rubric gives students the ability to check what they have written against a standard that is both visible and familiar to them.

It is also possible that students entered the classroom on a particular day after finishing a reading assignment begun in the previous day's block. The combination of what they read the day before and what they completed the previous night might be the basis for paired discussions or a piece of journal writing that could, in turn, serve as the basis for a class discussion later on. When students respond in writing or in student-to-student conversations to a prompt or a set of questions, the teacher's job is *not* to sit behind the desk or grade papers. Schmoker (2011) says teachers circulate to "listen, ensure on-task behavior, and scan student work so you can more precisely guide the next steps of learning and not leave students behind" (p. 82). My experience is that when teachers circulate constantly while students are working, the amount of on-task behavior increases a great deal.

In the preceding example, students completed a reading assignment begun in class the night before, about which they *knew* they would be writing in a journal or pairing up to discuss. It is important for teachers to model this with students by first having them read something in class and then discuss it or otherwise process the reading passage verbally in pairs or in their journals. A standing paired discussion of what they read (allowing them to move *and* talk) can be followed by the journal writing, and that can be followed by different pairs of students standing with their journals and discussing what they wrote. Once students have this entire process down, the reading not completed in class can be extended into the evening, and that can be followed in turn by the paired discussions and journal writing *with which they are perfectly familiar and totally comfortable.*

Their Questions and Their Choice

In the process of teaching a unit in science or social studies, teachers will often introduce into the mix a powerful graphic, picture, or other visual, something that may stir the interest of students too often subjected to a highly auditory classroom environment. Too often, the teacher will display the picture with the lights out (ostensibly for better viewing) *and then proceed to explain everything on the screen.* My observations at such moments make me believe that many students take this opportunity to open their minds to limitless mental avenues of escape while looking directly at the screen or the teacher. In this case, teachers get a real workout in the second level of the cognitive ladder (comprehension), because it is *they* who are doing the explaining, describing, and illustrating. Teachers will often ask questions of students, but rarely do the students get to ask questions of their own. The teacher asks questions as she searches for specific answers.

My suggestion is that teachers begin a unit with a particularly powerful graphic, and then have students stand in trios or quartets and discuss what they think is going on in the picture. What do *they* see? Then, with one student in each group acting as group leader, they can raise questions for the teacher after maybe two minutes of collecting those questions within the groups. The teacher can have someone write the questions on a chart or on the Smart Board. When the questions have been exhausted, the teacher announces that these questions will be posted on her teacher website by 5:00 p.m., and she will also have hard copies of the questions and the graphic on a table by the door at the end of the school day. She then asks her students to find as many answers as they can that evening, bringing them to class the next day.

At the beginning of the class period on the following day, the teacher puts the students into the same groups they were in the day before, and, with the questions now posted on the screen, they proceed to talk about what they discovered the previous evening. Some students will have researched (on the Internet most likely) a few questions; others may have researched a great many; still others may not have answered any questions at all the previous evening. However, if there are three or four students in each group, the new knowledge base about the topic will expand during the conversations, and students will get experience in that comprehension level of the cognitive ladder. It is *they* who will do the explaining, illustrating, and describing; they may also get a chance to defend a point of view based on their research. Once again, the teacher's job is to circulate and listen to the various conversations, gauging where they are in their understanding of this new topic of discussion.

In this case, the questions did not belong to the teacher; the questions were surfaced the day before from the *students*. The questions were *theirs*. It was *they* who did the research; it was *they* who may have raised even more questions in the process of answering others; it was *they* who did the talking and processing—not the teacher. They learned from each other, and they had a wide variety of questions from which to choose as they sat down at their computer keyboards and tapped into a convenient and much-navigated search engine of choice. This could properly be called homework not labeled as homework, and perhaps not labeled at all. Students were simply empowered to grab as many questions as interested them and find out what they could. It started with an intriguing visual, tons of unanswered questions of their own making, some time on the computer they were going to be on anyway that evening, and it ended with two discussions (one at the group level and one at the class level) that can now serve as a doorway into a new unit on slavery (beginning with a picture of a slave ship on what was known as the Middle Passage). It is not graded and it was not, strictly speaking, required, but enough interest was generated by what they observed on the screen and the subsequent questions that most students were willing to take a journey into cyberspace to find out what was going on in that picture.

In the pre-Internet era, this kind of activity would have been limited by the relative paucity of resources, but this teacher is asking students to shift their attention from whatever else they are doing on the computer long enough to find the answers to as many questions as they like—not labeled as homework. If there were thirty-some questions asked and posted on the chart—and eventually on the teacher's website—it is possible that most of the students hovering over their keyboards that evening asked at least one of them. A quick visit to the teacher's website (already bookmarked on his desktop) brings the questions back up, and the students' natural curiosity should do the rest—assuming the picture or graphic displayed was one that solicited substantial talk and at least several questions to begin with.

As any casual visit to a school's website will confirm, more and more teachers have their own websites to which parents and students have access,

> Students who did not contribute in class were willing to do so online.

and I truly can't imagine *not* having such a website in today's electronic environment. I could not possibly count the number of times one of my students asked me the following questions, all of which began with "Mr. Nash, when is our next major test?

what is included on that next major test?

when is that project due?

do you have another copy of that syllabus?

do you have another copy of the instructions for that project?

can you give me another one of those oral-presentation rubrics?

if we don't have school on Monday, will Tuesday's test be postponed?

[along with the ever-popular] what are we supposed to do????"

When I think of what I could post on my own teacher website today, it boggles my mind. Parents in many school districts can now check their students' grades online, chat with teachers via e-mail, and go to a teacher website to find out whatever they need to know about expectations and course requirements. Once there, they can locate checklists to determine what is to be included in a standard essay, find a short list of twelve proofreading marks their students have been taught to use, get the scoop on the upcoming field trip and print out the permission form, see rubrics of every description that would help them help their kids, and forever close the age-old gap between when their son *told* them the project is due and when it is *actually* due.

Classrooms Outside the Walls and Inside the Minds of Digital Natives

Traditional homework assignments are completed alone, done in paper and pencil, and handed in the next day or by a specific due date. Feedback may be delayed, and by the time some assignments are returned, students may have forgotten all about what they wrote what seems to them like eons ago. When today's students communicate with their friends online, they get immediate reactions and instant feedback. Students will work on an assignment with many lines of personal communication open, and they much prefer the immediacy of the personal to the paper-and-pencil demands of teachers. I hear teachers, particularly those who are admittedly digital immigrants, complain of the competition between Facebook and textbooks all the time, but for those willing to meet students where they are, there are alternatives.

Stacy Kitsis (2010) has her eleventh- and twelfth-grade English students post on a class blog their comments about works of literature they are reading. What Kitsis found was that students who were already connecting online at a personal level found it simple to shift their discussions into the realm of literature, and even students who did not contribute in class were willing to do so online. Students who rarely turned in paper-and-pencil homework assignments were regular contributors to the blog. Importantly, Kitsis found that "students learned to support their arguments and to communicate effectively and respectfully in a virtual environment, despite the absence of nonverbal cues" (p. 53). Feedback in this kind of environment is immediate, and this is what today's students like and expect.

Sarah Erschabek, a fourth-grade teacher, conducted a book club with her students over seven Saturdays. (Yes, Saturday.) Thirty-six of her forty-one students took part in these sessions, which took place at the homes of the students. Erschabek set up a blog to support the book club activity, and the blog is even open to students from *previous years,* so they can see just what is being read and discussed. A survey of her students at the end of the seven Saturdays told Erschabek that "78 percent of the book club members . . . said that reading was an interesting or great way to spend time, while that figure was just 39 percent for non-club members. Book club members also improved their writing scores over the course of the year to a greater extent than nonmembers" (Nash, 2011, p. 170). The Saturday book club, supported by the use of the blog Erschabek created and maintained, was a success, and she continues to make adjustments to the program. Her willingness to meet students where they are in cyberspace was matched by their willingness to give up seven Saturdays to discuss the books they read.

Final Thoughts

Meeting students where they are means a shift in our thinking about what a classroom actually is. When I was in school, we had blackboards on all or part of three out of four walls. We spent a good deal of time at those boards, working on math or diagramming sentences. Today's blackboard is electronic and limitless in size and scope; it has no walls. Teachers are increasingly learning how to meet students where they are, and where students are is a multidimensional world *that can be carried around wherever they go.* More than ever, teachers are shifting along a continuum from someone who provides information to someone who facilitates process in both traditional and virtual classrooms.

In a teacher-centered classroom, giving students laptops may invite them to seek out new worlds in cyberspace having little to do with the course content. From the front of the room, a teacher may have no earthly idea what students are doing while he is holding forth in lecture mode. Teachers who are willing to create performance tasks supported by several online sites shift the workload from themselves to students who are perfectly comfortable with using laptops, tablets, and cell phones.

Our choice is to fight the technology or use it, and more and more teachers and districts are having success with the latter.

In Chapter 3 we'll see that an enormous amount of brain research of the past two decades increasingly reveals the direct and powerful connections between exercise and learning. We'll see how teachers can put that knowledge to good use in classrooms.

3

Exercise and Learning

When I was a kid, we spent untold hours playing outdoor games. Every kid new to the neighborhood understood the rules for kick the can, red rover come over, and any number of other outdoor pursuits—winter or summer. On occasion we chased each other all over the backyards of our extended neighborhood for no particular reason, other than the fact that it felt good to move; it felt good to run. Although we certainly didn't realize it at the time, we were strengthening our cardiovascular and pulmonary systems for life, and this was supplemented by plenty of recess in elementary school and frequent physical education classes all the way through high school. But this is changing; as I travel around the country, I see physical education classes being reduced in number or simply made optional at the secondary level. Kids spend many hours indoors, looking at screens of various sizes, and the games they play increasingly call for electricity rather than physical exercise.

Today's neighborhoods may be less safe than those of the 1950s, and parents may be more reluctant to turn their children loose with as little supervision as we had back then, and I understand that. Safety is a concern today in a way that was not the case just four or five decades ago, and those opportunities for seemingly limitless outdoor activity are perhaps few and far between today. But parents need to make sure that their children receive as much physical activity as possible, and this may mean limiting the amount of time kids spend in front of the television or computer screen. Schools and school districts should work with parents to help them understand the importance of exercise for health and learning. This must be a priority for school districts all over the country; *students who are physically fit are more likely to perform better in school,* and every level of leadership from districts to individual schools ought to take every opportunity to impress on parents and students alike the importance of physical fitness.

This reduction in school-based physical activity is in response to the increased number and importance of end-of-semester or end-of-year standardized testing. Common wisdom is that the decks must be cleared for more seatwork, and that more time spent "hunkering down" will improve test results and allow more schools to become fully accredited and meet or exceed continuous-improvement goals from year to year. Physical education and fine arts programs in many districts are being pushed aside in favor of "increased rigor" and more seat time for students.

Reducing the amount of PE and recess in schools is counterproductive. Medina (2008) puts it this way: "Cutting off physical exercise—the very activity most likely to promote cognitive performance—to do better on a test score is like trying to gain weight by starving yourself" (p. 25). "Movement," says Hannaford (2005), "is not only essential for nerve net development and learning, but also for adequate heart and lung development to support brain function" (p. 158). Movement and exercise need to be an essential part of our curriculum, for the simple reason that it is in the best interests of our students.

Our PE teachers may be said to be our first line of *offense* against obesity and an inability to concentrate on the part of students. As reported by Ratey (2008), one group of Naperville, Illinois, high school freshmen arrived at school earlier than everyone else to take what was called "Zero Hour PE," an attempt to improve literacy skills. During this extra PE session, participants were "required to stay between 80 and 90 percent of their maximum heart rate" (p. 11). Those who took part in the program improved their reading and comprehension scores by 17 percent, compared with a 10.7 percent improvement among the other literacy students who did not take part in this early-morning program. According to Ratey, "Exercise provides an unparalleled stimulus, creating an environment in which the brain is ready, willing, and able to learn" (p. 10). In California, state education officials compared test scores for 800,000 students at three grade levels (5, 7, and 9) with their performance on six physical fitness standards: "The result was a clean, stair-stepped relationship: the more fitness standards a student met, the better the test scores" (Ratey & Manning, 2014, p. 109). Healthy kids are in a better position to learn, and teachers and administrators at the building and district level are in a position to increase, rather than decrease, the amount of exercise students get during the school day.

In this age of standardized testing and the pressure this brings on administrators and teachers alike, schools sometimes enlist the services of the PE teachers in assisting with core subject material. I understand the pressure, but I recommend that PE teachers be left to make certain kids are getting their heart rates up in an effort to improve health and academic performance. In cases where innovative PE teachers can combine a high level of exercise with core content, so much the better—but exercise should not be reduced for the sake of getting ready for standardized tests. PE classes ought to be about health, fitness, and improved cognition. These things are too important to overlook or to displace with other core-related information. Let the subject-area teachers take care of course content, freeing the PE staff to concentrate on maintaining fitness standards, keeping kids healthy, and improving cognition in the process.

While in an elementary school for a solid week, I had occasion to visit one particular PE class several times over the course of many days, and I noted that the PE teacher had students in every grade level in almost constant motion on every occasion. They danced, ran, scooted and skated, jumped rope, and otherwise exercised in a way that served to improve their overall health and get them ready to learn when they arrived at other classrooms in the building. *That PE teacher was doing his part by promoting the health and well-being of the students in his charge.*

> The combination of movement, music, and collaborative processing can be a powerful learning tool.

In another elementary school, two PE teachers used upbeat music constantly, and the kids at every grade level received tons of exercise during their time in the gym. While I watched, a second grader walked by, stopped, turned, and just watched the students as they exercised and had fun. I looked down and asked him if he enjoyed PE. He looked up at me, gave me a giant ear-to-ear grin, and said, "I love it!" Let's face it, kids gotta move, and teachers, building administrators, and parents ought to be going to bat for PE programs all over the country. They are critically important for many reasons, and provide a great feetwork alternative to seatwork.

Square Pegs in Round Holes

In my years in the classroom, I provided plenty of seatwork on a daily basis. Here were these teenagers, who liked nothing better than to be actively involved in everything from collaborative games like Monopoly and Twister to outdoor activities and school-sponsored sports, who entered my classroom only to be grounded for the better part of fifty minutes. My experience is that this is perhaps tougher on boys than girls, and the research tends to support this. At least through the age of ten, "boys may be more active than girls as a result of higher basic metabolism" (James, 2007, p. 49, citing Goran et al., 1998; Maccoby, 1998). Rather than build active strategies into instruction, teachers often simply choose to force boys into a passive environment, with predictable results. Boys *or* girls who feel the need to move and fidget in passive situations will find ways to do that, and this can lead to disruptions and even confrontations between teachers and students.

As more and more students are diagnosed with ADHD, the tendency of schools consumed with improving end-of-year test performance to increase the amount of seatwork (and sometimes *reduce* the amount of formal PE classes and recess) is actually "boosting symptoms" of ADHD (James, 2007, p. 93). By creating more passive classroom environments, and placing kids who need to be active—boys or girls—in those situations, we do them, and the cause of learning, a disservice. We are trying to fit the proverbial round peg in the square hole, with results that may be frustrating for students and teachers alike.

One result of decreasing interactive learning that involves standing and moving in favor of seatwork, is that sitting for long periods of time decreases the amount of blood going to the brain. Exercise *increases* blood flow to the brain, and triggers the release of BDNF, a protein that "supports the health of young neurons and encourages the growth of new ones" (Sousa, 2011, p. 34). While comprising only 3 percent of the body's total weight, the brain consumes fully 20 percent of the energy and fuel available. At any time, the brain needs oxygen and glucose, and "when it is working especially hard, as when solving a problem or doing a complex critical- or creative-thinking activity, it uses even more energy and fuel" (Smilkstein, 2003, p. 69). At the very time we want students to think, concentrate, or recall previously learned information, we reduce the brain's fuel sources by decreasing the amount of movement and exercise that would be available if teachers created lessons that were at once more active and interactive.

I have been in classrooms where students sit for most or all of a fifty-minute class period or ninety-minute block. I have seen elementary students sit for half an hour without getting up or moving in any structured way. Too often, students who realize there is no system in place to allow them to stand or move *will find ways to do so on their own*. A student who really does not have to go to the bathroom will nevertheless take advantage of the restroom pass to walk the halls—missing a large chunk of classroom instruction in the process. Another student will take the long route to the pencil sharpener to put a point on a pencil that was not dull or broken in the first place—just to be able to stand and move a bit. Still others may crumple a piece of paper into a ball and use the wastebasket—or a classmate—as a target. In the absence of any "legalized" system of movement and exercise, students will become understandably creative in finding ways to get up, get around, or even get *out* of the classroom.

Our brains crave novelty and movement. The reticular activating system (RAS), a collection of neurons connecting the brain stem to the cortex, acts, as Almarode and Miller (2013) put it, "like the venetian blinds for the brain. Just as venetian blinds can be opened or closed to let sunlight in, an activated RAS controls the brain's response level to stimuli" (p. 69). When students sit for long periods of time, they will gradually lose interest in what the teacher is saying or doing. The lawn mower outside the window and the sound from the HVAC system in the room will serve to activate the RAS of student after student, until many or most of them are what would be referred today as offline. They've punched out, even as they sit up straight and smile at the teacher. Teachers who do not understand what is going on here will sometimes carry on regardless; they will continue to describe something, explain something, or simply talk in a way that becomes monotonous to students who are relegated to being passive observers—they are *attendees.* There is one constant that reveals itself in even the most cursory inspection of classroom process: *Kids gotta move.*

Purposeful Movement in Classrooms

The happiest and most successful teachers I have observed over the past several years are those who purposefully and thoughtfully incorporate movement into their lessons. Many of these teachers look at movement and music as twin motivators for students—and for themselves. Movement can be used as a transitional piece between short periods of seatwork, and it can be used in conjunction with effective collaborative strategies to get excellent results. The combination of movement, music, and collaborative processing can be a powerful learning tool, and I have seen it used at every grade level from kindergarten on up. This leads us to explore options teachers have when it comes to harnessing the power of movement and student-to-student interaction.

Stand and Deliver. We have seen that standing sends more blood to the brain, and with it goes oxygen and glucose (the latter for energy). If there is a task that might have been done in the past while seated but can be done while standing, then I suggest teachers plan to have students stand and accomplish that task.

> Mrs. M. is about to read a short story to her second graders, and before moving them to the rug in one corner of her classroom, she has them stand behind their desks and pair up with a partner. She reveals on her screen a picture that is central to the story she is about to read, and she invites her students to share with their partners what they see and what they think the accompanying story might be about. While her students are talking with one another, Mrs. M. walks around the room and asks two students if they would be willing to share what they discussed with the entire class. She brings the discussion to a halt and asks those two students to

share, after which she gets two or three others to talk about what they discussed. She has them thank their partners for sharing and then—to the accompaniment of some upbeat music—she moves them to the rug.

In this scenario, Mrs. M. understood that her students had been in their seats for a few minutes and would be seated on the rug for a few minutes more. She chose to harness the power of prediction by having students share with each other, and in some cases with the entire class, what they saw in the picture and what they thought the story might be about. Having them stand for four or five minutes before shifting them to the rug served as a nice change of state, and she was able to have them provide their own "hook" into the story itself. Looking at the picture on the screen could have been done while students were seated, but Mrs. M. also recognized that nothing was lost and much could be gained by having them stand for a bit before moving to the rug.

Break in Place. Many teachers I know find that transition points are welcome opportunities for students to stand and stretch or even do some simple exercises, and in the case of the following teacher, it provides an occasion to check for understanding before moving to the day's next phase of instruction.

In his middle school civics class, Mr. B. has just completed a short but intensive review of the purpose and functions of the Federal Reserve System, and it is time to do two things: (1) get his students standing and (2) see if they are ready to move beyond what they have been studying for the past couple of days. Before getting them up, Mr. B. has his students reach into the plastic pouches on the side of their desks and take out three small, white 3 oz. cups, placing them on the desktop. The inside bottom of each cup is painted a different color: green, yellow, or red. That done, Mr. B. has students stand and stretch a bit to the accompaniment of some upbeat music.

He then has them pair up and discuss what they know about the U.S. Federal Reserve System, with some prompts on the board as a springboard for the conversations. While they are still standing, he has four or five students share with the class what they discussed, and he clears up a couple of minor points.

The students know what they will do next; they understand that soon Mr. B. will ask them to hold up one of the three cups so he can identify the color. A student who understands the Federal Reserve System well enough to explain it to someone else will hold up the cup painted green on the inside so Mr. B. can see it clearly. The student who needs more examples or a bit more discussion or direct instruction will hold up the cup with a yellow bottom. Anyone who simply does not understand will display the red-bottomed cup. On his cue, the students hold up their cups until Mr. B. can view them all. On this occasion there are no red cups in sight, but there are a few yellow cups mixed in with the green. Mr. B. has them put down their cups, thank their partners for sharing, and they take their seats, putting their cups back in the plastic pouches hanging from their desks.

Based on what he just heard from their paired discussions, and from what he saw when they displayed the cups, Mr. B. decided to incorporate one more review activity the next day before moving to the next economics-related lesson. He had been using the cups to receive some quick student feedback for several weeks, and he had picked it up from another teacher who, along with Mr. B., knew full well the futility of asking students if they understood something by requesting a show of hands. No one was willing to admit to a lack of understanding in this very public way, but the anonymous nature of the white bathroom cups with the colored bottoms allowed them to let Mr. B. know if they felt comfortable with the material.

Burst of Energy. The preceding vignette probably took a total of maybe five or six minutes, and it took that long because our Mr. B. combined the standing break with a quick check for understanding. Teachers don't have to wait for transition points to get students up and exercising for a minute or so.

Ms. D's fourth graders are hard at work editing the second draft of a paragraph. They have been working for about five minutes, and Ms. D. asks them to finish their thoughts and put their pencils down. She has them stand while she throws a stack of index cards into the air so that they fly all over the room. She instructs the students to grab a card—any card, and stand behind their chairs. On each card is a picture of someone playing a musical instrument (brass, wood-wind, or percussion). Then, she tells them to put the card down and get ready to "play" their instrument, at which point she hits the play button on her remote. Out of the speakers in the corners of her room comes Glenn Miller's *In the Mood*. Ms. D. also has a card, and she begins to "play" a trombone. The students get into the act, and "instruments" spring up all over the place. To the sound of general laughter and a good deal of hamming it up on the part of many of her fourth graders, she brings it all to a halt inside of a minute or so. One person collects the cards while they all sit down and resume work on the essay—with a good many neurotransmitters (think dopamine and serotonin) cascading in their brains.

Ms. D. learned the hard way that many of her students had a difficult time concentrating on a single task for any length of time, so she set about working with other fourth-grade teachers on these short breaks that combined exercise and music. She and her colleagues created at least two-dozen such burst-of-energy activities that they then began to use on a daily basis. Ms. D.'s students enjoyed the breaks and seemed to be able to focus when they sat back down. It took less than ninety seconds from start to finish, but it was worth the effort and certainly worth the time it had taken for all five fourth-grade teachers to brainstorm the activities and begin to put them in place.

This works with seventh graders as well. I can remember having some jazz music playing when the kids came into my classroom. One of them began to "play" the trumpet. I chimed in with another instrument, brought several students up front, and before long we had a great little jam session going. A little gentle high fiving took all the "band members" back to their seats, and I used that same little energy booster on several occasions with different classes that year. Oxygen, glucose, and laughter make a powerful combination.

Gallery Walk. Much can be accomplished in a relatively short time if the activity is both focused and timed. Students who have been sitting for several minutes working, perhaps on their own, may benefit from standing, walking, and sharing something in pairs, trios, or quartets. If students have been basically silent while they work at their desks, being able to walk and talk is a pleasant change. Teachers can create purposeful and thoughtful activities allowing students to review, brainstorm, or reflect with their peers in something that lasts several minutes.

> Mrs. G. has attached to her classroom walls six vertical cork boards to which she can attach posters, pictures, text, or anything else her students can contemplate in groups while traveling from board to board, and she has numbered the stations one through six on cards affixed to the frames that secure the cork boards to the wall. Today, after her fourth graders have spent part of the past several days on addition, subtraction, and multiplication, Mrs. G. has posted a large white sheet of paper on each board. One board has the number 26 at the top of the paper, while another has the number 85. Each of the six stations, in fact, has a different number. She has her students count off one through six, and she has each numbered group move to the corresponding chart. She gives each group a fine-tipped marker of a different color and instructs students to switch recorders as they move from chart to chart.
>
> Mrs. G. has the groups (quartets) face her as she explains that they will begin where they are and, when the music stops, finish what they started and move to the next chart in clockwise fashion. They have done this before and they have the process down, so she moves to the content piece. They are to face the chart and agree on any number of "questions" for the answers on

the chart. For example—and she models this using a number on her whiteboard—if the answer is 40, then one question would be "What is the sum of 20 + 20?" Another would be, "What is the sum of 15 + 5?" She records two "questions" relating to subtraction, and then instructs the recorder to check with everyone in the group before writing something on the chart. She also tells students they should check the math on the next chart before adding questions of their own. Finally, Mrs. G. moves to a chart and records a question to give them an idea as to the relative size of their entries.

Moving back to the front of the room, Mrs. G. asks if there are any process-related questions and then begins the music and tells the students to begin. She times each segment at about thirty seconds, at which point she stops the music, and tells them to go to the next chart. She continues this pattern until each group is back at its original chart. She then instructs them to check the math one more time, has them thank their group members for sharing, and has them return to their seats to the accompaniment of an upbeat piece of music.

A few weeks earlier, Mrs. G. had seen this gallery walk activity used in another classroom and simply adapted it to her fourth-grade math curriculum. This eight-minute activity allowed her students to practice their computational skills while standing and talking in a purposeful way. Mrs. G. traveled around the room and was able to follow each group's relative progress based on the different colors. If after two stations had been visited she noticed a lack of effort on the part of the group using the red marker, for example, she could work with that group or simply stand behind them for a few seconds until their output increased. The important thing here is that it is the students who were doing the work from start to finish; the task for Mrs. G. was to facilitate process and to use this activity as a check for understanding before moving temporarily past addition, subtraction, and multiplication to division.

The gallery walk Mrs. G. used in the vignette is a great way to get students up, moving, and sharing. In classrooms where wall space is limited, the posters or whatever else students need to see and write on can be placed on flat surfaces anywhere in the room. In one classroom I observed a few years ago, the elementary teacher had large sheets of paper at various counters and desks throughout the room when students returned from lunch. On each sheet of paper were several sentences or fragments. The students, traveling from station to station in pairs, were instructed to correct the grammar and turn whatever fragments they found into complete sentences. When the music started, they moved to the next station in clockwise fashion. The whole activity took no more than ten minutes, but students had an opportunity to ponder over and fix dozens of pieces of copy—and they loved it. There were enough sentences and fragments

> Consider what activities accomplished normally as seatwork can be done standing. . . .

on each sheet to ensure that each pair could get to at least four stations and still see new material. The teacher circulated around the room; when the students were finished, she had them take their seats while she went to the board to prepare a bit of impromptu direct instruction on several things she noticed when she walked around the room visiting the pairs as they worked. While they were engaged, she was checking for understanding by observing what they wrote and listening to the various conversations.

All of this, of course, could have been accomplished at their seats, working individually, in typical worksheet fashion, but here was a case of being able to pair students up, get them moving and sharing, play some upbeat music during the transitions, and check for understanding—all in ten minutes. If there is something teachers normally do while students are seated that can be done with them standing and moving, *the change is beneficial for the students.* In the case of the gallery walks, it does take a good deal of work up front for teachers who have to set up the charts or posters, but the results I have witnessed over the years make it well worth the extra effort.

Reflecting and Processing. I always recommend that video clips be kept short; students should always be given time after viewing a short clip to reflect on what they saw and then ask questions. There is no better time to have students stand, move, and talk than after they have been sitting for several minutes watching a video segment.

Mr. L. has his seventh-grade American history classroom arranged so that the student desks are clustered around the classroom perimeter, as shown in Figure 3.1. The desks are in quads, and each student has an automatic shoulder partner and face partner at all times. Each nine weeks, Mr. L. moves his students to different seats, but the furniture is left where it is, and the center of the room is always open for student movement and interaction. Notice that the teacher's desk is in the corner, not in front; this allows for even more student movement and interaction.

Figure 3.1
Created by Brian T. Jones.

On this occasion, Mr. L. has just shown a video clip dealing with the triangular trade of colonial times, one that stressed the conditions on the slave ships bound from Africa to the American colonies. As soon as the video is done, Mr. L. has everyone stand

and form a square around the outside limits of the open area in the middle of the classroom. Mr. L. shares something that struck him about the video clip and then throws a soft medium-sized ball to a student across the square. His instructions are to contribute something and then toss the ball to another classmate, at which point that student must share something different.

After several students have shared, Mr. L. takes the ball back and asks a question he has about the film's content. Having thus modeled a question, he has the students pair up in place and talk about questions they may have. Having thus primed the group so they are in question mode, he takes the ball and passes it to someone he knows came up with a good question during the paired discussions. The ball gets passed several more times, while Mr. L. charts the questions so they can work with them later on. Finally, Mr. L. has students give gentle high fives all around, and they return to their seats to the accompaniment of an upbeat song.

Here is something Mr. L. has discovered over the years: Students who just stare at a screen with nothing to do when the film clip is done are tacitly invited to sit passively and daydream during the video. However, he has found that when he follows the video clip with the kind of reflection and processing in the preceding vignette, his students pay attention to a much greater extent than before; when the clip is done, they have something to do that relies to a great extent on what they just saw and heard. Their questions give him direction for the next phase of the discussion. Importantly, his students moved from their seats to their feet and back again within a total of about thirty minutes. His experience has been that the processing his seventh graders do while standing helps them understand and remember what the film was meant to convey, and their subsequent questions allow him to go deeper into the subject material on all or any one of those questions—surfaced from *them*, not from the textbook.

Music as a Prime Motivator and Mood Lifter

While setting up for a workshop in a hotel ballroom years ago, I uncharacteristically waited to play some upbeat music until thirty minutes prior to the session. (Kicking off a playlist on my iPod is normally the first thing I do after entering the room to set up; in this case I simply forgot to turn on the music on my arrival.) At each of the doors connecting the ballroom with the hallway, there were students from the school district handing out brochures to teachers and administrators as they entered. A few people had come into the room at that point, and the students made sure they each had a brochure. They were polite, but they were not displaying much energy . . . until I played the first song from the playlist,

Happy, by Pharrell Williams. The students went from just handing out brochures to greeting people with a smile and singing and moving in time to the music. This one song, along with those that followed in the playlist, seemed to motivate them and lift the moods of over a dozen students. Their somewhat mundane task had been transformed with some feel-good music. It had the same effect on the hundreds of educators entering the ballroom. Music is a sure-fire mood lifter.

In one third-grade classroom, the teacher played some upbeat music while students entered the room, and she occasionally danced with them as they went through the mental checklist of things that needed to be done before class started. It was a snowy day, and students came in all bundled up and sniffling, only to be greeted by an exceptional teacher and some great music that set the tone for the day—snowstorms notwithstanding. In a middle school classroom, students transitioned from seatwork to a standing pair share by singing along with Aly & AJ's *Walking on Sunshine.* In two fifth-grade classrooms where teachers across the hall from each other team taught every day, students filed out of one room and into the other to *Pretty Woman,* by Roy Orbison. The driving beat that starts that song sent them from their seats into a single-file line, ready to cross the hall at a verbal cue from the teachers. The students often high-fived each other as they changed rooms, and they loved it.

Allen and Wood (2013) call this pump-up music, and recommend it be used as students enter or leave the room, as well as during transitions from one activity to another, or for cleaning up at the end of the class period or the end of the school day. If upbeat music like this can put students in a better mood at the front end of a long day, a class period, or a block, teachers would do well to try it. One Virginia middle school teacher told me it made all the difference in the way students entered her classroom. There is a physiological basis for this, according to Allen and Wood:

> When we hear a feel-good song, we get a rush of dopamine in the pleasure/reward centers of our brains. This is the feeling you get when your favorite song comes on the radio—it's like taking a giant bite of chocolate or the first sip of your favorite latte or parking all day without feeding the meter and not getting ticketed or . . . anything else that makes you feel good! It's an instant shot of pleasure. (p. 23)

I have observed in countless classrooms where this kind of feel-good music lifts everyone's mood, and that, by the way, includes the teacher.

Teachers often come to school dragging a bit, coming off a sleepless night or a longer-than-normal session grading tests or essays the night before. When I taught at the middle school level in Virginia Beach, I was normally the first one at school. The first thing I did when I got to my room was to play a dozen or so of my favorite songs. By the time my students began to arrive, I was in a good mood no matter what shape I was in when I arrived much earlier in the morning. Students have a right to expect their teachers won't start the day in a grumpy mood.

Just as the third-grade teacher I mentioned earlier uses upbeat music to begin her day with students, a British primary teacher, Holly Osborne, uses "a calming, relaxing CD, which calms them at the beginning of the day. I put the music on as I go outside to collect the children so that it is on as we enter" (as cited in Allen & Wood, 2013, p. 55). Teachers at every grade level can experiment with both upbeat and slower, calming music at various times during the day or class period.

My experience is that some students will say they think the use of music is silly; when teachers continue to use it over time, however, even students who claimed not to like classical music or other easy-listening tunes will learn to accept it, and even like it. I used to play a bit of Baroque classical music as my students worked in a twenty-minute study hall our middle school team set up at the end of the school day. During that time, students who needed help in a particular subject could to go the teacher who could assist them with whatever content they were struggling with at the moment, and everyone else used it to begin their homework or read. One afternoon I forgot to hit the start button on the cassette player (this dates me, I know), and one of my seventh graders asked me if I could play the Vivaldi. *A seventh grader asked me to play the Vivaldi.* I played the Vivaldi and followed it with a bit of Mozart.

I highly recommend the book I have cited in these paragraphs, *Rock 'n' Roll Classroom,* by Rich Allen and W. W. Wood (2013). It is, I believe, the definitive work on the use of music in classrooms, and contains gobs of research on the value and effect of using music with kids. Mood and energy levels are important no matter the grade level or subject area, and music has its uses . . . it's also not an expensive undertaking for class-room teachers.

Working Exercise Into the Curriculum

It is important for teachers to create and maintain an environment conducive to learning. A key learning-climate component is movement, and teachers should build opportunities for movement into their daily lessons. We are not always talking about the kind of exercise possible in PE or outside during recess. Making movement a regular part of classroom activities gives students a break. The teachers in the preceding examples have acted on this knowledge by purposefully incorporating movement into their lessons.

In *The Kinesthetic Classroom: Teaching and Learning Through Movement,* Traci Lengel and Mike Kuczala (2010) provide an entire chapter filled with simple exercises teachers can do in the classroom, and they list several "windows that present an ideal opportunity to prepare the brain for learning" (p. 44). These are either transition points during the school day or class period, or occasions when the teacher realizes it is time to give students a break and get them ready for whatever activity is next:

- At the start of the day
- Before diving into an academic goal
- Between academic activities
- When students show signs of boredom
- When students appear restless
- Before, during, and after testing
- While teaching and reviewing academic content (p. 44)

While observing in an elementary classroom several years ago, the students had just completed a fairly lengthy and rigorous writing activity, and the teacher realized it was time for a brain break. She went to her computer and brought up a video on the screen. Several teachers at the school had banded together to record a two-minute segment of exercises accompanied by some upbeat music. Every teacher in the school had access to the video, and the kids loved both the exercise and the opportunity to see their teachers letting go a bit. A fifth-grade teacher at another school had her students pause during a math quiz and do something called the Chicken Dance (yes, I did it, too!) before going back to the quiz. This math teacher had her students moving a great deal, and her math scores were through the roof.

Some teachers use natural transition points between activities to get kids up and exercising. Fifth graders in one Northern Virginia classroom were all standing as I entered the classroom with the building principal. They had been sitting for several minutes, and the teacher had moved them away from their desks, doing some simple exercises while some upbeat music played in the background. One of the exercises had them raise a knee as they tried to touch it with the opposite elbow. These cross lateral exercises are important because students cross the midline (an imaginary line running vertically down the middle of the body). There were perhaps a half dozen different common exercises these particular fifth graders did over the course of a couple of minutes, and it set them up for the lesson component that came next. Jensen (2005) affirms that movement and learning are connected: "Evidence from imaging sources, anatomical studies, and clinical data shows that moderate exercise enhances cognitive processing" (p. 67). Even a modest and impromptu bit of exercise can give students a break from the kind of seatwork that can ordinarily leave them a bit numb if it goes on too long.

Many teachers will have students identify permanent partners with whom they can pair during the school year whenever the teacher wants to use standing pair shares in the classroom. Tate (2010) recommends the use of the appointment clock at all grade levels. Students have a clock drawn or printed on a piece of paper, then stand and make four "appointments" with four different classmates. Once the appointments are made, each student has a permanent 3:00, 6:00, 9:00, and 12:00 partner. Students learn quickly who these four partners are, and teachers can move them quickly into standing pairs to discuss anything related to content. I have seen this used all the way from kindergarten to the twelfth grade. This is particularly useful in middle or high school settings, where teacher talk tends to predominate.

I can remember when districts around the country began the move to block scheduling, and I recall high school teachers who recoiled at the prospect of having to expand from fifty to ninety minutes. The whole idea of adding up to forty minutes to a single class period was particularly painful for teachers who were already lecturing for most of the shorter classes. Williams and Dunn (2008) encourage those operating on a block schedule to incorporate such strategies as having students work on graphic organizers together or simply stand and move a bit as they work on common tasks (p. 17). My suggestion is that high school teachers consider what activities accomplished normally as seatwork can be done standing, with students processing, reflecting, and brainstorming in pairs, trios, or quartets. In the space of a ninety-minute block, students could transition from standing to sitting several times. Once again, upbeat music can accompany those transitions.

Teachers can also seek out colleagues who already incorporate movement into their lessons as a matter of course. Additionally, it may be helpful for districts to bring teachers who use such strategies together at all three levels to brainstorm whole lists of strategies related to movement that can be adapted for any content area. I always encourage administrators to make it possible for teachers to observe other teachers, even for short periods of time, so that those observing can get a sort of balcony view, free of the need to actually teach the class and subsequently free to watch the students as well as the teacher. The idea in all these cases is to essentially go viral with strategies and content-specific activities that incorporate movement as a way to enhance learning.

Finally, the best way to model the kinds of interactive strategies that incorporate movement is in adult workshops run by teachers or administrators who can structure the time in such a way *that the workshop itself mirrors what ought to be happening in classrooms.* Too often, professional-development sessions amount to a series of "talking heads" who simply give teachers information and thus demonstrate to teachers what *not to do* in their classrooms. Building principals who schedule passive sessions where teachers become attendees rather than participants tacitly encourage teachers to follow suit, employing more teacher talk and less student interaction and movement.

Final Thoughts

The classroom vignettes in this chapter have at least two things in common. First, they incorporate movement or moderate amounts of exercise, or both, into the curricular mix. Second, students are actively and productively engaged in their own learning; the role of the teacher in each case is that of process facilitator.

The tools available to students and teachers today are far greater in number, to stay the least, than those available to us when I started teaching in 1971. However, one thing has not changed. To learn and remember, students must move up and down the cognitive ladder from knowledge to comprehension all the way to evaluation (and creativity and innovation) on a regular basis. It is simply not enough for students to sit and "pay attention" in any classroom at any level. It is they who must do the explaining, describing, summarizing, analyzing, and synthesizing. Students who want to be good citizens must be able to evaluate on their own what they see and hear in the media and online. The companies for which today's students eventually work may well value critical thinking, collaboration, and effective communication as part of the daily routine. One of the ways students can develop their social discourse and critical-thinking skills, and simultaneously deal with and understand important content, is by processing information collaboratively in pairs or groups; this is the subject of Chapter 4.

4

Reflection and Discourse

Algebra II in the tenth grade was my last stop on the math train, and as a high school senior, I was an indifferent physics student. I freely admit that I went to what I considered to be a better place in my mind on many occasions during those math and science classes, and perhaps in other subjects as well. Such interaction as existed in my physics class came in the form of an occasional lab. The information flow was basically one-way, unless the physics teacher asked a question and sought an answer from among the faithful. I can honestly say I did not answer too many of his questions, and on one particular occasion, I blurted out an answer whispered in my ear by one of my friends sitting right behind me. I had on my desk a list of the songs our garage band would perform at Friday night's dance, when I heard the physics teacher say, "Well, Mr. Nash, what is the answer?" This was, of course, the first I had heard that there had been a *question*, but from the seat behind me came a whispered, "Pi R squared." I obediently blurted out, "Pi R squared!" and immediately understood—from the considerable laughter in the room—that my answer in no way came close to fitting the question, and my friend had done me in and sold me out. The question had to do with why hot air rises, or something along those lines.

Thinking back on those years, the information flow in most of my classrooms was from the teacher to the students and from selected students back to the teacher. Our teachers filled the blackboard with notes while we, in turn, copied everything down in our notebooks. The idea of standing, moving into a pair or trio, and processing what we had just heard or seen was, I would have to say, extremely rare. While there were no end-of-year state tests to take, we covered the subject matter at a pretty fast clip, often driven by the textbook.

My favorite high school course was English, and I must admit I actually enjoyed going to the board and diagramming sentence after sentence. In doing this, I got to stand, move, and engage in a struggle with verbs, subjects, predicates, and prepositional phrases. I'm pretty sure not everyone shared my love of diagramming, but we learned sentence structure and the parts of speech that way—and we were engaged. Some classrooms had blackboards on three walls, so most of us could stake a claim to a small piece of the action, made easier by the fact that the English teacher placed a tall student between two shorter ones, thus maximizing the available space and giving her the chance to check our work as she circulated in her role as quality-control supervisor. When it appeared that most of us were done, she would ask us to check the work of those nearest us at the board. On those occasions when *math* teachers put us at the board, I approached this with all the anticipation of a sixteenth-century Protestant who found himself in the clutches of the Grand Inquisitor. The difference between my performance with diagramming and doing math at the board was my relative facility with sentence structure and equations. I loved one and hated the other.

In most of my high school classes, we were not really encouraged to reflect or process information with a neighbor. The expectation was that we would reflect on our notes and process the information at home. When it came to the ubiquitous worksheets in those courses, it was sink or swim and "do your own work." I swam in English and sank in Algebra. I knew it or I didn't, and if my class notes in English were a godsend, my notes in Algebra were gobbledygook. Many of my classmates, of course, were of a different view. For them, English was painful and math was a breeze. In math, I needed to slow down, reflect more often, and have the benefit of far more examples. In English, I might have helped some of my classmates had we slowed down enough to allow for such reflection and assistance. In Algebra, I have no doubt there are those among my peers who might have helped me shift that D to a C (something that would have qualified as a major accomplishment or at least a minor miracle). My senior English teacher came closest to understanding the value of collaboration when she had us work with a neighbor at the board while we diagrammed sentences.

College courses, with the exception of one philosophy course taught by a professor who constantly posed questions and gave us time to process and reply in a way I found refreshing, were simply an extension of my high school experience. One professor actually read from a set of yellowed notes while he chain-smoked his way through a ninety-minute class twice each week. We took our own copious notes and otherwise passed the time by counting the number of cigarettes he smoked. He rarely paused long enough to ask questions, and we were, as was the case in so many classes, simply attendees. We *attended* his class. We were not really participants in any meaningful sense of the word.

I'm painting a bleak picture here, and I should say that many of my high school teachers and college professors and instructors were quite interesting and, on occasion, entertaining. My favorite professor told wonderful stories and brought British history to life in countless ways. Many were possessed of a wonderful sense of humor, and most of them certainly "knew their stuff." Others, especially in graduate school, led us in focused class discussions of many different and eminently interesting topics. Absent most of the time, as I look back now, was student-to-student interaction and the opportunity to pause after a few minutes of teacher talk for a few minutes of interactive processing. We were expected to write it all down, take it all in, and spit it all out on quizzes and exams.

These (frequent) summative assessments marked the end of one chapter or unit, and then we moved on to another. I remember, and not fondly, all-night cram sessions where I tried to retain in short-term memory enough information to get me through whatever quiz or test was scheduled for the next day. With few exceptions, this was an individual effort; study groups were rare in my undergraduate experience. True understanding or long-term retention of the material took a backseat to getting ready for the test. Teachers and professors need grades; quizzes and tests give them those grades; therefore, they are scheduled at regular intervals and students tend to relax after the last one until the next one is on the horizon, at which point a flurry of "studying" (and cramming) pave the way for the next test and the next recorded grade.

Today, of course, we have a much better understanding of how the brain works and learns, and we know how critical to understanding reflection and processing can be. Whether those opportunities to process newly presented information are face-to-face or online through a structured blogging exercise, digital natives can be trained to speak clearly, listen actively, and draw new inferences based on the analysis of information that is deeper and more meaningful in the face of multiple perspectives and insights. Teachers at every grade level and in every subject must give students time to reflect on what they have heard or seen, and opportunities for processing in pairs, trios, or quartets must be provided on a regular basis. Simply "covering" the material is not enough; students do not learn by osmosis. The fact that students have immediate access to more information than ever twenty-four hours a day makes it even more important that we work with them to reflect on and process that information.

Classroom conversations are often limited to teacher-to-student discussions that often take place while the other students simply tune out. The teacher often asks a question (initiation), finds someone willing to answer it (response), at which point the teacher lets the responder and everyone else know whether the response was right on the money, just okay, or flat-out wrong (evaluation)—a process known as IRE. The initial question is often of the closed variety, seeking a single right answer. The object is to get the right answer, and teachers, affirms Hattie (2012), "can involve all students in IRE, but it is usually through a choral answer, and many students learn to 'play the game' and thus are physically present, passively engaged, but psychologically absent" (p. 81). This means that at any given time in the IRE cycle, very few students are actively engaged. The rest have learned how to hide in plain sight.

What Doesn't Get Tested Gets Left Out

In our hurry to cover the curriculum (much of it now dictated by the ubiquitous state standards), we as teachers often don't take the time to slow down and make certain students truly understand the material. Other important skills and information are left out altogether. As we saw in Chapter 2, as companies compete in an increasingly global and ever-more competitive marketplace, they value communication skills, including those related to oral language. One might conclude, therefore, that it is important for students to be trained to be articulate speakers and careful listeners, but my experience is that students often do not get a workout on the comprehension rung of the cognitive ladder (where one cements understanding by explaining, describing, or summarizing) for the simple reason that these skills are not reflected in the end-of-year, multiple-choice testing. Teachers often admit that the reason they do not focus on the oral components of the communication skill set is for this very reason. What is not tested often does not get taught.

Yet it is critical that students learn to communicate effectively, and oral communication is important. When I was a sales manager, I interviewed dozens of prospective sales applicants, and those who spoke in an inarticulate manner were simply not hired. As a manager I had no remedial program; I needed sales people who could communicate clearly and effectively with clients and potential clients. Today's companies—and there are many more sales and service-oriented firms than there were when I was in sales in the 1980s—look for people who can both speak and write effectively.

Herein lies a problem. When I was growing up in the 1950s and 1960s, McDonald's was still a relatively new phenomenon, and most meals were prepared and eaten at home, and attendance was mandatory. This meant whole families spent a good deal of time at the breakfast, lunch, and dinner table—and we learned to converse with adults, siblings, and anyone else who showed up for dinner. At my best friend's house next door, the conversation *began* at the dinner table (and lasted at least forty minutes), and then moved to the kitchen as I helped wash or dry (my choice as a guest) the dishes. Breakfast and lunch (on weekends and during the summer) were also opportunities for these extended conversations with adults and friends. The fellowship at these meals amounted to valuable training by way of communication skill development.

More and more meals today are eaten on the run, in the car, or not at all. Every school year sees more students eating breakfast not at home, but at school. Some students now eat three meals a day at school. As each year passes, opportunities for students to have conversations around the dinner table diminish. (An architect recently told me many homes are now being built with no dining rooms at all, because formal dining on a semiregular basis is a thing of the past.) All this means that schools are going to have to step up to the plate (no pun intended), and teachers are going to have to provide students with opportunities to talk with each other in structured ways—in pairs, trios, quartets—in focused classroom discussions. Students need to be able to articulate well in oral conversation, and Keene and Zimmermann (2007) suggest that teachers "must help them develop the language to define and describe their thinking" (p. 40). If the development of oral language contributes to reading, as students talk about books they have read, and to written language, as Keene and Zimmermann affirm, then we as educators need to set aside time for student-to-student conversation and dialogue. Students must learn to articulate a position clearly and defend that position, even as they see merit in the points of view of others.

> It is the students who need to be doing the talking, for the simple reason that talking is learning.

In the interest of assisting students to be better communicators, teachers must set aside time in class to let students discuss what they have seen, read, or heard in small groups or class discussions led by a teacher who models the kind of communication skills she wants students to develop. This means teachers must *model* the kinds of listening skills (eye contact, appropriate body language, not interrupting, pausing for reflection, asking for clarification when necessary, and paraphrasing in a way that lets students know we are trying to understand what they are communicating). These skills then surface for the teacher to post on the classroom wall as part of the classroom routine. This does take some preparation on the part of teachers. Schmoker (2011) reminds us that "a good discussion is not a free-for-all" (p. 85), and I would add that classrooms must become laboratories for respectful and focused communication between and among students and teachers.

It is not just communication skills students are developing when they talk. Talking is thinking, and when students simply sit quietly in passive mode, they are not able to process information. Students encounter new information in classrooms all day long, and they need time for reflection and interdependent processing with other students. Many teachers will not take the time to make these conversations happen; the perceived pressure of time and a brimming curriculum may work against such collaborative efforts. This has consequences. According to Allen and Currie (2012),

> Preventing students from talking prevents the likelihood of them embedding the new material in long-term memory. Transferring information from our short to our long-term memory requires *processing.* For some students, figuring out the worksheet will be sufficient processing to encode the memory. But for many students, this level of processing only occurs when they talk. Working in silence deprives them of this critical processing step, resulting in them quickly losing all memory of the new material. (p. 5)

For many teachers and students, collaborating in even the simplest of paired conversations marks a great leap forward, but such conversations enhance memory and facilitate the development of good communication skills.

The Common Core State Standards (CCSS) for Speaking and Listening provide a framework for teachers who want to help students develop their communication and collaboration skills. Divided into Comprehension and Collaboration, along with Presentation of Knowledge of Ideas, these standards have kindergarten students participating in conversations with peers in pairs and in larger groups. The students learn to seek clarification by asking questions and follow agreed-upon rules for these conversations. Although these standards are under the Language Arts umbrella, these skill sets for communication, collaboration, and critical thinking can be—and should be—used in every K–12 subject area. States not currently using the CCSS have their own oral language components, and all these standards, if used, can help students become effective at communicating and collaborating in school, in the workplace, and in life.

Ramp Up Administrative Support

If students are to become more actively engaged in their own learning, and if collaboration is an essential component of classroom life, then communication skills are important facilitators of the continuous-improvement process. "Students who have well-developed vocabulary, listening, and speaking skills," asserts Zacarian (2013), "are far more likely to be successful than are students who do not possess these much-needed school language skills" (p. 73). Furthermore, if students are not coming to school with these oral language skills, then teachers and their administrators must clear the decks for their successful development. We should do this not only in support of other content; learning to master these important skills *is* the content.

Administrators should encourage the institutionalization of efforts to improve the oral communication skills of students and teachers alike. This should include professional-development sessions where someone skilled in initiating and facilitating teacher- and student-led conversations models exactly what needs to be done, and then has everyone participate over and over again in the process, using concrete examples from various subject areas to connect with those who teach those subjects. This should also include taping in classrooms where teachers regularly incorporate student-to-student conversations where those students explain their thinking, process information, ask questions or paraphrase to clarify understanding, and demonstrate appropriate body language and facial expressions as a matter of course.

My suggestion is that once these clips (short . . . just a few minutes at the most) are edited and all the permissions are obtained, teachers should be brought together in small groups to view the tapes. Facilitators can, once teachers have viewed the clip, ask the teachers to discuss in pairs or groups what they just saw and heard. It is, I believe, important to begin with *the teachers'* facilitated discussions, rather than by saying something to the effect of, "We want you to view these tapes and do what *these* teachers do!" Let teachers simply watch the video and then reflect on and process in small groups what they have seen and heard, followed by a general large-group discussion of what was effective, why it was effective, what can be used, and where it can be used in content areas. The district (or a principal) can also take the time and spend the money to train coaches who can visit various classrooms and model strategies like pair share, paired verbal fluency, and other powerful instructional tools intended to improve the communication skills of students and increase their understanding of material. The teachers can then have students practice the strategies themselves.

Whether it is through training, classroom tapes, or the use of coaches—or all three—it is necessary that students get to practice these oral-communication and listening skills. Students cannot be *told* what makes a good listener; they must actually get plenty of experience at listening against a rubric that constantly reminds them of the standard. Students cannot be *told* how to describe and articulate their thinking; they must learn through experience how it is done. Students cannot be *told* how to summarize, clarify, or otherwise seek to understand; they must have plenty of opportunities in all their classes to do just that. However, having students share in pairs or talk with each other in larger groups will not happen unless at least three conditions are part of the mix from kindergarten through Grade 12:

1. The teacher must create an environment conducive to student interaction. Students who feel that it is not safe to share will not do so.

2. A set of ground rules for sharing and some sort of basic rubric for the skills related to listening must be put in place the first week of school.

3. Teachers should model what it is they want students to do, and to avoid confusion and wasted time, directions for activities should be chunked.

Create an Environment Conducive to Student Interaction

When teachers ask students to discuss something in pairs, trios, or quartets without first creating a safe classroom climate, confusion and chaos can result—and quickly. Teachers must model the following in their classrooms:

- A calm demeanor, even and especially in the face of provocation
- Respect for students and for other adults who come into the classroom
- The absence of sarcasm or humiliation, along with a refusal to accept either on the part of students
- Listening without interrupting and responding without judging
- Modeling good eye contact, neutral or supportive facial expressions, and positive body language

This is a lot to think about, perhaps, but if teachers really want students to successfully interact with peers, then modeling appropriate social behaviors must be job one during the first weeks of school. The teacher who posts a wonderful and carefully thought-out set of social norms on the wall and then proceeds to act contrary to many, most, or all of them during the first week of school, might as well take the list off the wall and consign it to the trash can. Students are nothing if not perceptive, and they will see the contradictions right away. Whoever said that if we don't model what we teach we are teaching something else was right on the money.

Teachers must be careful and thoughtful about their responses to what students say in the classroom. If the teacher asks a question and meets a student's answer with sarcasm, a rolling of the eyes, or hostility or humiliation, the interactive game is over for that student at least, and perhaps for a large segment of the classroom population. Teacher responses must be neutral or supportive in a way that encourages further participation on the part of the student. Bluestein (2008) says it well: "Teacher responses that interfere with children's ability to own, feel, express, or process their feelings can block communications, teach children to mistrust their own feelings and perceptions, and interfere with the development of their problem-solving capabilities" (p. 225). Remember, the idea is to have a classroom full of participants and not a classroom jammed with attendees. This means that from the moment a teacher first meets and greets his students at the classroom door on day one, he is modeling the kind of social norms and listening skills he will expect from them.

Teacher–student relationships are incredibly important, and the effect size of powerful relationships is high (.72); Hattie (2009) says the establishment and maintenance of such relationships "requires skill by the teacher—such as the skills of listening, empathy, caring, and having positive regard for others" (p. 118). In one incredibly student-centered classroom where we interviewed all the students at length, they all agreed that being with the teacher and each other every day was like being with family. I've been in teacher-centered classrooms, by contrast, where one could cut the tension with a knife. Working relationships in environments like that are largely nonexistent. Classroom climate has an enormous impact on learning and the continuous-improvement process, and working relationships between and among teachers and students are critical components of a positive climate.

Excellent teacher–student relationships are fueled by teachers who take the time to find out what makes those students tick. Excellent teachers go out of their way to find out—and connect with—what actually *interests* students. The three teachers to whom this book is dedicated did that with me. Good teachers, like good mentors, don't just say, "My door is always open!" and leave it at that. "Indeed," says Gordon (2006), "students tend to be highly attuned to those teachers who initiate and cultivate positive relationships with their students, as opposed to those who deem it sufficient to make themselves available" (p. 158). Teachers who have taken the time to build those connections with their students are much more likely to find them willing to take risks like collaborating in pairs or groups.

Standards Related to Listening and Speaking

When I was in sales in the 1980s, a school principal once shared with me why I did not get the yearbook contract for his school. He told me that all I did was *talk* during almost the entire half hour he had set aside for me to meet with him and his yearbook adviser. He said I never once asked either of them any questions that might have told me what they wanted in a yearbook representative; I thought selling (and getting the contract) depended on my ability to *talk,* whereas in reality selling is *listening.* That principal's feedback was painful in the short run, but priceless in the end. Thereafter, I paid much more attention to the company-sponsored seminars dedicated to developing listening skills, because effective communication is the lifeblood of sales. In making that critical mistake on that—and other—occasions, I was repeating the mistakes of several years of teaching prior to that; I was under the mistaken impression that teaching was telling and talking was selling.

In our headlong rush to get through a curriculum or a textbook, it is often difficult for teachers to slow down and do less talking and more listening. It is the students who need to be doing the talking, for the simple reason that talking is *learning*. Listening can be an effective teaching tool because it leads to understanding. My experience is that students—and adults—*know* instinctively and through experience what makes a good listener; they know, for example, that one should not interrupt the speaker, and they know that eye contact is important. Teachers, beginning in that first week of school, can enlist the students' help in surfacing the attributes of active and effective listening, and then model those skills every day. Students must see that the list of powerful listening skills posted on the wall is what the teacher is actually *doing*. Once the standards, perhaps in the form of a rubric, are in place, students can be brought actively into the process as participants. Before that can happen, though, the standards should be clear, and must be modeled by the classroom teacher.

Having been in hundreds of classrooms in the past couple of decades, I can say with certainty that there is one important communication skill that teachers need to support through practice, and this has to do with speaking. When teachers ask students to answer a question or otherwise articulate something in the classroom, student voices are often so soft and tentative that many in the room cannot hear them. On occasion, teachers will simply repeat what the student said and by so doing serve as an ad hoc amplification system. At other times, a teacher simply assumes everyone in the room heard the student's response or comment, nods her head, and moves on. Neither of these actions is good policy. Teachers who spend time repeating what students say are wasting that time; they are not helping students develop a speaking voice that is confident and effective. It may not be clear to the teacher standing right in front of the responder that no one else heard the response, but teachers who take the time to visit other classrooms or have their own classes videotaped from time to time will soon discover the problems here.

I encourage teachers to work with students to raise their volume and speak in a more articulate fashion. A teacher who models both is on the way to getting students to successfully and naturally mimic them, but I recommend that teachers have students respectfully say the following when they cannot hear a student's response or comment: "Louder please." Students should be encouraged to say this when peers are speaking too softly. A student trying to improve his listening skills relies on peers who are willing to speak clearly and loudly enough to be heard, and students should hold themselves and their classmates to a high standard.

Students need to learn how to communicate effectively in pairs and quartets, and in front of the entire class on occasion. When concentrating on processes during the first week of school, teachers can ask students to assist them in developing a checklist of effective speaking skills. As it is with listening, eye contact is critical, and students can work on keeping their gestures to a minimum while not holding on for dear life to a lectern or standing at attention. Hoff (1992) reminds us that speakers need to move and gesture: "When a speaker doesn't move, that's really making it difficult for any well-meaning audience to pay wholehearted attention. Static speakers produce listless audiences" (p. 84). Many teachers have had professors or high school teachers who leaned a little too heavily on a lectern and produced a listless student audience.

> One key to this entire process is that students are doing the work.

Teachers and students can work together to create a rubric that helps students understand just what a quality oral presentation entails. I used a rubric in my middle school classes in the early 1990s, and it worked well. It can contain items related to eye contact, body language, and gestures, and matters related to voice (volume, pitch, timing, and the use of the verbal distracters "um" or "ah"). Students can be taught to pause on occasion for emphasis, or ask questions of the audience. At the secondary level at least, students can practice stopping long enough to let classmates turn to someone else in a pair or trio and process what the speaker has said so far. My experience is that students can get better quickly, for the most part, if the standards are clear and there is plenty of time to practice and make mistakes in a safe classroom environment.

Structured Interactions

I have seen classrooms where the social chemistry is such that teachers are able to get students to pair up or work in groups with no problem at all; by this I mean that the students have done this enough that they are used to talking together as a matter of course. In these classrooms students feel perfectly comfortable sharing with peers and teachers alike. On occasions when I observe this, I know this did not just happen; teachers put in the frontloading necessary to ensure success and began laying the foundation for this during the first five days of school. In these classrooms, I often see a written list of behavioral norms for listeners and speakers alike, and it is much more than just a sterile listing—the norms have been successfully incorporated into the daily routine. In many cases, checklists and rubrics provide necessary scaffolding until students are proficient at speaking and listening.

I have seen students seriously discussing something they have just read or seen on a video clip, while sitting or standing. I recommend that if students have been sitting for several minutes, watching a video clip or listening to a short period of lecture, teachers move them into standing

Figure 4.1 Norm as a Distracted and Distracting Listener

Created by Brian T. Jones.

Figure 4.2 Norm as a Supportive Listener

Created by Brian T. Jones.

pairs or trios to process the information. Once again, given the right environment and the right training, this will not only give students a chance to process what they just saw or heard; it will provide them with a welcome *physical* state change as well. To practice specific skills like summarizing or asking for a point of clarification, however, teachers may want to provide more structure in a strategy called *paired verbal fluency* (PVF). I first encountered PVF (Lipton & Wellman, 2000) in 1995, when Laura Lipton and Bruce Wellman introduced it to central-office coordinators in the school district where I was employed at the time.

In PVF, students decide who will be "A" and who "B." The idea is for A to explain something for maybe thirty seconds, at which point the teacher says, "Switch!" At that point, B (the listener) proceeds to summarize what A said. The teacher then reverses the roles, and B talks while A listens. On cue, A summarizes what B has said. In this way, both partners get a chance to explain something and summarize the explanation. These two verbal skills (explaining and summarizing) both live in the comprehension level of the cognitive ladder. In the process of doing this, both get to practice using supportive and appropriate body language, facial expressions, as well as eye contact. This same structured conversation strategy can call for the listener to ask for a point of clarification: "You mentioned _____; tell me more about that." The job of summarizing or asking for a point of clarification each calls for the listener to actually . . . well . . . *listen!*

When two students are facing each other, body language can make or break the interaction. Both the speaker and the listener can drive each other crazy with off-the-wall gestures that can derail the conversation and serve as a distraction to other nearby pairs of students who are themselves trying to concentrate. Body language and facial expressions can also serve as barriers to a good discussion. Figure 4.1 shows Norm in distracting mode. I have had teachers tell me they feel comfortable standing with their arms crossed, and I hasten to tell them that while that is normal for many people, in this case, it is not about them—it is about the speaker; the closed nature of the crossed arms, along with a slight frown or a furrowed brow, can send a strong and negative message to the speaker. Figure 4.2 shows Norm in full supportive mode, with his hands comfortably at his sides and a smile on his face as he listens to his partner, Fred. Visuals are powerful, and teachers should make certain that students support each other completely; many students are naturally shy anyway, and need all the visual and auditory support the listener can give.

The key here is for teachers to model every step of PVF. If there is another teacher or teacher assistant in the room, the two adults can model the correct stance (Figure 4.2), decide who is A and who is B, and model it the whole way through twice. This gives students two chances to see PVF in action and to ask any questions they may have about process. The very first conversation they have, by the way, should be about something with which they are completely familiar (favorite vacation, favorite meal, etc.). *Only after students have the process down* should teachers shift gears to course content. Process comes first, with content introduced into the mix only when students know exactly what they are doing. Occasionally, a student will balk at taking part in these structured conversations. Rather than forcing him into it, instruct him to watch two other students who don't mind an observer; it may be that the reluctant participant actually gets drawn into the conversation, and I have had teachers confirm that. It may take a while, but most students will probably agree to participate in these conversations down the road a bit.

Once students get to the point where teachers can introduce course content into the PVF structure, I suggest those doing the speaking be allowed to bring a set of notes related to what they are going to discuss in pairs. Remember, this is not a quiz and students are not being evaluated on this; the idea is to get them used to working in the comprehension level of the cognitive ladder (explaining, describing, illustrating, summarizing). The time may come when the notes can be left behind, but for students to feel comfortable with the process, allowing them to have the notes with them may make the difference between success or failure during the discussion. The listener need only listen and summarize or ask for a point of clarification *based on what the speaker said*. When it is their turn to speak, the notes can come out of the pocket or off the desk.

It may be useful, once they have spent eight or nine minutes in a PVF activity, to have students connect with their own feelings about how they just did in a reflective journal. Reflective journal writing "provokes more reflection and encourages students to take charge of their learning and their feelings" (Burke, 2009, p. 112). A question for students who have gone back to their seats after a PVF discussion might be, "What is the easiest or hardest part of summarizing what the speaker said?" Burke distinguishes between reflective journals and reflective lesson logs, the latter of which "help students select key ideas from a lecture, discussion, or video and write down important facts, insights, or questions that will lead to better understanding" (p. 112). The combination of a learning log, in which students take down a few notes from a short teacher lecture, followed by a PVF activity where students can explain what they just heard (and summarize), followed by a reflective journal entry on dealing with the process-related issues surrounding this most recent PVF experience would accomplish the following:

- Writing in the reflective lesson log allows students some individual processing time to pull together what they just heard.
- Standing to go meet with a partner somewhere in the room gives students a break and the movement sends more blood (oxygen and glucose) to their brains.
- Being able to talk about what they have just heard and subsequently written into their learning logs gives them another opportunity to make connections and make sense of what they have just experienced.
- Writing in the reflective journal allows students to revisit the metacognitive side of the PVF experience. They can sort out their feelings and emotions in the journal and truly think about their thinking, perhaps in response to the question about the relative ease or difficulty of summarizing what someone else said.

One key to this entire process is that students are doing the work. The teacher begins with a short lecture on whatever the topic is, while students take a few notes or simply get ready to write in their learning logs.

Make Time for Reflection

If we want students to get better at explaining, summarizing, inferring, drawing conclusions, defending those conclusions, and solving sometimes complex problems, then we need to give them time to think about—and perhaps write in their reflective journals about—their thinking. Providing time for reflection is critical to understanding and memory, and, according to Williams and Dunn (2008), "For some students, it is only when time is allowed for reflection that lasting connections to the material are made" (p. 28). To teachers faced with going from a standard seven- or eight-bell format to a block schedule, chunking instruction becomes critical. High school students need to be able to get up and move, and shift instructional gears in a way that provides powerful metacognitive strategies. "Group discussions, metacognitive questioning, logs and journals, and graphic organizers are helpful processing tools and, perhaps, can be most efficiently employed during extended time blocks" (p. 28).

Simple pairing of students at their seats, standing pairs, PVF, journals and logs, and questions that go to process are all ways of giving students time to reflect, no matter the grade level. I observed a kindergarten class where students were paired up on the rug in the corner of the room. The teacher read part of a story to them, after which they turned to their partners and retold the story; the teacher then proceeded to tell the rest of the story, at which point the partner who had done the retelling became the listener. I watched another group of kindergartners travel in pairs to posters around the classroom, where they discussed with each other what they saw and what they liked about what they saw. In both cases, students were given the opportunity to develop their social skills and work at the comprehension level of the cognitive ladder.

We have seen that videos can be stopped frequently so that students can discuss what they have seen and heard. Teachers, according to Baloche (1998), can provide the structure of questions students have to answer or problems that need to be solved—all related to the video, lecture, or story. Teachers can also put students in pairs or groups to discuss the topic they will see in the video or hear in the story. The conversations help to surface prior knowledge and get students focused on what they will see or hear. Teachers can also, says Baloche, ask a question "that helps students summarize and synthesize the material that has been presented and provides closure for the lesson" (p. 101). Videos or lectures that are too long simply overwhelm students who may begin to feel like they have been trying to sip from a fire hose.

Success with collaborative reflection and processing requires at least two things. First, it requires planning on the part of the classroom teacher, who must be willing to set aside time for reflection and writing, reflection and paired conversations, or a more formal structure such as PVF. Second, the teacher must provide students with plenty of opportunities to practice what it takes to succeed in these conversations. Listening skills must be surfaced, discussed, and practiced. In one classroom recently, a first-grade teacher had students share with each other using regular voices and whisper voices. They had it down, and they did it right, but this did not just happen. That teacher committed to creating a community of learners in which students are used to working with everyone in the room on demand.

Go Vertical With the Planning

I can't count the number of times I have heard a middle school teacher pose the question, "What are those elementary teachers doing down there?" High school teachers say the same about their middle school colleagues, while college professors wonder what is happening in

> The blame game is rampant, but it solves nothing.

high school. The blame game is rampant, but it solves nothing. Time spent playing the blame game could be put to good use planning across grade levels in critical areas like reading, writing, and the development of skills related to oral communication, collaboration, and critical thinking.

Here are some questions that might help teachers plan vertically:

1. Exactly what do we want students to be able to do at each grade level related to meeting in pairs, trios, or discussion groups?

2. Who on staff is having particular luck with using collaborative techniques in the classroom, and how can we go viral with that in the building?

3. How would reflective journals and learning logs help with continuous improvement for students? Also, who uses reflective journals or learning logs regularly and to great effect in the building or district, and how can we tap into that success to benefit the rest of the students?

4. What specific speaking and listening skills ought to be introduced at each grade level, or, if that is already laid out in the state standards, what are some activities that would allow students to practice and improve those skills?

5. How is it that oral language skills reinforce writing, and what could we do to make sure that students enter the next grade level ready and able to take the next step?

6. What role does questioning play in cognition, and are there some questioning techniques (e.g., wait time) that could be used and improved at each level?

7. Is there a particularly effective classroom-based brainstorming model that could be introduced at a particular grade level and used thereafter, so that succeeding grade-level teachers don't need to reinvent the wheel?

8. What graphic organizers have proved effective in the building or district, and which can be introduced at what grade levels after some professional development to ensure they are used properly and effectively?

9. Because problem solving is going to be critical in the lives of today's students, both on personal and workplace levels, who on staff can research some strategies and activities that can be made part of the curriculum in a way to ensure students at every grade level are engaged in problem solving?

10. How can new best practices in the way of technology or graphic organizers be introduced on a regular basis with an eye toward improving communication, collaboration, and critical-thinking skill sets?

11. Finally, what resources can we consult that would contain best practices that might help us improve our delivery methods at each level?

Prepare, Practice, and Persevere

There is no question that if teachers want students to have any kind of deep understanding of a particular concept or topic, those students have to be given time to work with it. They have to reflect on what it means. They have to think about it, write about it, talk about it . . . *or they will forget about it.* Students cannot simply listen to the teacher or watch the video and have any hope of remembering or deeply understanding much, if anything, of what they saw or heard. The problem here is that many teachers don't think they have the time to stop and let students wrestle with the [proverbial] alligator. The students have to do the work, and in this case, it means they have to be provided with enough time to reflect, discuss, and ask questions.

Teachers must be willing to look at their lesson and unit plans with an eye toward removing some of the direct instruction (teacher talk) in favor of student interaction (student talk). This frightens some teachers, for a couple of reasons. First, they are afraid they will not be able to cover all the material. Second, they are not sure what students will do when given the chance to hold a conversation with a partner or in a trio or quartet. The train will go off the track. The car will swerve into the ditch. The world (read order and control) will end. My experience is just the opposite. When students are given the chance to talk about something and ask questions *on a regular basis,* especially if this replaces the passive nature of sitting and "paying attention" to the teacher, they will respond favorably. However, teachers need to stick with it and not run for the exits if it does not work the first time. Students who are not used to having these conversations, asking these questions, summarizing what another student says, or asking for a point of clarification when they don't understand are going to experience difficulties up front. This is to be expected. This is normal.

I would suggest the following for teachers unsure about how to proceed with at least some student interaction in the classroom:

- Take the time to ask your students if they remember more when they have the opportunity to pause and talk about something, than they do when they simply take notes for an entire block.

- Have a conversation about what listening really entails. What do we do when we actively listen? How do we act? What do we say? How should we stand?
- Create a checklist of listening skills, post them on the board, and discuss them one more time. Model active listening with another adult or with a student. Let the student talk while you model, and then lead the class in a discussion of how you did with the items on your listening checklist. Do the same with speaking skills.
- Let students stand, pair, and talk about something with which they are totally familiar (favorite restaurants, movies, books, etc.). While one partner talks, the other practices listening in an active manner. If they have reflective journals, this would be a great place for them to capture how they think they did as a speaker and as a listener.
- Cut the next lecture short, allowing students to stand and partner with someone with whom they can talk about what they just heard. Or stop the next video after just a few minutes, letting students stand and talk with a partner about what they just saw. Tell them they can take any notes they took with them for the conversation. (If they know they can do that, they may take more notes!)
- After the conversation, have the pairs look at the checklist and see how they did with each skill category (eye contact, positive body language, supportive facial expressions, asking questions when they don't understand).
- Finally, keep at it. Give students multiple opportunities every day or every class period or every block to discuss something with a partner—something they just saw, read, or heard in class.

I have been in scores of classrooms where teachers simply say, "Turn to your partner and. . . ." or "Talk with your face partner about. . . ." or "Face your shoulder partner and. . . ." In these classrooms, students are no longer shy about sharing. They are rarely befuddled when asked to talk with another student about anything. It is so ingrained in the standard practice in that classroom that they just do it; they process information, ask questions, offer suggestions, and disagree respectfully—all within the framework of student interaction. The teacher's job is to model and then facilitate process by circulating and listening to the conversations. Much can be learned from doing that; teachers who hear a good deal of misinformation can take the opportunity to clear some things up later on.

Teachers should *prepare* lessons that have opportunities for student interaction. Next, have students *practice* the art of respectful speaking and listening until they have the process down. Finally, teachers should learn to *persevere* in the face of obstacles. The teacher who gives in when students don't interact well in pairs or groups the first time is letting the students set the standards low. The idea is to work with them so they rise to a set of high standards.

Final Thoughts

We can no longer avoid taking time in class to allow students the opportunity to reflect individually and discuss content in pairs and groups. We need to get them out of their seats and into interactive lessons that will move them down their own continuous-improvement highways when it comes to the process skill sets that will be critical to their collective futures. This requires us to plan both horizontally and vertically in the schoolhouse and in the district at large. There are success stories out there that are not being shared, and we are losing kids in classrooms where the status quo is both powerful and obstructive. Unless teachers are willing to challenge and disrupt the status quo, students who are used to being highly interactive on their *own* time are no doubt feeling increasingly underserved on what they perceive as *our* time.

Finally, there are many ways listeners and speakers discussing something in pairs or participating in class discussions or student presentations can support each other. Appendix A is devoted to this mutual support on the part of students who may think listening is a largely passive role.

Two closely related elements of communication and collaboration can either serve as barriers to progress or become ingredients for understanding and continuous improvement. In Chapter 5 we'll explore perspective and empathy.

5

Perspective and Empathy

The context of our lives forms our perspectives; when we interact at a party, in a meeting, or in a classroom, our perspectives and points of view are often on display as we discuss politics, sports, course content, books, or movies. In paired conversations in class, or when communicating socially via the Internet, students run headlong into different perspectives from one or more friends, fellow students, or written sources. John Chaffee (2012), in *Thinking Critically* (10th ed.), speaks to the importance of perspective in life:

> To increase and deepen your knowledge, you must seek other perspectives on the situations you are trying to understand. You can sometimes accomplish this by using your imagination to visualize other viewpoints. Usually, however, you need to seek actively (and listen to) the viewpoints of others. It is often very difficult for people to see things from points of view other than their own, and if you are not careful, you can make the mistake of thinking that the way you see things is the way they really are. (p. 63)

Taking the time to consider the personal perspectives of others is all part of the critical-thinking process, and by doing so we can learn "to 'think emphatically' within other viewpoints, particularly those of people who disagree with our own" (Chaffee, 2012, p. 495). In classrooms where teachers are doing most of the talking, and where paired or group interactions are rare or nonexistent, students don't have opportunities to encounter and grapple with the points of view and perspectives of classmates in an academic setting. Opening the door to student-to-student discussions does present problems that teachers need to confront and deal with.

Content-centered conversations are often difficult for students, especially when they encounter a classmate's fiercely held point of view or a perspective different from their own. Students who have recently shifted to active mode have to learn how to process and then react to what a classmate has just said. "Unlike writing or passive listening," according to Zwiers and Crawford (2011), "conversation requires the skill of quickly processing and responding—without being able to push a button to forever delete a weak point or to move text around" (p. 15). The student who can learn to pause for a few seconds before responding can accomplish two things: She can use the time to process what she just *heard* before responding, and she allows the speaker to process what he just *said*. Taking the time to think before responding, come to think of it, would on many occasions save us all a great deal of trouble.

Teachers must model the kind of patient listening that lets students know their perspectives and points of view are respected. They can also demonstrate ways to seek out the perspectives of others as a way of increasing understanding. After a student has offered one perspective or point of view on something, a teacher might pause, look off to the side for a few beats, then look back at the speaker, saying, "What is another way to look at this?" or "What reasons do you have for thinking that?" or "Why might someone disagree?" (Marzano, Yanoski, Hoegh, & Simms, 2013, p. 43). That pause gives everyone time to think and reflect on what was just said.

Teachers can take the time to model this kind of out-loud thinking: "Having said what I just said, I can think of at least two other ways to explain this." or "Let me give you two reasons why I think this may be so." A teacher might also say, "Another point of view could be..." Students need to hear the language teachers and other adults use; students who have spent many years as passive observers may have no clue as to how to articulate what they may be thinking. They may need more than a little modeling, and then lots of practice in a safe classroom environment.

Student-to-student conversations in pairs, trios, or quartets require students to think on their feet. Perspectives and points of view naturally surface during discussions on various content-related topics or books students are reading. Such conversations, according to Keene and Zimmermann (2007), "can focus on the content of a book, the comprehension strategies children are using to understand it more deeply, their real-life connections to what they read, their personal stories, or a combination of all of the above" (p. 40). These real-life connections and the personal stories students share in the course of these conversations reveal perspectives that may be new or unfamiliar to peers. These interactions offer students opportunities to learn more about classmates who may not be in their immediate circle of friends, and the perspectives of other students can be both interesting and enlightening.

In planning paired and group conversations at any grade level, teachers must provide structure in the form of scaffolding that will facilitate successful student-to-student interactions. It begins with building plenty of time into the daily routine for conversation.

Time and Structure for Out-Loud Thinking

In *Creating Cultures of Thinking*, Ron Ritchart (2015) tells us, "A chief goal of instruction, right alongside the development of content understanding, is the advancement of thinking." One of several *kinds* of thinking Ritchart identifies is "examining things from different perspectives and alternative points of view to discern bias and develop a more balanced take on issues, ideas, and events" (pp. 32–33). The CCSS Anchor Standards for Speaking and Listening calls on students to "Prepare for and participate effectively in a range of conversations and collaborations with diverse partners, building on others' ideas and expressing their own clearly and persuasively" (National Governors Association [NGA], 2010, CCSS.ELA-Literacy.CCRA.SL.1). Diverse partners bring diverse perspectives to structured conversations, and students willing to fully attend to another's contribution can facilitate—and advance—their own thinking.

It may be useful—and less threatening—to have students practice this kind of discourse with a *single* partner in a standing pair share, away from 24 other pairs of eyes. One of the two students in the pair can probably come up with "another way to look at" whatever point of view the teacher or a student has stated. The teacher is free to walk around and listen to the various conversations, and she may well pick up on one or two things she wants shared. I always recommend teachers get permission from students to share later on. Some teachers will share the information themselves, crediting the student. Students need to get into the habit of doing the sharing; the teacher already knows how to articulate her thoughts in a cogent fashion. It's the kids who need the practice.

Once these paired conversations become routine, *new* students will have to be worked gently and slowly into a system now embedded in classroom practice. When a new classmate realizes the environment he has just entered is less passive and more active than the one he left last week, he may find himself somewhere on a continuum from mild confusion to outright panic. I watched as an eighth grader new to a social studies class whispered to his teacher with some anxiety and urgency, "We don't do this!" What he meant, of course, was that at his former school this kind of face-to-face interaction was not on the menu. He was anxious and unsure of himself; *he simply did not know what to do.* The teacher instructed him to stand next to a pair of students and simply listen. I was watching all this from the sidelines, and I smiled as, within a couple of minutes, the new student was contributing to the conversation he had started out observing. The teacher did not force him to do something with which he was completely uncomfortable. He observed another pair of classmates; when he felt comfortable he joined the discussion.

When working with students on various activities related to developing these communication skills, I recommend giving one-at-a-time directions. Before students have any idea about what the topic of conversation is, get them up and into standing pairs. If it is early in the school year, take it one step at a time.

> **Direction 1**: "Close your books." (Wait while making sure it gets done.)

> **Direction 2**: "Stand behind your desk and push in your chair." (Wait.)

> **Direction 3**: "In a moment, when I say go, raise your right hand and move to the center of the classroom. Go!" (Wait until everyone is standing in the open area.)

> **Direction 4**: "Raise your right hand. When I say go, shake hands with someone with whom you have not met yet today. Go!" (Wait until all the hands are down; you should already know whether you have an odd or even number of students, and if there is an odd number on that day, pull one student aside until all the pairs are formed, asking him to stand with another pair to form a trio.)

> **Direction 5**: "Face me." (Wait until each pair of eyes is on you.)

At this point the students are ready to take on whatever task you have in mind. I have seen this done with marvelous efficiency, and I have seen it take forever. The key is not to move to the next verbal instruction until every student has done everything you asked. If after the first direction there is a book open, look at that student until he gets the idea and completes the task. If one student is still not facing you when you have instructed them to do that, make it a point to make that happen.

Getting students to stand behind their chairs, push their chairs in, face you, and move into the center of the room are all procedures. Procedures are either effective or ineffective, explains Fred Jones (2007). To become effective, they must become routine; if little time is invested in turning procedures into routines, the resulting chaos will get in the way of learning. Transitioning from desks to standing pairs is either going to run smoothly or it isn't. When a teacher, during the first few weeks of school, allows some students to NOT push their chairs under their desks, or NOT face her when she asks, or NOT move quickly and quietly from their desks into standing pairs, chances are this will escalate until there is a breakdown in routines and—in all likelihood—severe discipline problems not too far down the road. The standards for routines need to be high, and they need to be enforced: "The standards in any classroom are defined by whatever the students can get away with" (Jones, 2007, 148).

If procedures become effective routines over time, then it should be possible down the road to reduce the number of directions:

Direction 1: "Close your books and stand behind your desk."

Direction 2: "When I say go, come to the center of the room and find a partner with whom you have not met today, and then face me. Go!"

The key is to make directions crystal clear, and then practice it until it is right. Teachers must invest the time in processes up front that support the content later on.

Teachers who try to give too many directions at a time should not be surprised by the resulting confusion. I once saw a teacher give six verbal directions all at once, and then spend the next fifteen minutes walking around the room cleaning up the mess she had created. She may have wondered how she got all the slow kids, but the

> Giving one verbal direction at a time can help avoid confusion and misunderstandings among students.

confusion on their part was understandable. Getting process right at the beginning will prevent problems later on.

Something to Chew On

Once necessary procedures have become routine, it is time to give students something worthwhile with which to wrestle in pairs, trios, or quartets. Ritchart (2002) asserts that if we want to facilitate the thinking of students, "there must first be something that engages students mentally, something that necessitates a discussion, something that exposes students to new ideas, uncovers other perspectives, and pushes thinking forward" (p. 117). Big ideas or concepts often provide fertile ground for student-to-student conversations (followed by or preceded by a writing exercise), and it helps if students have, as part of the context of their lives, something to share.

I served for a few years as middle school social studies coordinator, and had the pleasure of working with the middle school language arts coordinator on some interdisciplinary units. One of these units had as its big idea the subject of immigration, something that is always topical. It is a major thread that runs through the history of the United States, but we needed an entrance point to classroom conversations for middle school students. We needed something on which they could chew substance-wise; we needed something that was familiar and part of the context of their lives.

We found that something in the transitory nature of life in an area with a huge naval base and various other military installations—our students moved a lot, and many of them had lived in other states and countries. They knew what it was like to pick up and move, sometimes in the middle of a school year—sometimes twice in one year. They understood the pain of leaving friends behind on their way to new neighborhoods, churches, and schools. In a sense they were all immigrants, especially, of course, those who lived overseas for years at a time. These experiences gave them perspective. Those perspectives opened the door to conversations about Irish immigrants of the 1840s or indeed anyone coming through Ellis Island in its heyday.

For social studies teachers and those who teach literature or science, there are gobs of big ideas (change, conflict, power, or the whole concept of citizenship, life cycles, energy) that can serve as the focus of substantive student-to-student interactions or whole-class discussions. When I taught U.S. history at the junior high and middle school levels, I entered the study of World Wars I and II through the front door; that is, by telling them about the causes of the wars, or the major players and battles. In the role of chief information officer, I told them. I informed them. I explained to them and described for them. And I bored them silly.

It never occurred to me that the student who knows little, if anything, about the war in Vietnam, *does know something about conflict.* Students see it—and its effects—every day. The location of Saigon or the date the first American advisers went ashore may elude them, but the whole idea of conflict allows a social studies teacher to enter a study of the war in Vietnam not through the front entrance, but through the *side door.* A student who has experienced conflict in some way is in a position to offer up a perhaps unique perspective in a series of journal entries or in standing pair shares with multiple partners. The causes of conflict in general can then lead to an analysis of the causes of a specific war or wars in general.

If students can accept, deal with, and build upon the perspectives of classmates, they are in a better position to recognize and understand the perspectives of Jews in World War II or frightened soldiers in a foreign land. When teachers are skilled at facilitating academic conversations between and among students, thinking is advanced. Ritchart (2002) again explains: "Given the importance of such talk to thinking, it's not surprising that thoughtful classroom environments are dominated by discussion, writing, and a general sense of reciprocity in conversation" (p. 117). I used to think talking was teaching; it took me many years (and many lectures) to understand that talking is thinking, and thinking is learning.

The entire set of Speaking and Listening Standards calls for interactions that become more sophisticated through the grades. In schools where teachers collaborate vertically through the various levels, everyone can get a sense of what is meant by student presentations that include "multimedia components" (Grade 6; NGA, 2010, CCSS.ELA-Literacy. SL.6.5) and the "strategic use of digital media" (Grades 11–12; CCSS. ELA-Literacy.SL11.12.5). Just as students can benefit from the perspectives and ideas of peers, so can teachers profit from the perspectives and ideas of colleagues in the building and in other schools. Trying to unpack and understand the speaking and listening standards on one's own can be as lonely and frustrating an exercise as Norm trying to understand the notes he took on Tuesday morning by staring at them that evening.

By listening respectfully and attending to what the partner in a paired discussion is saying, a student can pick up on that person's perspectives. Through multiple conversations in the classroom, students are exposed to the perspectives of many classmates. Beginning in kindergarten, the Speaking and Listening Skills section of the Common Core State Standards recognizes the importance of listening and seeking to understand—and thus begin to empathize with—one's conversation partner or partners. "Conversations," affirm Zwiers and Crawford (2011), "encourage students to get to know each other and expose them to a range of opinions, ideas, and worldviews. A student can and should learn from every other classmate's opinions, experiences, and ways of thinking" (p. 16). This can only happen if teachers provide opportunities for students to have these content-laden conversations in the classroom.

Anyone who has taught for any length of time knows that students will often discard the opinions of others out of hand, simply because they do not fit neatly into their own world view. This can carry over into adulthood as well, and this egocentric thinking can become the habit of a lifetime. This can result in a metaphorical hardening of the arteries when it comes to understanding other points of view, and it can lead to conflict. It takes time and effort to listen to what others have to say, and then reflect on what they are really saying—and *why* they said it. The whole idea of taking the time and making the effort to understand someone else is something that needs to begin early in life; understanding others starts with taking turns and attending to one's partner in a simple conversation. Getting into the habit of listening and reflecting in order to understand someone can have positive consequences, according to Zwiers and Crawford (2011), who maintain that "when students understand each other at deeper levels, many of their conflicts become smaller and fewer" (p. 16).

When we reach a point where we can both understand and accept the viewpoints of others, we can be said to be empathetic. Empathy is putting oneself in someone else's shoes, and can often result in a supportive action that benefits someone else. I experienced that years ago when I was taking part in some customer service training at the Ritz Carlton Hotel in Atlanta. Having arrived at the hotel at 7:00 in the morning on the second day of training, it dawned on me that I had left all my training materials and several other important items at the hotel where we had stayed the night before (when one works for a school district, one may not actually *stay* at the Ritz Carlton). The doorman observed my frustration and immediately informed me he would take care of it. Sure enough, by 8:30 all my materials were in the training room, several minutes in advance of our start time.

Empathy is built into the customer service framework at the Ritz Carlton. In my case, the doorman looked at things from my perspective and saw a way he could solve the problem to my satisfaction. I have never forgotten that supreme act of empathy on my behalf, and I have told this story hundreds of times since it happened perhaps fifteen years ago. The doorman could have patted me on the shoulder and provided some words of sympathy: "That's too bad, Mr. Nash. How unfortunate. May I take your bags?" He didn't do that, however; he told me he would solve the problem, and proceeded to do it—even though it took him away from his station (and his tips) for an hour.

A Powerful Brew

Again, what the Ritz Carlton doorman did qualifies as empathy—not sympathy—and it was something that required first a registering of my frustration, followed by a commitment to remove the source of that frustration. "Empathy," says Keene (2012), "is more than compassion; it involves effort. It demands conscious deliberation focused on the thoughts and emotions of another. It is a powerful brew of thought and feeling" (p. xvi). Empathy is, according to Keene, "often present when we understand deeply" (p. xvi). If the commitment is one of time and effort, then teachers need to provide the time and model the kind of effort necessary for deep understanding—and empathy.

This confluence of perspective and empathy is important as students read about historical figures and ponder the statements of political candidates, bloggers, and commentators. "A student's ability to take on different perspectives and empathize fosters in-depth learning because," asserts Zwiers (2014), "in order to be able to think in the shoes of another person, one must learn much about that person and his or her circumstances" (p. 94). The more students know—and take the time to find out—about other people, the more they learn and understand about them and their points of view. This may begin with very personal conversations with classroom partners as they take part in structured pair shares beginning at an early age. Every set of oral-language standards I have seen over the years, including the Common Core State Standards, calls for these types of student-to-student interactions on a regular basis.

When students are paired frequently, and when they work with classmates on a regular basis, they get to know a good deal about each other. They talk on many occasions with those they might ordinarily avoid, and this helps them build relationships they might not ordinarily build. Zwiers and Crawford (2011), in their work with fourth through eighth graders, speak of a "leveling of social status" among students who took part in peer discussions. One of the students with whom they worked said, "I made friends with kids I never thought I would even talk to, or want to talk to"' (p. 20). Students who take part in frequent, structured conversations with classmates not only become better speakers and listeners, but they lose their reluctance to talk to people outside their own sometimes small circle of immediate friends.

I had occasion a few years ago to observe a class full of second graders using a strategy (introduced in Chapter 4) called paired verbal fluency (PVF), where one partner talks while another listens and responds in some way. In one variation of PVF, the listener is then required to continue the conversation without repeating what his partner said, or he may be asked to summarize or ask a question in search of clarification. These second graders met with partner after partner for several minutes, and I realized after a few minutes of PVF in action that they were good at it—and they could change partners without missing a beat. I wondered aloud when debriefing with the teacher after class what levels of understanding and empathy students could reach if they spent a good deal of time in every class and at every grade level in these types of academic conversations.

> Students who take part in structured conversations on a regular basis may well overcome the fear of meeting new people in a diverse world.

Students who take part in structured conversations on a regular basis may well overcome their fear of meeting new people in a diverse world. Gardner (2010) speaks of "the respectful mind" as something that will help human beings thrive and survive in a world where they may well come into contact with people (and fellow workers) from other countries and cultures. "A person possessed of a respectful mind welcomes this exposure to diverse persons and groups. Such a person wants to meet, get to know, and come to like individuals from remote quarters" (p. 20). Students who are used to talking with and sharing ideas with classmates representing diverse backgrounds are in a better position to meet and interact with fellow citizens and workers down the road.

Allyn (2013), in *Be Core Ready*, includes the thoughts of a cardiologist commenting on the importance of listening and empathy in medicine:

> The artful parts of good medicine—some of which are innate, but many of which can be learned, modeled, and taught explicitly— include the ability to asses the knowledge and literacy of the patient, tailor the verbal and written communication accordingly, and actively listen to make sure that the communication was successful. The other part of course is the ability to convey empathy and caring. (p. 16)

In my workshops I often have participants discuss in pairs what professions require skills related to listening and empathy. When they report out they begin most often with teachers and health professionals, and it isn't long before someone points out that almost every modern profession requires empathy to a greater or lesser extent. With Boomers like myself heading for retirement villages and then rest homes in ever-increasing numbers, the health care industry is growing rapidly. (My old high school is now a senior citizens' center. I could go back to school . . .) When I'm in an assisted-living situation, I want all the empathy those doing the assisting can muster. I go back to Ellen Oliver Keene's (2012) observation that empathy requires effort; it focuses "on the thoughts and emotions" of other people (p. xvi).

Listening and Empathy From the Top Down

In forty-plus years in education, I have often seen new principals (or those new to the building) who try to hit the ground running in August, and wind up hitting the wall instead. Most often, I have observed, this is because they don't *listen*. There are professionals in the building— teaching and nonteaching—who have experiences to share and stories to tell. There are brand new teachers and those who have been in the business for two or three decades—maybe in that very building. There are teachers who came to teaching after many years in another profession. There are custodians who were in the military, and cafeteria workers who are single moms. Every one of these individuals has something to contribute and something to say. They all come to the table with different perspectives.

The best administrators I have known over the years have been effective listeners; they are leaders who understand they are dealing with people first and curricula second. Costa (2008) says, "We want students to learn to hold in abeyance their own values, judgments, opinions, and prejudices so they can listen to and entertain another person's thoughts. This is a complex skill requiring the ability to monitor one's own thoughts while at the same time attending to a partner's words" (p. 24). Costa goes on to say that listening in this way does not mean that we must agree with what the speaker is saying. We can, however, demonstrate "understanding of and empathy for an idea or feeling by paraphrasing it accurately, building upon it, clarifying it, or giving an example of it" (p. 24). If we as educational professionals want students to become powerful listeners, there is something to be said for modeling empathy and understanding at the staff level.

The same kinds of working relationships that help create a supportive classroom environment need to be present at the building and district level. Leadership at every level of the organization is more than simply diagnosing problems and handing out prescriptions. Teachers who feel left out of the continuous-improvement process in a school will naturally come to be dependent on decisions administrators make. Making teachers partners in the planning, execution, and evaluation of the school improvement plan (SIP) is what effective administrators do. There are valuable perspectives and years of experience available on every staff that can be tapped on the continuous-improvement highway; whether it surfaces and provides value added from year to year depends on the administrators whose job it is to work in tandem with those closest to the kids:

> In other words, effective leadership involves not only the task of decision-making but also the facilitation of staff discussions and the nurturing of trusting relationships that lead to shared solutions and good decision-making. In short, if leaders do not get the relationships right, it will be problematic for them to accomplish the task. (Smith & Smith, 2015, p. 12)

Every stakeholder across the educational landscape from teachers to students to parents has something to contribute—provided those in a position to extend the invitation are willing to do so in ways that harness the power of "we."

Final Thoughts

A classroom filled with diverse students is also filled with diverse perspectives and points of view, products of a lifetime's worth of experiences and learning. Students who understand the role active listening plays in learning can successfully navigate the often-difficult waters of communication and collaboration in a classroom setting (or in life or the workplace, for that matter). Students who take the time to try and understand what someone else must be feeling have made great strides on the road to empathy. "Empathy," says Daniel Pink (2006), "is a stunning act of imaginative derring-do, the ultimate virtual reality—climbing into another person's mind to experience the world from that person's perspective" (p. 159). This will not happen, however, if students while away the hours in school largely in passive mode, listening to teachers talk (or pretending to do so while going elsewhere in their minds). Diverse perspectives and differing points of view can be an integral part of the learning process at every grade level.

In Chapter 6 we'll take a look at the effects of competition and collaboration on the learning process.

6

Competition and Collaboration

I am not a particularly competitive person. This proved somewhat of a handicap when I was in sales; I tended to want to spend my time servicing existing accounts and left the cold calls I needed to make (for the purpose of generating new business) for another day. Although I counted among my friends many of the salespeople in my company, we tended to compete against one another for the sales prizes that typically went to the top performers. Already in direct competition with our external competitors, we were, given the nature of the reward system in place at the time, also in competition with each other. While many of us were not driven by external rewards, for those who were it set up internal competition that was not, perhaps, in the best interest of collaboration on the part of the sales force. This was sometimes uncomfortable for those who might have otherwise helped each other far more willingly. Those in leadership positions finally changed this policy, allowing anyone who got to a certain level of sales to get the same reward. While it probably did not completely do away with internal competition, it certainly helped.

The same can be true of students who perceive themselves to be in direct competition with their peers. This happens if students see their relative advancement in school as a zero-sum game (e.g., the race for valedictorian or salutatorian). As is the case where workplace rewards are few and coveted by many, competition in schools can work against cooperation and collaboration. "In competitive situations there is negative interdependence among goal achievements; students can perceive that they can obtain their goals if and only if other students in the class fail to obtain their goals" (Johnson, Johnson, & Holubec, 1990, p. 3). Even in classrooms where teachers grade on an absolute scale, so that technically everyone could receive an A if he or she met the standard for an A, students may still want to outscore their peers, and this may work against any kind of cooperation.

For teachers who want to use collaborative strategies in the classroom, competition can serve as an impediment to learning because there are students who are highly competitive and take every opportunity to put the emphasis on competition rather than cooperation. I saw this again and again as a classroom teacher on those occasions when I tried to review for upcoming tests using a game that divided the students into teams. Boys tended on the whole to be more competitive, and James (2007) and I agree that "in the presence of girls, boys are more likely to engage in direct competition" (p. 132). Boys were much more likely to shout out an answer without consulting their teammates, and it was a constant struggle on my part to get some boys to come down to earth long enough to talk it over with the other four or five boys and girls on their teams before coming up with an answer.

Whatever the reasons for this phenomenon, it can have negative consequences for those boys unable to shift from a direct-competition mode to one of cooperation. The communication skills they need in life and in the workplace may not become well developed, and, according to James, the boys "may spend a good deal of their adult life frustrated because they are not included in the few who attain the top positions" (p. 132). There are those who may be driven to succeed in a competitive environment, but there are many more who are simply turned off by competition. Students "who believe they don't have a chance of winning," according to Kohn (1999), "are discouraged from making the effort; having been given no reason to apply themselves except to defeat their peers, and convinced that they cannot do so, these people are almost by definition demotivated" (p. 56). If students get the idea that winning takes precedence over learning for its own sake, we may be sending the wrong message. Successful collaboration and teamwork requires working *with* others, not against them. Education should not be seen as a zero sum game.

Sometimes It's Just About the Dot

Aiming for a less competitive classroom is not to say that students cannot and should not work toward individual peak performance, competing, in essence, against their earlier best on the track or in the classroom. Some of the most effective teachers I have met over the years have students use simple run charts to track progress over time. My experience is that surpassing one's personal best in the 3200-meter run or moving from a Level 3 essay to a Level 4 essay are both powerful motivators—and the motivation that results is essentially intrinsic. For students, plotting a *new dot* on the run chart each week as the trend is either upward and positive (spelling quiz grades) or downward and positive (fewer edits on a succession of multipa-ragraph essays) is proof that they are improving, and the knowledge that they are capable of making steady progress is its own reward. Students who see such progress on a run chart as the dots are connected—revealing improvement—normally feel good about that. A good friend and out-standing educator once told me, "Sometimes, it's just about the dot!" She and I agree that students loved seeing improvement over time, and several data points going in the right direction can be motivating.

This is also true when teachers harness the power of the entire class by creating a chart on which *class* progress can be plotted over time. I worked with a pair of middle school teachers who did this, and the results were positive. Students loved the idea that, working together, they could shift that series of run-chart dots or bar-graph bars ever upward. In another case, a high school teacher led her students in an analysis of just why the dot went up this week, or why it went down. In this way, students got used to looking for root causes; she explained to them—and I saw firsthand that they understood this—that going up or down is not about good or bad, right or wrong. A shift in the line has one or several root causes that provide feedback to the group. The only form of competition at work in this high school science classroom was built around *improving the performance of the entire class.* This involved students helping other students, in part for the good of the group. When direct competition can be replaced with cooperation on the part of students as members of the group, good things happen.

Whatever the course subject or content, getting students to cooper-ate collectively is a plus. In fact, according to Gunter, Estes, and Schwab (1999), the ability to work in cooperative fashion with peers "may be the most critical social skill that students learn, when one considers the importance of cooperation in the workplace, in the family, and in lei-sure activities" (p. 264). In traditional classrooms, "the modes of learner interaction are," as McInnerney and Roberts (2004) affirm, "pri-marily learner–instructor and learner–content, with almost no learning taking place between the students, at least as part of the formal learning process" (p. 204). In classrooms where teachers have moved beyond this traditional mode of instruction to one that consists of a more multidirectional flow of information and interaction, my experi-ence is that students enjoy it more and on many occasions shine in the role of teachers as they work with their peers.

> Teachers who have spent the first week of school on process will find the going much easier.

In a Virginia elementary classroom, I watched students work cooperatively in pairs. Their first task was to read a short passage on their own and then discuss what they had read. Holding his place in the reading with his finger, one boy asked his partner what a particular word meant. His partner asked him to read the sentence that contained the word, offered a tentative opinion, and finally grabbed a dictionary and looked it up. Satisfied, the first boy said, "Thanks!" and they went back to reading. I wish I had a video of that exchange. Here were two students *confident enough in their ability to sort this out* that they did not have to interrupt the teacher, who was working with a group of five or six students in a corner of the room. This happened enough during the time I was in that particular classroom that I concluded the teacher had spent a great deal of time turning her students into cooperative and interdependent learners.

"Do Your Own Work!"

I wish I had a nickel for every time I uttered that command over my teaching career. Really, I do. Add to it "Sit up straight!" as well as "Hunker down and think!" and you have a pretty good idea that cooperative learning was not in my bag of instructional strategies. My student desks were in six rows of six, with students facing me in perfect parade-ground order. I obsessed about how straight the rows were (picture little pieces of tape on the floor against which the right front leg of each desk was placed) and I "ran a tight ship." If my students could find a job on an assembly line, in a machine shop, in the military, or in any number of industrial-age positions, then dressing properly, getting to work on time, paying attention, following instructions, and getting the job done was pretty much what they could expect to have to do. Mine was the language of compliance, not of thinking or learning. That was what my freshmen must have realized I valued above all, and I think they may have been on to something.

Because I placed a high premium on order and discipline in my early classrooms, I believed that straight rows of students who listened, took notes, and generally "did their best" qualified as an excellent classroom. Many administrators felt the same way and often looked askance at classrooms where the noise level was too high, and cooperative-learning sessions can get loud. I put my students in teams for competitive review games and publicly acknowledged the attainment of high grades in hopes of getting others to try to catch those high performers. I always thought in terms of "Norm can do better!" on his own if he just "put his nose to the grindstone." (I may actually have written that on a report card at some point.) It never really occurred to me that by harnessing the power of cooperation and truly effective collaborative learning, I could have improved performance for Norm and most of his classmates.

One reason I used to give—and I was not alone here, by any stretch of the imagination—for not having students work in groups was that one or two students might wind up doing all the work, while Norm went along for the ride or threw a monkey wrench into the works. Rather than think this through or work it out, I used it as an excuse to maintain the individualistic status quo. On rare occasions when I tried what we then called "group work," I never made an effort to do what was necessary to keep Norm or anyone else from taking a free ride, which could upset and even anger the rest of the group members. The chaos that resulted from my failure to train my students to be cooperative members of a functioning pair or group simply kept me from repeating the exercise more than a couple of times. It was simply easier four decades ago to remind everyone to get to class on time, take notes, and pay attention. Forty years later and well into a new century, things have changed.

The language of compliance I demonstrated every day in my early years in teaching (*Pay attention! Are you taking notes? Where is your textbook? Hunker down!*) did little to create a culture of thinking. In Lisa Verkerk's classroom (related in Ritchart, 2015), she "asked students to look closely, notice details, observe carefully, make interpretations, build explanations, reason, generate alternatives, provide evidence, make connections, and raise questions" (p. 70). This is the language of thinking. Students who participate in the fabric of classroom life become confident learners even as they begin to understand that working together in collaboration with classmates beats staring at a worksheet while the teacher admonishes everyone to "do your own work!" This constant cooperation and collaboration on the part of students creates a sense of community that I have found is present in the classrooms of the best teachers I have seen over the years. Collaboration beats compliance any day of the week.

The intense pressure of the global economy requires that our educational system support the communication, critical thinking, and collaborative skills that help keep companies innovative and competitive. "Workers with these skills can perform tasks that require higher-skill human action not easily codified into computer software" (Karoly & Panis, 2004, p. 201). Pink (2006) tells us we have moved well beyond the industrial age "to a society of knowledge workers. And now we're progressing yet again—to a society of creators and empathizers, of pattern recognizers and meaning makers" (p. 50). This new society and economy are "built more and more on people's *right brains*" (p. 50). The only way to get students ready for their future in the workplace and in an increasingly complex world is to give them a workout up and down the cognitive ladder from comprehension to evaluation, and then on to the kind of creativity and innovation that is driving global progress. "Increasingly in the twenty-first century," says Wagner (2012), "what you know is far less important than what you can do with what you know" (p. 142). Companies like Google and Apple thrive on the kind of teamwork that relies on reflection, cooperation, and collaboration.

The goal of cooperative learning can be the completion of a specific task or project—a report or a video presentation of some sort—and there is certainly value in putting student groups to work on that sort of collaborative exercise. Often, students are put to work on solving problems in a fairly generic way, so that those skills can be transferred to other problems in other situations. Dede (2010) tells us, however, that we need to go to the next level with this and help students develop "expert decision-making and metacognitive strategies that indicate how to proceed when no standard approach seems applicable" (p. 54). As workplaces become less geographic and more virtual in nature, Dede says we need to go beyond what he sees as the current "gold standard" of face-to-face communication in the classroom and give students experience "in mediated dialogue and in shared design within a common virtual workspace" (p. 54). Once again we are looking at creating a hybrid system, where students can get valuable experience at collaborating in the classroom and online.

In Search of Cooperation and Collaboration

On my high school track team, I discovered what some refer to as "the power of we." I was a sprinter and an alternate on what today would be called the 4 × 100 meter relay team. Any relay race is an excellent example of what can be done when four sprinters or distance runners work interdependently toward a common goal. In these races, runners pass the relay baton to the next runner, and in the 4 × 100 meter relay, a split-second miscalculation can cost the team the race. A false start by the first runner may cost the team a medal. A runner who leaves too quickly before getting the baton firmly in his hand may go out of the zone and cost the team the race. Coaches must decide who will go first and who will take the baton for that last leg. Everything must go perfectly, and everyone must commit to being part of this highly collaborative activity, one that demonstrates "the power of we."

In these situations, it is the responsibility of the coach to make certain that every member of the relay team understands exactly what his or her role is. The first runner must understand that there can be no miscalculation out of the blocks if a false start will end the race for the team. Subsequent runners must not only do their best in terms of speed; they must be careful not to step off the track or, in the case of distance relays, get boxed in or go out so quickly that they run out of steam near the end of their leg of the relay. Over four decades, I have seen scores of relay races at the Pennsylvania state high school track meet, and I can say with confidence that these races are exceptionally collaborative efforts, and interdependence is the name of the game.

It is no more possible for students in the classroom to operate automatically in teams than it is for coaches to throw four sprinters or distance runners together on a relay team and expect them to function as a unit *without a great deal of structure, preparation, and training*. Johnson and colleagues (1990) remind us that children must be taught how to interact in a cooperative way with others. Teachers who do not take this into account are in for a rude awakening if they put students into pairs or groups and expect them to function as a team. "Interpersonal and group skills do not magically appear when they are needed" (p. 87). Teachers who want students to benefit from the power of peer collaboration must frontload those skills in the first five days of school. Once again, the process horse comes before the content cart; the context for introducing content into the collaborative mix comes from teaching students how to cooperate when working in pairs or groups. It is during that first week of school that the processes related to basic social skills and productive collaboration should be put firmly in place.

Begin With Basics

During the first five days of school, teachers ought to spend a good deal of time doing nothing but establishing and rehearsing procedures, to the point where students can clean their work areas or transition from one activity to another, and move quickly and efficiently into standing pairs, trios, or groups. By the end of the first day, teachers should have rehearsed their operational norm for getting their students' attention dozens of times in an elementary classroom or several times during a class period or block. What students do when they enter the room, *how* they enter the room, how they leave the room, how they walk down the hallway in elementary school, and how they conduct themselves when others are explaining something or asking questions. Social skills are a critical part of all this, and there is no substitute for turning processes into routines—*and during the first week of school*. Jones (2007) underlines the importance of going from "practice to mastery" and "teaching the students that you are the embodiment of two timeless characterizations of a teacher:

I say what I mean, and I mean what I say.

and

We are going to keep doing this until we get it right. (p. 150)

No subject-area content is so important that it cannot wait until these process-related preliminaries are out of the way. I can't stress this enough; there is no shortcut here, and it is not enough to have posters all over the room that tell students what they need to do and how they need to act in the classroom. It is not sufficient simply to explain to them anything related to process—they must *do* it. They must *practice* it. They must, as Jones says, *master* it. Wong and Wong (2009) maintain that down the road, it may be necessary to make some corrections, at which point a teacher should remind students of the correct procedure and then "have the class EXPERIENCE the procedure" (p. 179) once again. It is not necessary to scold, threaten, or punish, says Jones (2007); it is only necessary to practice, practice, and practice again (p.150). Teachers who have spent the first week of school on process will find the going much easier, and my experience is that when it comes time to put students in pairs, trios, or groups for collaborative work, the preparation for that will be much easier for everyone. Process comes first; content second.

In the same way that students learn basic classroom procedures by practicing them over and over again, Kagan (1994) says, "The ability to adjust one's behavior to work effectively with others and to communicate with others can be learned only in the process of working and interacting with others" (p. 3:2). Outstanding coaches and teachers understand the nature and utility of corrective feedback, and my suggestion is that when students are paired or put into trios or quartets, it is advisable initially to give them something relatively easy to do in the way of a task or goal. In the same way that coaches build up to a scrimmage with the basics, teachers can do the same thing by working through what is necessary to make a group click. Once students are able to function as a group—no matter whom they are paired or teamed with—teachers can fold subject-area content into the mix.

A classroom that is *safe* (students can share and ask questions without fear of sarcastic responses from anyone in the room), *fully functioning* (all processes have been explained and rehearsed to the point where they are routine), and *feedback oriented* (students do not see criticism as criticism, but as feedback that will help them make adjustments on their continuous-improvement journeys), the context is there for good group dynamics. For students to collaborate in pairs or groups, teachers must allow for and plan for what Kagan (1994) calls *simultaneous interaction*. In paired work, for example, at least half the kids in the room will be talking at once, as they share something with their partners. I always recommend that during the first week of school, students meet in several paired structures before moving to trios or quartets. I also recommend that groups be kept at four, if possible. Larger groups, I have observed, are harder to manage, partly because in desk groupings of five, one desk is always at the end, and that student is simply not close enough to the others to function well as part of the group.

Surface What They Know, and They Know a Lot

In Chapter 4, I introduced a basic face-to-face structure called *paired verbal fluency* (PVF), and I suggest that during the first week of school—and before moving into cooperative structures that involve more than two students—teachers establish the norms for paired discussions and practice, practice, and practice some more. This gives students the opportunity to work at the comprehension level of the cognitive ladder by explaining, describing, sum-marizing, and asking for a point of clarification (questioning). It also allows students to become familiar with appropriate and supportive body language and facial expressions. By the time teachers and students move into the second week of school, students should be comfortable with functioning successfully in pairs, as speaker and listener. As I said in Chapter 4, listening must be defined. It is not enough for teachers to say, "Pay attention!" or "Listen carefully!" Those phrases mean nothing until it becomes clear to students exactly what it takes to be an effective and active listener.

> By the time teachers and students move into the second week of school, students should be comfortable with functioning success-fully in pairs, as speaker and listener.

After the first five days of school in the fall, teachers can create opportunities for students to work in trios (e.g., in a gallery walk) or quartets (doing a card sort at their desks). Having observed small-group activities over the years, there is one student behavior that can derail any group effort very quickly: Students are quick to judge. They quickly measure what someone else said against their own opinion or understanding—and they pounce. The other partner or group mem-ber gets defensive, and the pair or group is off topic and off to the races. This is difficult for adults and for students, and it is important that teachers model nonjudgmental behavior during that first week of school. Students are perceptive, and they will pick up on every phrase, comment, and nuance of what a teacher says or does during those first five days.

Costa (2008) reminds teachers that they need to accept what students say and what they do in nonjudgmental fashion:

> When they accept, they give no clues through posture, gesture, or word as to whether a student's idea, behavior, or feeling, is good, bad, better, or worse, right or wrong. In response to a student's idea or action, acceptance of it provides a psychologically safe climate where students can take risks, are entrusted with the responsibility of making decisions for themselves, and can explore the conse-quences of their own actions. Nonjudgmental acceptance provides conditions in which students are encouraged to examine and

compare their own data, values, ideas, criteria, and feelings with those of others as well as those of the teacher. (p. 212)

This is not easy, and it goes against the grain, frankly, to adopt the kind of body language and verbal response mechanism that says, "I'm not judging here." The fact remains that if a teacher expects students to refrain from judging right out of the gate when they are in conversations with their peers, that teacher must model this during the first week of school, and model it often.

The Business of Brainstorming

One collaborative activity where judging can become a process-halting monkey wrench is in brainstorming. During the first week of school, teachers can lead students in brainstorming sessions that surface speaking and listening skills, but before attempting to brainstorm in class, teachers must first set some ground rules for this activity. Because the idea is to get students to open up and contribute during brainstorming sessions, everything possible must be done to create a classroom climate that encourages input from everyone. There don't have to be many ground rules here, but they must be followed.

First, students must be allowed to contribute an idea without fear of being ridiculed or otherwise judged by classmates. This also means that teachers and others should not say things like, "Oh, that's a good one, Sandy! Well done." Whoever comes after that is going to be disappointed unless the praise is even more effuse. Any kind of criticism or praise paints teachers into a not-very-comfortable corner. Second, whatever ideas are put forward should be accepted and charted. The purpose, after all, is to surface ideas. Finally, the teacher or someone needs to facilitate the exercise to keep it moving and help paraphrase input if necessary. Criticism and praise may be *out,* but clarity is definitely *in.* What goes on the chart should be what the student intended.

Many students are not outgoing, and they may simply tune everyone out during a wide-open, classroom-level brainstorming exercise. There are a couple of ways to ensure that everyone is involved. One exceptionally effective strategy is called *Brainstorm and Pass* (Lipton & Wellman, 2000). Teachers can divide the students into small groups of four or five and have each group choose a recorder. Once the recorder has a piece of paper and a pencil, the person to his or her right begins by contributing something that the recorder then writes down. The next person to the right then contributes something and this continues for a set number of minutes. Students who can't think of something may pass; my experience is that once it has gone around once, students start to make connections and piggyback on the contributions already recorded.

Another way to get everyone involved is to have each student find an empty journal page and write the topic at the top: skills for listening. The teacher can tell students that the purpose of the exercise is to surface as many listening skills as possible. She can then give them an example or two and discuss with them why they think those are important. The students can begin their lists with those two critical skills, writing them down and continuing to add as many as they can. While they do this, the teacher can walk around the room and ask one or two students to share something later on. Once she calls time, the teacher can call on those two students to share, and everyone can add those two things to their lists. That done, the teacher can have them stand and partner up in pairs or trios, talking about what they have written down. Pencil in hand, as they discuss what they have, they are adding to their lists. The teacher can use some music to move them into one or two more pairs or trios, and the process continues until each student's list is pretty well developed. Everyone participates and everyone contributes in some way. Once they are all seated, a master chart of listening skills can be constructed on the Smart Board or whiteboard in the front of the room. The key here is that students who might not want to give input in front of twenty-eight students may well contribute in writing, in pairs, or in trios.

Successful brainstorming relies on a substantial knowledge base. Brainstorming speaking and listening skills should be successful, providing the ground rules are followed, because students understand the basics here (eye contact, body language, facial expressions, gestures, speaking clearly and loudly enough). Most students have been annoyed when someone keeps trying to talk when they are talking. Many, perhaps most, students have felt the pain of ridicule or sarcasm. Students who have been in dozens of classrooms by the time they get to the eighth grade can certainly help brainstorm a list of rules that need to be followed if a class—or team—is going to function successfully.

The ground is familiar, and the knowledge base is deep. When students know little of the content or topic they are asked to brainstorm, it may be best, according to Drapeau (2009), to give students time to do some research before the brainstorming begins. This might mean a trip to their computers that evening—and they are going to be at the keyboard anyway.

The important thing here is that wide-open brainstorming can generate lots of ideas on the part of students, and as they listen, they make connections. "Research indicates that students become more fluent in their thinking if they practice brainstorming," says Drapeau, and "student improvement in fluency supports the notion that creativity can be taught" (p. 109). Students enjoy brainstorming as long as it is completely safe to throw out the ideas and provide the input without being judged by anyone.

This whole matter of judging needs to be tackled during the first week of school. I would encourage teachers to have students do some journal writing with the following prompt at the end of the first five days of school: "Record in your journal what, if anything, you have noticed about how I respond to your ideas, comments, and input." Once they have something in their journals, ask them to stand, grab their journals, pair up, and discuss (using the listening skills established and practiced all week long) what they have written. While they are having these paired discussions, walk around and listen carefully. When you bring an end to the discussions—and have them thank their partners for sharing—choose three or four students and have them share. If you have modeled nonjudgmental acceptance of what students said or shared during that first week of school, the resulting class discussion should be rich and insightful. It should allow you to come up with a posted list of nonjudgmental behaviors that can serve as the model for subsequent collaboration efforts in your classroom. The important thing here is that you are not telling them how they should behave in groups; *you are modeling it and then surfacing their observations and conclusions*. If students do not learn to withhold judgment, cooperation will come to a screeching halt as others on the team become defensive or openly hostile.

Model and Model Again

Teachers can never model enough what it is they want students to do. My experience is that when two adults model paired conversations, students really do observe and listen. I have seen or taken part in this kind of modeling many times, and in each case, students, no matter the grade level, closely observe what is happening. My recommendation is that during the first week of school, teachers should find another adult willing to participate and model PVF. Decide who will be A and who B, and A explains something while B listens and then summarizes. Then, B explains something while A listens and then summarizes. This whole PVF sequence can be repeated, with the listener asking for a point of clarification. Finally, partners shake hands and thank each other for sharing.

Next, the teacher and the other adult can pause and face the students, asking them to talk with a partner about what they observed during the structured conversations and how, specifically, each partner interacted with the other. Questions could guide the discussions: *What body language did the listener in each conversation display? What did the listener do when the speaker was done? What did they do when they were finished?* Again, rather than telling students what to do in paired conversations, let them observe one and then reflect on what they saw, talking about it with a partner. Students could also answer the questions in their reflective journals and then share what they wrote with a partner or a table group. Telling is not teaching; modeling something and giving students time to reflect verbally or in writing—or both—on what they observed allows them to analyze and come to some conclusions on their own.

Back to Those First Five Days Again

If the following is accomplished during the first five days of school, the stage is set for cooperative learning groups down the road:

- Basic classroom procedures are explained and rehearsed until they become routine.
- Paired conversations are modeled, and students have an opportunity to reflect on what made the conversation work.
- The teacher responds to student comments or answers in a way that is nonjudgmental, and students have a chance to reflect on how and why that is conducive to cooperation and collaboration in the classroom.
- Students begin to understand that this classroom is safe and free of sarcasm, bullying, and any sort of intimidation from any source.
- Students have the opportunity to pair and share, learning to summarize and ask for a point of clarification when they do not understand.
- Plenty of sharing opportunities during the week allow students to meet with everyone in the room and to understand that they will be meeting with everyone during the course of the year, not just with those whom they would prefer to meet.
- Students begin to understand that this is one superbly organized teacher who knows what she is doing, and she is not going to be doing all the work in this classroom for the next several months.

This last point is critical and has to do with the expectations of students. I often have teachers tell me that students resist having to stand, move, pair, and share. This attitude is at least in part due to the fact that they have become used to sitting in straight rows, minding their own business, and going to a better place in their minds—while others in the class do the heavy lifting. They rely on the teacher's fan club to answer her questions and volunteer when a volunteer is needed. Being able to hide in a classroom full of students becomes their very comfortable status quo. If cooperation and collaboration in pairs and groups is going to have any chance of success, this battle needs to be won decisively and early on—during those first five days. If the teacher decides serendipitously in week six to have students get into groups and "do group things," *it will not work.* If any students truly do not feel comfortable pairing and sharing right away, let them observe another pair or group until they realize they can do this. My experience is that they will eventually take part in the conversation they are observing, paving the way for their own participation later on.

When students are working in groups on a project or attempting to do some problem solving, the time is going to come (and early) when they will disagree; different perspectives, as we saw in Chapter 5, should be treated with respect, because it is through those varying perspectives that collaborative groups often arrive at a consensus or make a decision that is better than one arrived at easily and without controversy. I have always been of the opinion that if a group arrives at consensus within a few minutes, not enough questions have been asked and not enough answers have been questioned. If collaborative groups are doing outside research, that research is going to surface evidence that is contradictory, and students must be taught how to listen nonjudgmentally, question the research (not the researcher), and stay focused on the goal in objective fashion. Johnson and colleagues (1990) affirm that "conflict is an inherent part of learning as old conclusions and conceptions are challenged and modified to take into account new information and broader perspectives" (p. 63). Differing points of view and research findings make for a richer product in the end, and this is something well worth discussing in the classroom early on. Students should not be turned loose on a collaborative effort before they know where the minefields are.

Once the foundation is laid, students who have some experience working in pairs and know how to make that work can move into working in groups. They will make mistakes and experience conflict, but teachers should not shrink from collaborative activities and cooperative groups because of this. It is important that students move from what may be a passive role to a more active one, and one way to accomplish that is to make the flow of information in the classroom less one-directional and more multidirectional. Teachers need not fear this shift if they have done the necessary groundwork up front. Replacing competition with collaboration puts teachers and students on the same side, says Kagan (1994). "Further, in the properly managed cooperative learning classroom teachers are freed from many of the problems of management inherent in keeping most students quiet most of the time" (p. 3:6). Teachers who frontload the collaborative learning experience with the right prep work can move students up the cognitive ladder from comprehension to analysis, synthesis, and evaluation throughout the course of the school year.

There is something else teachers need to make sure happens regularly, beginning when students start working in pairs during those first five days of school: Students need to evaluate process by asking questions like *What did we do that helped us do what we set out to do?* and *What things did we do that got in our way?* Evaluating process in pairs, trios, or groups should be the responsibility of the students, although, once again, this can be modeled by the teacher and another adult or two who set up a situation where things go smoothly much of the time in the work they do together, but then derail briefly before getting back on track. Students can observe this vignette and then discuss with each other what behaviors they observed that helped and hindered progress. Providing feedback to one another within the group should be a regular part of the routine; feedback is the lifeblood of improvement.

Collaborating Online

Students working on projects or solving real-world problems have at their disposal an electronic universe full of information, examples, and ideas that would have been unheard of a couple of decades ago. Students taking part in a book club at school can take advantage of a blog set up specifically for that particular group, and they can sit at home and contribute to a rich discussion related to the book they are all reading. I know of several schools doing the same thing with books or articles related to the teachers' professional development. The idea that the classroom is no longer confined to the space between the four walls of Room 222 is one that may scare teachers used to a traditional face-to-face learning environment. There is, to my way of thinking, plenty of room for both venues, and this is a case of younger teachers being able to mentor those with little or no experience with wikis, blogs, or website development.

There is no reason why collaborative student groups should not have all the advantages that the Internet provides, and face-to-face collaboration norms (summarizing and asking questions to understand, being nonjudgmental and respectful of the opinions of others) can certainly be transferred to situations where students are doing a good deal of their collaborating in the virtual world. Graham and Misanchuk (2004), in speaking of the disagreements among authors as to what constitutes cooperative learning and what constitutes collaborative learning, hit the nail on the proverbial head:

> We are less concerned with the fine distinctions among these ways of working than we are with emphasizing the need for students to work together in small groups, in order to exchange ideas, challenge their own ways of thinking and create synergy to produce something that goes beyond what any of them could have done working separately. (p. 187)

My guess is that most CEOs would not only agree with this statement but would also encourage teachers all over America to harness the power of collaborative groups as a way of enhancing and improving the future workforce. Additionally, our country needs citizens who can think critically, value and encourage the opinions of others, examine their own beliefs and understanding frequently, and seek feedback from peers and adults on a regular basis. While we certainly want students to be able to operate independently when the occasion demands, we also want them to understand that interdependent learning is a powerful tool in the twenty-first century.

In This Together

Years ago, when I was working as an organizational development specialist in central office, several of us (principals, assistant principals, teachers, and curriculum coordinators) filled two vans for a trip to a school district in a neighboring state. Once there, we divided into small groups, visited several classrooms at several grade levels, and observed some amazing things going on in those classrooms. Problem solving, higher-order thinking skills, and truly learner-centered classrooms were displayed in what was an incredibly rich day of observations; the ride home in the two vans consisted of nonstop analysis based on what we had seen and heard. We often saw the same things, but from different perspectives, and the three-hour ride home provided time to do tons of processing and planning. That visit was one of the highlights of my educational career to that point, and it demonstrated to me how important it is to see how others in this business do what they do on a regular basis.

> Competition between school districts should be replaced by cooperation and a "We're in this together" attitude.

What was even more amazing was that the principal in the elementary school we visited that day agreed to come to our district with his assistant principal and six of his top teachers so that they could share—and we could videotape—a great many of the wonderful things they had accomplished over the past few years. Think about this: The principal *and* his assistant principal came together, and they took six of their finest teachers out of their classrooms for a day—*all to help us*. To me, this was an eye opener. It was pure cooperation; they *wanted* to share how they did what they did. Not only did they open their doors to us; they came to us to share and work with our staff. The idea, to them, was that we were all in this together.

In sports, of course, no coach would ever think of handing over his playbook to the coaching staff at another school. He would be fired on the spot. We have to be careful, though, not to let our "They are the enemy!" attitude in sports spill over into the academic arena. Districts should be working cooperatively with other districts, schools with other schools, grade levels with other grade levels, and teachers with other teachers. Teachers who are particularly good at getting students to work in cooperative groups with positive results need to open their classroom doors to others who would most certainly benefit from that success. Schools that have shown over the years that they can consistently produce graduates who excel in math ought to be inviting leadership teams from neighboring schools to see their playbook. This "We're in this together" attitude should also extend to the district level.

On the way home after our visit to that district a state away, those vans were alive with the rich conversations of administrators and teachers who had seen some wonderful things and met some extraordinary educators. That district was willing to share, and we were eager to learn. The nexus of people willing to share and others eager to learn is often a powerful and synergistic place to be. Teachers who work with students during the first week of school on the basic skills related to listening, cooperating, and collaborating may find their students willing to share. If students deem the classroom climate as safe, the teacher may discover they are eager to learn as well—the triumph of collaboration over competition.

Final Thoughts

The same competitive nature that drives students to shun cooperation on occasion also drives many schools within a district to avoid the kind of intraschool cooperation and collaboration that would help lift all boats. This is unfortunate, and it is a result of a system that advertises how individual schools are performing and, by so doing, sets them against each other in ways that are not productive. This also happens in schools where teachers used to working in isolation year after year look askance at collaborative efforts; teachers who see the value of collaboration among colleagues in pursuit of a common goal might also come to understand that synergy is synergy, wherever it is created. The same synergy that comes from students working together in collaborative ways could be put to good use in school districts all over the country. The same collaborative norms that support excellent student groups could support groups of teachers and administrators working districtwide to improve performance and help make lifelong learners out of those involved in these improvement efforts. Turning groups into high-functioning teams can and should be job one at the classroom, school, and district levels.

Building administrators can make certain, as part of their continuous-improvement plans, that the adults in the building model cooperation and collaboration as teachers and support staff work in teams on goals that are part of the ongoing improvement efforts. Administrators who train teachers to be good listeners and effective team members are modeling the kinds of behavior and cooperation the students in the building need to become skilled at during the school year. Students are nothing if not perceptive, and they can tell when a staff has it together in a cooperative and collaborative sense . . . or not. I have been in buildings where evidence of teamwork is everywhere, and I have seen situations where teachers close their doors and tune the rest of the world out. When positive attitudes, teamwork, and cooperation are embedded in the culture of the school, that culture is likely to exist at the classroom level as well.

In Chapter 7, we'll continue to look at the importance of frontloading success and facilitating process throughout the school year.

7

Frontloading and Facilitating

My first teaching position came as a result of a one-semester leave of absence granted to an eighth-grade history teacher. I took over at the beginning of the second semester, and I can still, after forty-three years, remember walking into my classroom on the second floor of that junior/senior high school in Pennsylvania. I was excited, yet anxious, and I can remember sitting at the small desk in our dining room, pondering lesson plans for the first few days and weeks with those eighth graders. I had done my student teaching in that school with seventh graders the year before, and I recognized many names as I pored over the class rosters prior to my debut.

My role, as I saw it, was that of the one person in the room whose job it was to deliver important information on the history of our country. I did that, and I served as the keeper of the answers to the questions posed by me and by the textbook with which we had all been provided. My past heralded my future at that point, because my conception of that role was forged in all the classrooms I had attended in high school and college. My role back then was identical to that of the eighth graders in my first classroom as a new teacher; I had been largely an attendee, and those students were attendees—not participants. I lectured, asked questions, showed videos, assigned homework almost every night, and handed out worksheets that were intended to get my students to search the textbook for the answers with which they could properly fill in the blanks or answer the questions so conveniently provided by the textbook publisher. I dispensed knowledge and justice in that room on the second floor and kept as tight a lid on the proceedings as I could during the winter and spring.

We lived only a few doors from the school, and I walked up the hill each afternoon pretty well exhausted from the day's labors. I can honestly say that I was more tired than my students. The reason for that, I now realize, is that I was the one doing most of the work. I talked and called it teaching. My students came to school to watch me work, and work I did. Looking back on it from a distance, I really did not need much preparation for my classes; a few lecture notes, a transparency for the overhead projector, some dittoed worksheets, and a stack of video ordering forms were all part and parcel of the set of processes that composed my system of delivery in those several months.

For many years after that, no matter where I taught, the system remained pretty much the same. A few minor tweaks here and a few medium adjustments there, but no matter the subject (world history, geography, U.S. history, civics), my students *attended* my classes in much the same way one *attends* a concert or ballgame—but without the fun. It wasn't until the early 1990s that I began to realize that perhaps being a participant is more interesting—and more rewarding—than being an attendee.

The more I learned about how the brain functions, the more I realized that he who does the participating does the learning. I had been the chief participator in my classrooms, and I can truly say that I learned a great deal about all my subjects over the years for the simple reason that I did all the talking, explaining, illustrating, describing, summarizing, inferring, analyzing, and synthesizing in the classroom. I understand now that talking is thinking, and thinking is learning; he who does the discussing and processing does the learning. Teachers in the pre-Internet age had a virtual monopoly on the flow of information, and it flowed one way. This was, for the most part, simply the way it was.

But today's students are used to an information system that is incredibly and increasingly diverse and multidirectional. The social networking provided by Facebook or Twitter literally makes it possible for anyone with access to the Internet to get in touch with anyone, anytime, anywhere. The power of this social networking even fueled and accelerated a bottom-up revolution in Egypt. Textbooks are out of date the moment they are written, and more so by the time they are proofed and printed. Wikipedia can be updated almost immediately, and the click of a mouse gives us access to knowledge about anything one cares to mention. The amount of instantly available information is mind boggling, especially to digital immigrants like me who can remember homes without television, offices lucky enough to have an *electric* typewriter, and telephones that came in every color as long as that color was black.

What students are used to *outside* the classroom must affect and inform what teachers do *inside* the classroom. Students who are actively engaged at home in their pursuit of action and interaction when it comes to things electronic are going to become increasingly dissatisfied with classrooms where they become decidedly passive observers—with little or no control over the proceedings. Teachers used to doing most of their work during class must learn to do their work in *preparation* for class, committing themselves to shifting the workload *during* class to students who essentially *want* to be active and, for the most part, interactive.

Taking the Time to Take the Time

We as educators often tear through the curriculum and the textbook at breakneck speed, fearful that if we slow down or drop our guard for even a moment, our students will miss out on something. The truth is that *because* we tear through the curriculum quickly, our students are missing out on a great deal. We feel the need to cover the material, whether or not students actually learn anything in the final analysis. Teachers must be given the flexibility and latitude to build into the overall structure strategies and activities that will engage students in their own learning. Darling-Hammond (1997) encourages such flexibility:

> Research has shown that teachers who plan with regard to students' abilities and needs and who are flexible while teaching are more effective, especially at stimulating higher-order thinking, than teachers who engage in extensive preplanning that is tightly focused on behavioral objectives and coverage of facts. (p. 72)

A strict pacing guide that does not provide teachers with time to experiment and take risks on behalf of kids is going to prove counterproductive, if well meaning. The if-this-is-Tuesday-everyone-must-be-on-the-same-page approach to learning presupposes that every child in every class is ready to wrap it up and move on, having understood what came before and being ready to dive into whatever comes next. Part of creating a culture of thinking, according to Ritchart (2015), means, "We need to call into question the underlying assumption present in schools, organizations, and society at large that doing more and doing it faster are always better" (p. 105). We feel the need for speed as we look at the calendar and see time slipping away. If we don't slow down and allow time to reflect both independently and interdependently, it is the students who will be slipping away.

The problem here is that it is inconceivable that all students in all classes or sections will arrive at the same point at the same time in terms of their learning progression. When teachers are focused on the pacing guide at the expense of learning and deep understanding, this is invariably going to lead to problems for students who are simply not ready to move on. The important thing is not how quickly we cover the material; the important thing is how deeply and completely students understand the material. In terms of skills related to writing, listening, speaking, analyzing, synthesizing, evaluating, creating, and innovating, students improve at different speeds and process information in different ways. This may mean teachers have to reteach something that did not "take" the first time through; the whole class may have to pause long enough to reinforce a particular skill. If, however, the pacing guide is always looming, teachers may feel the need to push on regardless, at the expense of learning. This is not to say that teachers should pay no attention whatsoever to pacing guides, but if the choice is between moving on before kids are ready or pausing long enough to ensure they understand or even extend their learning in some way, the kids should take precedence.

Above all, if we want students to be engaged in a way that leads to deep understanding, they must be given time to think, write in their reflective journals or learning logs, and do some out-loud thinking or structured brainstorming with a partner or other group members. All this requires not only time but also an understanding of what it takes to cooperate, communicate, and collaborate in pairs or groups. Once students understand how to do this effectively, my experience is that they can move up the cognitive ladder from knowledge to comprehension, analysis, inference, and evaluation as a matter of course. When planning lessons, time must be provided for students to analyze, individually or in groups, and to infer and draw conclusions in ways that will follow them into life and the workplace. If, as Drapeau (2009) points out, "it is important for teachers to actually teach students how to become good inferential thinkers," then those teachers must build such opportunities for this kind of higher-order thinking into the school day (p. 52).

Preparing the Work for the Students

There is what economists would call an *opportunity cost* for getting students actively involved during the class period and, in an extension of what takes place in class, at home. Getting ready for class when most of the class period consists of teacher talk takes relatively little time or effort, provided, for example, a science teacher has a good foundation in the subject matter. I used to look over some notes, put the salient points on an overhead transparency, arm myself with some interesting stories and historical anecdotes, turn off the lights, turn on the overhead projector—and give my students the benefit of four years of undergraduate and two years of graduate work as I entertained, elucidated, and otherwise did 80 percent of the work done in my classroom. But shifting the mental workload to students does require time on the part of teachers in terms of quality planning.

Teachers who want to move students from seatwork (sitting up straight, taking notes, and "paying attention") to feetwork (individual reflection, student-to-student communication, collaboration, checking progress using checklists and rubrics, and processing information in a timely fashion) must decide what advance preparation will be necessary to facilitate process and progress in the classroom. For example, one of the best teachers I know has her students work in collaborative groups to edit multiparagraph essays one day per week. Each group of four students grabs an envelope that holds an essay, and they set about working together to find the grammatical flaws and inconsistencies inserted by the teacher. Those fifth graders love being thus engaged and challenged, and that activity, together with many other writing strategies, has helped lead to a 100 percent pass rate for those students every year. They love writing, they improve at it, and they deal with all forms of assessment in stride. Not coincidentally, they love coming to that classroom every day.

For this particular teacher, most of her work is frontloaded days, weeks, or months ahead of time. She writes the essays in advance, and the mistakes are then inserted for students to find and correct in their groups. Some of the essays are informational, while others are persuasive; they are excellent pieces of writing that simply need editing by her students. She then laminates them and saves them from year to year; the frontloading in this case was considerable, but the outcomes made it all worthwhile, for the simple reason that her goal is to get students deeply and meaningfully engaged in collaborating with their peers. She models, and *they* do the work. At that point, her job is facilitating process, making sure things run smoothly. Her work, considerable in this case, was done up front, much of it on her own time.

In another elementary classroom, a teacher had stations set up around the room when students came back from lunch. At each station was a clipboard and sheet of paper that doubled as a graphic organizer and a set of instructions. Four sets of small bags containing various items sat at each station when the students arrived in the room, and the whiteboard at the front of the room told students who was in each trio or quartet. This was a lesson on probability, and the students spent almost twenty minutes working at analysis and synthesis; I can attest to the fact that they were totally engaged. *They* did the work in class; the *teacher* had frontloaded the process so that it was possible for them to do the work and the hypothesizing on their own. When her students asked a question, she simply asked another question; it was up to them to provide whatever answers were within reach. They could do this, by the way, at any location in the room, including sitting on the floor. This bit of choice provided novelty and allowed for more movement. Setting all this up in advance of the lesson took a good bit of her time, but once again it paid off in the end.

For educators of every stripe who think telling is teaching, frontloading may be as simple as making a few notes in advance of "giving students the information" from the curriculum. That brand of frontloading is easy, but the payoff is normally not there. Students who serve time in passive mode are learning little and may travel elsewhere in their minds. In the case of the teacher who had her elementary students working on an engaging lesson on probability, she let them *uncover* the curriculum, and their interest level was high. I observed that when a student somehow got off task, others soon pulled that student back in. They had been trained to facilitate process when in groups, and it showed. It does take far more preparation *outside* class to guarantee that students will be actively engaged *inside* the classroom. There are, as it happens, no shortcuts here; however, if success is measured by results, and if the results are good and getting better, it is worth the time spent.

Preparing the Students for the Work

Spring is my favorite time of the year. We have lots of gardens on our property, along with almost seventy azaleas. As soon as the weather turns warm in March or April, my wife and I busy ourselves getting the garden beds ready for more than thirty yards of hardwood mulch. We understand, however, that if time is not spent preparing the beds in a certain way, a good deal of the mulch will wind up on the driveway or in the lawn. Specifically, the leaves and debris need to be cleared out, and we need to edge deeply around the borders of all those garden beds and the edge of the driveway to keep the newly spread mulch from straying during the predictably heavy spring rains. Our considerable investment in the materials involved will be for nothing if the necessary preparation is not forthcoming.

Many teachers will commit to spending hours in advance of a block or class period preparing a lesson of some complexity, and seeing to it that everything is in place for a successful classroom experience, only to be disappointed when students prove incapable of functioning collaboratively in pairs, trios, or quartets. The best-laid plans can unravel in the face of students who are not used to working in pairs or groups, and this can be disheartening for teachers who have committed a great deal of time, effort, and (perhaps) their own money in the creation of what should have been an excellent collaborative adventure for those elementary, middle, or high school students.

The lesson must be prepared for the kids, but the kids must also be prepared for the lesson. This requires frontloading of the processes of student collaboration and student-to-student communication, and there are, once again, no shortcuts here. In every classroom where I observe successful interaction among students at any grade level, I know that the teacher in that classroom took the time to think not just about the content and not just about the components of the lesson; that teacher

spent the *first week* of school having her students practicing pro
could subsequently call on for the rest of the year. In fact, there i
key processes that can make or break a classroom system.

Learning to Listen. Students must discover with their teacher,
what listening is all about. I hear teachers say (and I used to s , uus),
"Pay attention!" or "Listen carefully when your partner is speaking!"
or "Listen up now!" What do those things mean? What does it mean to
"pay attention" when someone else is talking? When I was teaching in
those early years, I would have been satisfied if the student at whom
I directed that command had simply sat up straight in his seat. He
could have done that and gone to a better place in his mind, not listening at all, and I would never have known the difference. My focus was
on compliance, not thinking. Effective teachers lead their students in a
discussion about what listening is all about (eye contact, body language,
facial expressions, asking questions, paraphrasing) and then have them
talk with each other as they practice those components of active listening. Once again, it is not enough for students to *know* what it takes to
actively listen—they must work on this regularly beginning the *first day
of school.*

Another way to approach the whole idea of listening as part of the
communication process involves an activity that gets students up, moving, and sharing as they try to discover what the next lesson (active
listening skills) is all about. Frontloading this activity involves the components of active listening written in complete sentences and printed on
cards. Teachers should give no clues as to content; students should not,
for example, be told that this is the opening salvo of a lesson on active
listening. The idea is to let them sort it out as the activity unfolds. They
need to make the connections and do the discovering on their own.

Each student will eventually receive one card up front; each of these
several cards contains only one sentence. Here are some that might be
included:

- Greet your partner.
- Stand straight but in relaxed mode.
- Ask questions to increase understanding.
- Make and maintain eye contact.
- Avoid distracting gestures.
- Paraphrase when the person is finished talking.
- If seated, avoid doodling or writing.
- Ignore distractions.
- Attend fully to your partner.
- Smile and use supportive body language.
- Avoid judging the person or his or her ideas.
- Don't look at your watch.
- Keep your hands at your sides, palms in.

- Avoid sarcasm.
- Pause before responding.
- Nod when appropriate.
- Thank your partner when the conversation is over.

There are many more of these components that could be placed on index cards or printed up, laminated, and saved from year to year.

Without telling students what this is all about, the teacher places a card face down on each desk; she then instructs her students to pick up the card and stand with a partner somewhere in the room. (Furniture arrangements that open up the center of the room are more conducive to activities like this.) Each student should then share the sentence on his or her card with that partner and discuss what the sentences have in common. Once that is done, students in the pair thank each other, *switch cards,* hold their new cards in the air, and look for another classmate who has his or her card in the air, approaching that person. Newly paired, the process begins over again until the teacher is sure that everyone has paired and shared several times. At this point, the teacher can ask them to thank their current partners for sharing and take their seats, to the accompaniment of some upbeat music.

During the multiple pair-share conversations, students had the opportunity to compare many of the components of active listening, once again without being told what the topic was. It was up to the students to analyze and infer together; when they are back in their seats, the teacher can have them record their thoughts in their journals and then facilitate a class discussion concerning what *all* the cards seemed to have in common. Again, rather than having students write down the components of active listening off the board or from the screen up front (as I would most certainly done early in my teaching career), *they must try to figure out what is going on by themselves,* first in rotating pairs and then as part of the larger group. The teacher can facilitate this whole-class conversation, perhaps with a newly revealed list of all the sentences displayed on the screen. The important thing here is that the list came *after* the thinking, the sharing, and the journal writing.

Having established that active listening is the topic alluded to by the cards, the teacher can then begin to facilitate process once more by having the students *practice* the art of listening in pairs and groups. What the students did during the initial activity—along with a reduced list of seven or eight key components of active listening displayed permanently on the wall as a checklist of sorts—can serve as the foundation for their collaborative efforts. Teachers who believe that students bring listening skills into their classrooms along with their backpacks are in for a rude awakening during paired or group activities. The skills related to listening are important—get to it on the first day of school; this bit of front-loading should pay off handsomely during the school year. Students need to understand what it is to listen, practice the skills frequently during the first week, and then have it introduced into the context of course content as a matter of course.

Improving Transitions. If at the beginning of an activity students fail to move quickly and uneventfully into standing pairs, trios, or quartets, the entire activity can unravel. Teachers who frontload their lessons with plenty of practice in transitioning from seatwork to feetwork during the first five days of school are investing in a smooth-running classroom. These teachers properly put the process horse in front of the content cart. On the other hand, the best lessons in the world can be brought to a halt by transitions that don't work because time has not been spent training students to shift gears efficiently. Transitioning from one part of the overall lesson to another should not take long, and simply *telling* students how they should accomplish these transitions is not enough. The first five days of school must be used to explain and rehearse those basic transition processes until they become routine. I know teachers who use a stopwatch to cut down on the time involved in shifting gears in their classrooms.

In some classrooms, transition points are chaotic for the simple reason that students are not sure what to do; nor are they aware of how much time has been allocated to shifting gears from one activity to another. I have seen classrooms where students took entirely too long to get ready to go to PE or lunch; the teachers let the students set the pace . . . and the pace was slow. Multiply several slow and chaotic transitions during the day by the number of days in the school year, and the time wasted can be substantial. Time, after all, is what teachers will tell you is their most precious commodity. If inefficient processes take too much of that time, valuable instructional time can be lost on a regular basis. Again, frontloading requires practicing transitions until students can clean up, set up, stand up, move about—and out—quickly and efficiently. Anything else should be unacceptable.

Using a Single *Way to Get the Attention of Students.* Teachers need to make sure that when they want to get students to stop, look, and listen, it is through the use of *one* procedural norm that combines both the visual and the auditory. For example, one teacher I know raises her hand and says, "Pause, look this way please!" and then waits until everyone is looking at her. She understands that if she proceeds before the last person is looking directly at her, she is giving everyone permission to continue talking or looking at someone else. Another teacher uses music to get the attention of her students; if students are in pairs discussing something, she will bring the volume of the music up and cut it off. At that point her students pause and turn toward the teacher. They do this because she spent time during the first five days of school practicing this over and over again. She frontloaded success by establishing and rehearsing a necessary procedure until the students mastered it. The teacher kept it simple by using only one way to get their attention, and she spent a good deal of time on the first day of school getting her students used to finishing what they were discussing with a partner quickly and turning to face her *on that one signal.*

Working the Crowd. In classrooms where a teacher puts students to work on an assignment and then retreats behind her own desk, the likelihood is that there is going to be much less work done by students who are basically unsupervised and—in their minds—forgotten. When I am in classrooms, I watch students closely. In those classrooms where the teacher puts things in motion and then goes behind the desk, or works on a bulletin board, or rearranges files in a cabinet, things tend not to stay in motion for as long a time as they might if the teacher is actively circulating among her students. In one classroom where the teacher told students to begin something that she said should take five minutes, the students expanded the work to fill about fifteen minutes, for the simple reason that the teacher used that time to grade papers at her desk.

There are at least three reasons why teachers need to get into the habit of circulating throughout the room any time students are doing anything—collaborative or otherwise. First, it says the teacher is interested in what is going on. Second, it allows the teacher to check for understanding, whether by reading what students are writing in their learning logs, for example, or discussing something with a partner or partners. Third, it is an excellent management technique. Jones (2007) uses the wonderful phrase *working the crowd,* relating it to comedians working the audience during a performance, and explains the dynamics of doing so as it relates to classroom management: "Natural teachers instinctively work the crowd. They have an innate sense of being 'in contact' with the students. They use the proximity of their bodies as an instrument of management. They *move*" (p. 31). The very first time a teacher has students write or collaborate in any way, he or she should be on the move, working the crowd for all it is worth.

Creating a Safe Classroom. It is wonderful to walk into a classroom where students are relaxed and where the relationships between and among teachers and students are strong and positive. Speaking specifically of reading, Keene and Zimmermann (2007) admire and applaud teachers "who create the environment and provide the tools students need to read deeply and thoughtfully, so they can contemplate ideas alone and with others, and write persuasively about what they read" (p. 252). Tools introduced in an unsafe or unstable classroom environment will have no power; attempts to introduce student collaboration into this kind of climate will simply not work. Teachers who do not realize the root cause for the failure of the collaboration may blame the strategy. The best way for teachers to see the contrast between the use of a strategy in their own and someone else's classroom is to take the time to visit that classroom to see another teacher use it successfully. Another way for districts or schools to provide this contrast is through the use of video segments that highlight the effective use of engagement strategies. Unless an individual teacher has some perspective, and unless administrators can work with teach-

> Part of the frontloading process for teachers is to take the time to create a physical climate that stimulates the curiosity and imagination of the students who will spend an entire school year there.

ers to break the hold of isolation, teachers may shy away from effective collaborative strategies that would help their students.

Students must be able to speak in the classroom without fear of a negative response on the part of the teacher or their peers. Students must know they can make a mistake without fear of being judged; as we'll see in the next chapter, mistakes are the lifeblood of continuous improvement for the simple reason that they provide feedback to those who made the effort in the first place. Classrooms where students are left to bully their classmates will never be ready for the kinds of engagement and collaboration that feed the continuous-improvement cycle. Students will ever remain attendees in classrooms where it is simply not safe to speak or volunteer something; before students can become true participants in their own learning, teachers have to create the conditions under which participation is possible.

Encourage the Asking of Questions in Pursuit of Solving Problems. When kids are young, they ask questions by the ton, and they do so because they are trying to make sense of the world around them; they are trying to understand. They are, in fact, immensely interested in the *why?* of their worlds. Somewhere along their educational highway, we as educators substitute the why with the what—things they need to know marked by us as important. Pacing guides and an ever-increasing body of knowledge (each year adds a chapter to history books) tend to squeeze out the why in favor of the what (and how fast), and the what is easily tested through the use of multiple-choice testing.

The problem, of course, is that life is not a multiple-choice test. Life throws us curve balls and interesting diversions in the form of problems that need to be solved. Asking questions is part of the problem-solving process; I want my doctor to ask me lots of questions on the way to a diagnosis. Today's global economy and an ever-increasing amount of competition require that we prepare employees capable of critical thinking and problem solving. Trilling and Fadel (2009) affirm that "puzzling problems that demand fresh ideas in the pursuit of new and better solutions can lead to creative, even breakthrough results and have been the source of useful inventions and innovations great and small throughout history" (p. 93). When students have the time to reflect individually or in pairs or groups, and when they are provided with time to write in a reflective learning log or journal, there is an opportunity there for them to articulate and then ask questions that can later be shared with their team or their classmates in general.

Teachers, administrators, and curriculum coordinators for large school districts need to let up on the gas a bit if it will give students the time to reflect, share, and *ask questions*. Problem solving should be part of any curriculum, and open-ended questions should replace closed questions in an attempt to "engage children's imaginations and help motivate them to explore, discover, create, and learn" (Trilling & Fadel, 2009, p. 94). Understanding the power of reflection, problem solving, and asking questions, two men founded Google, and expect fully 20 percent of employee time to be "dedicated to personal research of their own choosing" (Girard, 2009, p. 64). Google, by any measure, has been incredibly successful, and much of that success is due to the time they allow for personal and team reflection and inquiry.

Recognizing and Harnessing the Power of Curiosity. When I was teaching U.S. history or world history, the most interesting and productive classes were those where students asked a great many questions. On many of those occasions, their interest was piqued by stories or original documents related to the subject matter. The drummer boy who was captured by the Confederate Army on its way through Pennsylvania in June of 1863, or portions of primary documents concerning slavery, or the true story of a station on the Underground Railroad a friend and I discovered in his grandmother's basement, or short video clips showing blocks-long bread lines during the Great Depression, or the plight of orphans on trains headed for homes in the Midwest—all these rarely failed to get the attention of my students, and the whole concept of the Underground Railroad, along with the Fugitive Slave Act and Dred Scot, to having my sixth-period, seventh-grade class write a play on a runaway slave set in the late 1850s. I was able to pique their curiosity and work it into something tremendously creative and fun for my students.

The brain makes connections; that is what it does, and the richer the context for a particular subject, the more connections the brain is likely to make. These connections, according to Gunter, Estes, and Schwab (1999), provide the key to curiosity:

> Teaching in ways that make information interesting to learners helps them see the connections between what they are learning and what they know, between what they are learning in school and the world, and between the same information in different disciplines. (p. 371)

Today's students can, at the click of a mouse, connect to more sources of information than was even remotely possible only a couple of decades ago. Teachers who frontload their lessons with stories, anecdotes, interesting pictures and graphics, and intriguing questions can send their students home or to the computer lab with any number of answers to find, connections to make, information to uncover, or problems to solve.

I was recently in a wonderful, vibrant elementary classroom that was absolutely brimming with color, replete with pictures and graphics, and chock full of books to read and puzzles to solve. I know there had to be some walls there somewhere, but I'm not entirely certain what color they were—I know they were covered with wonderfully interesting things that stimulate curiosity and the imagination. On the other hand, I have been in classrooms where the walls are bare and beige; in one high school geography classroom, the only map on the wall was almost torn in half and just hung from the single bulletin board in the room. *It just hung there.* I have seen factory walls more interesting than those in that high school classroom. Imagine being a student in classrooms as physically different as those two. The message from the elementary classroom décor was, "I love being here and you will, too!" The message of the high school classroom was, "Yeah, whatever."

Howard (2006) cites a study conducted at the University of California, Berkeley, where two groups of rats were placed in different cages. One cage was "dull," while the other was a "Disneyland" cage; the result over time was that "the brains of the highly stimulated rats grew larger and developed denser concentrations of synapses" (p. 522). Another Berkeley study showed that "synaptic structures show growth from enriched environments throughout the life span, including old age" (p. 522). The brain loves such rich environments, and teachers can choose what kind of physical environment their students walk into on that first day of class—one that contains something to intrigue the curious, or one that is sterile and dull. Part of the frontloading process for teachers is to take the time to create a physical climate that stimulates the curiosity and imagination of the students who will spend an entire school year there.

Taking the Time to Rearrange the Classroom for Student Interaction and Collaboration. I sometimes wonder why I had a teacher's desk. Really. It served, as I think back on it, as a large, wooden depository for stuff—lots of stuff. Stuff piled on stuff. It was an archaeologist's fantasy. I had bookcases that contained books I rarely used or referenced. There was a four-drawer file cabinet that I could have replaced with a much smaller cabinet had I taken the time to throw out old tests, out-of-date curriculum documents, old handouts, big binders, medium binders, little binders, and any number of other unnecessary forms, materials, and pieces of paper. My room, not to put too fine a point on it, was crammed with stuff, much of which served no apparent purpose.

When a teacher requests it, I will help rearrange her classroom with an eye toward the number one goal for an active classroom where collaboration is the name of the game. Seated students should be able to turn to a partner whenever the teacher calls for a paired discussion, and there should be a large open area for students to meet in standing pairs, trios, or quartets. I recommend to teachers that they find six spaces on class-room walls—evenly spaced all around the room—for posters, charts, or graphics that can be part of gallery-walk activities for students working in trios or quartets. One teacher purchased six cork boards that she had fastened on the wall, making the placement of blank sheets of chart paper easy. She also had clips that held markers at each station; all this was put in place in the summer, and it helped facilitate the frequent gallery walks that were part of an extremely interactive classroom system.

Teachers at any grade level can look through their lesson plans to see which activities that their students normally do while seated can be done while standing, moving, and working together. Teachers need to think like students and then think about that night class where they wanted to get up and move well *before* the break. I often say that kids gotta move, and teachers anticipating a new school year should take the time to think of ways to get students up and moving frequently. Classroom arrange-ments that facilitate such movement can be set up easily, if teachers are willing to get rid of a lot of things they don't use. In one classroom, the teacher simply put a table in the hallway with a sign that said, "Take what you want!" in big, bold letters. When we were done with our remodeling effort, the center of the room was opened nicely, and every student had a shoulder partner in the adjacent desk and a face partner in front.

Final Thoughts

A teacher would do well to make a list of all the process-related com-ponents in her classroom system. This system, composed of myriad processes that work or don't work at all, will make or break an active, engaged, and collaborative classroom. When students feel safe and com-fortable sharing and asking questions in a rich environment that stimu-lates their curiosity, they are in a position to be able to make progress regardless of the subject matter. Great teachers spend the first week of school frontloading success by getting the processes—and the standards connected to those processes—down cold. At the end of the first week of school, students should be able to stand, sit, move, share, and ask ques-tions in an atmosphere conducive to learning. They should understand what listening involves, and active listening should be part of their social-skills repertoire. The frontloading of a rich, safe, and exciting class-room environment involves time and effort on the part of the teacher, but my experience tells me it is well worth the effort.

In Chapter 8, we'll take a look at the critical role feedback plays in the continuous-improvement cycle.

8

Feedback and Praise

The bell sounded for the last lap of the state finals of the 3200-meter run. Curt, who was currently in the lead by a few yards, remembered what his distance coach had said about the runner who was three back at the moment, and not far behind. "He'll pick up speed coming off the last turn, and you need to be well ahead of him by that time." Curt knew he had to increase the lead enough to keep it in the face of that kick his coach was sure would come. He increased his stride a bit and began to pull away on the straight stretch going into the final turn. Curt felt good in spite of the heat, and going into the turn he could see his lead was increasing with every stride. Curt did not have much of a kick, but he did have a good lead now, and he gave it everything he had coming down the final stretch toward the finish line. He could hear the kid in second place breathing hard and coming fast, but Curt crossed the line two strides ahead and took home the gold.

Curt's teammates met him at the tent they had set up outside the fence surrounding the track, and he wasted no time in thanking his coach, whose assistance over the course of a long track season had played a big role in leading them to this moment and a big victory. The year before, as a junior running on this same track, Curt had found himself boxed in for much of the race, and had to settle for third place. On the bus on the way home, his coach had asked him how he might have avoided that situation. Curt had offered up a couple of solutions, his coach asked a few more questions, and they came up with some ideas on how to keep from getting boxed in in the future. Reflecting on the conversation once he got home, it occurred to Curt that his coach had basically let him think it through and work it out; he had answered Curt's questions with more *questions, and they had arrived at a solution together. This year Curt stayed clear of the box, kept the lead during the last 400 meters, and took home the gold.*

Good teachers and coaches need to know more than their subject or their sport. They need to know their students and athletes; they need to know what makes them tick in the way Curt's coach understood both his strengths and his areas of opportunity. Curt didn't have, and would never have, a good kick at the end of a long race like the 3200. But Curt had strengths, including the ability to pad the lead against his opponents during the eight laps around the track. His coach had both knowledge and experience; he also knew what to say to Curt when it came to giving feedback, along with when it would do the most good. He appreciated the uselessness of phrases like, "Well done!" or "Good job!" as stand-alone praise after a race. Curt's coach recognized that good feedback is task-oriented. He had also developed a working relationship with Curt and the other distance runners on the team that made the feedback both welcome and powerful. Together they set goals, identified benchmarks along the way, and partnered in a totally satisfying effort.

While teaching social studies at a middle school in Virginia, I served as yearbook adviser. We chose to compete not against other schools, but against a set of standards published by the Columbia Scholastic Press Association (CSPA). Continuous improvement was our mantra, and we took advantage of every bit of feedback available. Every double-page spread was designed to standards provided by CSPA, and the drafts of stories and captions had to be read by at least three staff members before heading to my desk. We were *guided* by the standards, but we were *driven* by our desire to write stories worth reading and to take pictures worth reproducing. When the boxes loaded with yearbooks were finally delivered, I did not open them immediately. The staff gathered at our house after school one evening, and the editors were each handed a pair of scissors. They opened one of the boxes and everyone on the staff saw the books for the first time together. We celebrated the hard work, the late evenings, and finally the Gold Crown award we received from CSPA. More important, we had produced a book that would serve in future years as a history of that school year.

In the case of the distance runner and the yearbook staff, feedback was a critical and indispensable component of the continuous improvement process. As yearbook adviser, I was careful to let staff members know that feedback is, as Shute (2008) asserts, "information communicated to the learner that is intended to modify his or her thinking or behavior for the purpose of improving learning" (p. 154). My staffers understood that feedback should be task- and goal-oriented; it was not personal.

We spent a good deal of time during the summer reading award-winning yearbooks from other schools. At our early meetings we talked about what made the copy, captions, layouts, and pictures in those books extraordinary. We attended workshops where instructors displayed—and showed us how to create—page design that met the most rigorous standards. As the year progressed, we had a clear picture in our minds of what we wanted to produce. Along the way we compared what we were creating with the "anchor" yearbooks that served as the standard for journalism. I can't remember how many times staff members would go to the shelf containing these great yearbooks, pull one or two down, and talk with other staff members about what made the stories, captions, pictures, and layouts outstanding. Their increasing knowledge of what makes a good yearbook allowed them to provide each other with what amounted to a steady stream of formative assessment—freely given and entirely welcome.

Challenge and a Sense of Urgency

As with distance runners or yearbook staffs constantly trying to improve, for students there must be a challenge in the form of a goal that can be reached over time. Challenging goals, says Hattie (2012), "inform individuals about the level of performance desired, meaning that these individuals can then track their performance toward these targets" (p. 131). Absent the challenge, "the feedback is probably of little or any value; if students already know the material or find it too easy, then seeking or providing feedback will have little effect" (p. 131). Teachers need to make sure students understand what the goal is—and how they can get there.

For students who are learning something where they have little prior knowledge or experience, feedback should be immediate. The same is true for teachers traveling on their own continuous-improvement highway. As Nagel (2015) points out,

> Most teachers state that feedback from an administrator after a classroom observation is most useful if it is specific and they can apply it right away. The specificity and timeliness of the feedback is what makes it effective and useful. Teachers also often state that when feedback from their administrator either lacks specificity or arrives too long after the observation to be useful or applied, it is then usually very ineffective and basically useless. (p. 120)

There is a sense of urgency that can serve to drive administrators and teachers alike to provide task-oriented and timely feedback that can be used immediately to improve performance. Teachers who regularly return assignments with little or no specific feedback, or who wait days or even weeks before getting the work returned, send the message that the assignments are not that important. The administrator who waits days or even weeks before meeting with a teacher after a classroom observation sends the message that the observation wasn't high on her list of significant events. Feedback is as important in buildings and classrooms as it is on the track, the playing field, or the basketball court. Useful feedback provided in a timely manner keeps the process going, allowing students to make adjustments, correct mistakes, and move toward the goal.

However, feedback *can* be delayed on occasion. Delayed feedback, according to O'Connell and Vandas (2015), "tends to be more effective when students have a solid foundation in a concept or skill and are working to deepen their learning. As we transition from surface to deep learning, delayed feedback is often more effective" (p. 102). In these situations, students have enough context, content, or skills for them to wrestle effectively with what might come next in their continuous-improvement journey.

The Power of Internal Feedback

We think of feedback as something that is external, and it is certainly true that such feedback can be incredibly effective. External feedback can arrive from many sources, including teachers, peers, parents, standards, check-lists, and rubrics. But I have often felt that the greatest accelerant to learning may well be internal; for my yearbook staffers, the pride that resulted from one of their own stories well written or a double-page spread layout that really clicked was internal, and it drove us all the way to opening the boxes at our home when the books arrived in the spring. There is an immense feeling of satisfaction from a job well done, and it is wonderful for any adult adviser, coach, or teacher to see that sense of pride etched on the faces of young people who continue to improve over time.

This feeling of satisfaction even has a name: the IKEA effect (Hattie & Yates, 2014). In an attempt to see how something someone creates affects the perceived value placed on the finished product, one group of university students was instructed to assemble a small IKEA storage box. They were then asked what they would pay for the completed box; the average was 78 cents. Members of another group of students were each shown one of the completed boxes, and asked what they would pay; the average was 48 cents. We place a high value on what we have accomplished.

The best athletic coaches and teachers I have known in well over four decades in education are those who have constructed a *system of continuous improvement* comprised of exceptionally efficient and ultimately effective processes that facilitate progress on the basketball court or in the classroom. Those coaches and teachers understand that the satisfaction resulting from a job well done is the precursor to future success. A cross-country runner who may not have won the meet, but who just improved

on her personal best time, looks forward to the next ɪ
better time. The math student who just solved a particul
lem feels a sense of satisfaction, and the language arts
look at his portfolio of essays and see steady progress aɡ
may well develop the kind of confidence that will leac
improvements down the road. For the runner who just
it may be personal. For the yearbook staff experiencing ʋ̴ɪe joy of seeing
the product of their collective efforts over several months, it is a shared
satisfaction.

The *finished* product for the yearbook staff or the distance runner
serves as an evaluation and is therefore summative; it shows how they
did. But the *path* to the finished product is formative; the system is—or
should be—set up to provide continual assistance and guidance. Feedback is not separate from the improvement process; it is an integral part of
the process. For runners and yearbook staffers there are benchmarks to be
reached, standards to be consulted, and adjustments to be made. It is the
job of the coach, the band director, the classroom teacher, and the building
administrators to establish and maintain a supportive system that acceler-
ates improvement on the way to the completed product, task, or goal. In
the classroom, this system of support cannot be haphazard; it should be
constructed in such a way that students always have at their disposal the
kind of feedback that will help close the gap between where the student is
and where he wants to be. The improvement system must also encourage
and indeed celebrate mistakes that serve as the lifeblood of improvement.

Mistakes as Feedback

I sometimes think our educational system is obsessed with what might
be called *rightanswermania*. Students sit down to take a hundred-point
test composed of multiple-choice questions, and they know up front
there is only one right answer among the four possibilities in each case.
Correctly selecting the right answers on computerized assessments may
result in a smiley face or some happy music, a reminder to students that
we celebrate right answers and discourage mistakes. One elementary
teacher told me that in one online assessment, a big red X appears over
the answer when it is wrong, accompanied by a loud buzzing noise.
Mistakes count against us when it comes to the final tally. Right answers
are welcome, while mistakes are to be avoided at all costs. After all, the
student's grade depends on it.

Students, especially as they get older, don't want to be wrong, and
they can be embarrassed when caught out being wrong. I frequently hear
teachers say, "Who knows the answer to this question?" Norm doesn't
know the answer, but sits quietly, safe in the knowledge that Mary does.
Mary always knows the answer. If the teacher in Norm's class throws

ut that question and can get no one else to volunteer the answer, she can turn to Mary and the circuit is closed. The teacher gets her answer, acknowledges it, and moves on to the next question. Norm sits tight, watches the clock, and prays the teacher doesn't remember she has popsicle sticks with everyone's names on them.

Many students won't volunteer the answer, even if they are fairly certain they know it, because they don't want to be wrong. They don't want to trigger the negative reactions of classmates quick to make fun of the wrong answer and the unfortunate student who volunteered it— out loud. From the standpoint of most students, then, the best course of action is to clam up and let Mary do the heavy lifting. This negative dynamic can squeeze the cognitive life out of a classroom. Bluestein (2001) says, "Even when teachers offer encouragement and are very tolerant of mistakes and errors, it may take kids a while to catch on— especially if they've had a history of being shamed or humiliated for past mistakes" (p. 221). The teacher who wants to overcome this tendency for students to disengage when what she wants them to do is *fully* engage needs to take some actions to convince students that making mistakes and errors is acceptable and expected:

1. The classroom climate must be emotionally safe, and part of that is to model—and teach to students—excellent listening skills. "Some students ridicule, laugh at, or put down other students' ideas," affirms Costa (2008). "We want our students to learn to devote their mental energies to another person and invest themselves in their partner's ideas" (p. 33). When teachers interrupt students or respond in ways that may be interpreted as ridicule, it is unreasonable to expect students will act otherwise. Teachers must make it clear that such behavior is not tolerated, *and then they must not tolerate it.*

2. The whole idea of the efficacy of errors should be introduced and discussed during the first days of school. A teacher can have students stand and pair up, facing the screen. On the screen is the following question: *How can mistakes be part of the improvement process? Discuss one or two examples with your partner.* Having given them the cue to start their discussions, the teacher can then walk around the room and listen in on various conversations. When he hears something he wants shared with the whole class, he can simply ask the person who brought it up in the paired conversation if she will share it later on. The teacher doesn't have to remember the question, but he needs to remember the name. While students are talking, the teacher may identify three or four students whom he wants to share; he gets their permission and remembers the names. Students are all engaged during the pair share, and it is the teacher's job to listen, observe, and choose

three or four students to share with the whole class *what they have already discussed with a partner.*

3. Most questions asked by teachers in classrooms are convergent in nature, meaning they have only one right answer. All roads lead to that one correct response in the manner of summative assessments and standardized tests. Teachers can, however, pose questions that are more divergent; they may have several possible answers. A middle school teacher could, for example, have students circulate among a half dozen wall charts, providing possible answers for the question at the top of each. For example, *What are some ways we can deal with the severe drought in western states?* and *What might result from <u>not</u> dealing with a severe drought situation?* This kind of brainstorming in trios or quartets (often called a gallery walk) provides students with the opportunity to work together on possible answers, without concerning themselves with seeking "the one right answer."

Improvement requires the taking of risks. Risks invite mistakes, and students won't take those risks if the classroom climate is not safe.

Mistakes that are painful in their consequences often trigger corrections that prove to be effective and lasting. The distance runner in the 3200-meter run who finds herself boxed in by several runners for a couple of laps may ultimately lose the race because she could not move around and in front of other runners at will. The runner's own experience may provide some internal feedback that provides a workable fix. If she does not know how to keep that from happening as she reflects on the race, she will seek feedback from the coach or a more-experienced runner on the team. We often experience things, make mistakes, then reflect on those mistakes as we determine to avoid that particular error or lapse in judgment. Perhaps Hattie (2012) says it best:

All students (as all teachers) do not succeed the first time, nor do they always know what to do next, and nor do they always attain perfection. This is not a deficit, or deficit thinking, or concentrating on the negative; rather, it is the opposite in that acknowledging errors allows for opportunities. Error is the difference between what we know and can do, and what we aim to know and do—and this applies to all (struggling and talented; students and teachers). Knowing this error is fundamental to moving towards success. This is the purpose of feedback. (pp. 129–130)

Teachers have to give the whole idea of error in classroom settings a good deal of thought. What is most important is not what the teacher knows or intends, but what his students perceive. Teachers who understand the role of mistakes in continuous improvement should see to it that students arrive at that same understanding. A student who believes mistakes provide opportunities to improve will not be obsessed with avoiding them, provided the learning environment is safe and supportive. We want students to *seek* feedback and view errors as part of the improvement process. If they view feedback and errors as useful signposts on their continuous-improvement journeys, they are likely to welcome both.

Peer Feedback

Earlier I recounted the experience of a student who asked his shoulder partner to help him with the meaning of a particular word. His partner did not dismiss him out of hand; indeed, he put down his own book and proceeded to collaborate with his friend to solve the problem. The whole episode was a perfect example of what can happen when students are not afraid to approach a classmate, and the classmate's natural inclination is to be helpful and not dismissive. This all happened within a few feet of the teacher, and she could have said what I have heard said many times in classrooms: "Don't bother Fred. You have a dictionary!" Her students were quiet, cooperative, collaborative, and ultimately successful . . . without interrupting the teacher or the teacher assistant. When I spoke with the teacher after class was over, she said she encouraged them to do just what those two boys did: "If you want to find something out, I'm not your only source of information." The student who needed the help was not afraid to ask, and his partner wasn't afraid to provide a bit of assistance.

Some teachers use what I employed on my yearbook staff: *three before me.* This meant, as I stated earlier in the chapter, that three staff members had to edit a story *and sign off on their edits.* When it finally got to me, I saw not only the original draft, but the edits as well. "What students say or write about each other's work," notes Heritage (2010), "can show how well they understand the learning goals and success criteria, and the depth of their thinking about the task at hand" (p. 92). Teachers who use online-learning platforms like Edmodo can see the drafts of documents and the edits from students in the class. This provides, as Heritage has said, valuable feedback to the teacher. If the teacher observes edits or comments that are simply incorrect, she can deal with it in class the next day.

Another powerful advantage to providing opportunities for peer feedback is that the students giving the feedback are in the position of reinforcing their own learning. In editing a piece of copy, a student may sense something is not right, but feel the need to check on it with another student, the teacher, a printed source, a textbook, or online. In doing so, that student has taken another step on his or her continuous-improvement journey.

A Word of Caution

While peer feedback can be positive and effective, it can also be destructive on occasion. The student who writes on someone's paper, *This is just stupid!* may not accelerate the continuous improvement process. Teachers can model the kind of feedback students might give, using, as Heritage (2010) suggests, some sentence starters such as "Have you thought about. . . . ?" or "I wasn't clear what you meant when you said . . ." (p. 114). Teachers can work together to help develop peer-feedback skills by doing the following:

- Role playing with other teachers how to give feedback on a piece of student work and then demonstrating this to students as an exemplar, along with a discussion of what was effective about the feedback
- Observing other classrooms to see how the teacher organizes opportunities for peer feedback. Listening to or reading peer feedback and reflecting on what was effective, or how students might be helped to improve
- Teachers inviting colleagues to observe them and their students when peer feedback is part of the lesson, and debriefing afterward about what was successful, what could improve, and how to help students become more skilled (Heritage, 2010, pp. 114–115)

If the teachers in a building or on a particular middle school team are willing to work together to help students with their peer-feedback skills, the continuous-improvement process—and student achievement—will be well served.

Praise Is Not Feedback

Our property sits on a quiet side street, and when my wife and I are working out front we often say hello to neighbors and joggers passing the house. We take great pride in our yard and gardens, and passersby will pay us compliments along the lines of "Looks great!" or "You always have such a nice yard!" This praise is always welcome, frankly; it makes us feel good and we do appreciate the comments. The praise is, if anything, more summative than formative, and does not provide anything in the way of task-oriented feedback designed to help us make adjustments on our continuous-improvement journey. We appreciate it, and understand it for what it is—praise.

One big difference between our work in the yard and what students are doing in the classroom is this: My wife and I know what we are doing, where we are going, and how to get there. Our experience and our research into what works and what doesn't when it comes to creating the kind of yard and gardens we want informs us along the way, but we know at any given stage in the operation *exactly what to do next*. We have been over this ground (pun intended) many times before, and we have benchmarks along the way on a long Saturday outside: *This* garden comes first, followed by *that* garden or the planting of those bushes or flowers. After doing this for decades, we have a roadmap in our minds and we follow it. There is an inner satisfaction (the IKEA effect) that kicks in as each of several short- and intermediate-range goals is successfully completed.

Students, on the other hand, even if they know exactly where they want to *be* with a particular task, may not know what to do next in order to get there. This is new and unfamiliar territory, and they don't possess a mental roadmap based on the experience of years. The teacher's job is to help the student understand where he is now, where he wants to be, and what he needs to do next to move him along. Saying "Good job!" or "Well done!" to a student, and then walking away, provides no clue as to what to do next. It doesn't even tell the student—specifically—to *what* the teacher is referring when she says, "Good work!" Ritchart (2015) asserts that a teacher's words to the student must be instructionally oriented, directly related to the task with which the student is wrestling at the time:

> Furthermore, this information has to be received and actionable, guiding future learning. This suggests that our comments should identify what has been done well as much as what still needs improvement and then give guidance in helping the student achieve that improvement. If our words don't achieve this, then our comments are probably best understood as evaluation rather than feedback. (p. 81)

The implication of "Good job!" for the student who hears this from the teacher is that everything he is doing or has done is correct. As Ritchart says in the preceding passage, this has an evaluative feel, and therefore is more summative than formative. "Feedback must be very specific," asserts Erlauer (2003), "to assist the learner in knowing exactly what to keep doing and what to change" (p. 128). Good coaches and good teachers understand this, and they know the difference between praise and feedback.

The teacher who says, or writes, "You do good work, Norm!" is speaking directly to ability or effort, and it does not address the task itself. It is different if the teacher says to Norm, "Notice how in this second draft you followed this procedure and it worked. The only difference between the outcome yesterday and today is the use of the procedure." This reminds Norm that the use of that particular procedure in the second iteration of the task led to his success. "The way in which teachers give feedback to students about their use of strategies," affirm Hattie, Biggs, and Purdie (1996), "will probably influence their attributions for success or failure more than will feedback regarding either ability or effort" (p. 131). Telling a student he "did a good job" doesn't really give him any useful information that can help close the gap between where he is now and where he wants to be.

Teachers can aim well-intentioned praise at students and do them no good at all. Teachers may, on occasion, say something like, "Everyone congratulate Sheila on having the best paper in the class. In fact, let's give Sheila a hand!" This may leave Sheila wanting to crawl under her desk, and it may leave her open to ridicule in the hallway after class. If the idea of giving public praise is "to show someone who did a good job that this has been noticed, there is no need to do so in a way that may stir up others' resentment and possibly even embarrass the person being publicly praised" (Kohn, 1999, p. 111). Praise that is given in private—and is specific and timely—can serve a positive purpose, but doing so in public may cause problems for the very person the teacher is attempting to applaud.

Dweck (2007) suggests using "process praise" as a motivator. Providing praise related to improvement, for example, can have a positive effect: "This second draft of your paper demonstrates you understand verb/subject agreement. Your work with Sandy on this last week really appears to have helped. Well done." This praise is not about how intelligent the student is; it is instead related to a specific improvement made as a result of effort and a bit of collaboration with Sandy, the student's classmate. "Process praise," says Dweck, "keeps students focused, not on something called ability that they may or may not have and that magically creates success or failure, but on processes they can all engage in and learn" (p. 37). The tagline "Well done" at the end of the specific feedback above means something; it refers to the process that made the difference in the second draft of the paper.

Improvement by Wandering Around

Zwiers (2014) uses the term *academic encouragement* to describe specific language teachers can use to highlight something the student has done. He recommends some "starters" teachers can use to get a conversation going with students:

"I liked the way that you added supporting details to your . . ."

"Wow, I didn't know that . . ."

"You really synthesized the information from different places very well."

"Excellent interpretation of the antagonist's actions."

"I like the way you systematically solved this problem." (p. 270)

The suggestions here are conversation starters that allow the teacher and student to focus on one particular bit of work, and they can lead to a larger discussion in a mini-conference at the teacher's desk or as she makes her rounds while students work. "An environment with helpful feedback emphasizes that students don't have to learn everything the first time" (Zwiers, 2014, p. 271). Teachers willing to engage in relatively short feedback-laden conversations can let students know they are on the right track in a meaningful way, without simply patting student after student on the back as they work, saying, "Good job!" to everyone in sight.

On one of my coaching visits to a high school classroom, I sat at the teacher's desk only to realize I could not see over the desk without putting some of the *stuff* from the desk onto the chair to raise me up a bit. Some teacher desks seem to be about the size of small aircraft carriers; they provide teachers with a homeport and serve as a repository for everything from teacher editions to coffee mugs collected over long years in that same classroom. These often-formidable pieces of furniture may serve teachers well after hours, but during class it is more productive to be up and moving while students are working individually or in standing pairs, trios, or quartets (Chapter 4). Teachers who sit at their desks while students are employed at some task are sending this tacit but powerful message: *What I'm doing at my desk is more important than what you are doing out there.*

Some teachers are veritable feedback machines as they move about the classroom: One teacher "hunkers down" next to his students as they write or work on math problems. He is in constant motion, talking with and coaching his students. A high school biology teacher who had his students write often in his classroom used to travel from desk to desk using a green pen to circle or underline those things that were correctly done (grammar or content). This gave him the opportunity to have frequent—and private—face-to-face conversations with his students, providing specific and timely feedback that accelerated the continuous-improvement process. When time in classrooms is of the essence, and this is always the case, it should be used wisely. Face-to-face conversations provide feedback for students and teachers alike.

As Burke (2009) affirms, "Oral communication is a critical component of the assessment process. Often teachers find out more about what students know in a two-minute conversation than from their answers on a forty-question objective test" (p. 158). These conversations can be formal in the form of an interview or informal as teachers move about the classroom while students work on a task. These informal meetings serve as two-way streets; the teacher can use them to provide oral feedback and she can use what she hears from students as feedback that will help her improve instruction. Such conversations also help teachers build rapport and "probe for deeper understanding or areas of misunderstanding" (Burke, 2009, p. 160). These occasions also provide students with an opportunity to practice their speaking and listening skills, even as they give teachers a chance to model those same skills.

Formal conferences can serve as opportunities to elicit information from students concerning their progress on a specific project. These can be, as Chappuis and colleagues (2005), in Burke (2009) assert, short, three-minute meetings where "teachers confer with students as a way to offer feedback on their work by asking them to do some thinking prior to the meeting" (p. 159). Rather than try to deal with an entire research paper, for example, the teacher can focus on some small aspect related to quality. Several three-minute conferences with individual students would give the teacher multiple opportunities to provide valuable feedback over the course of a week. Such individual conferences also provide students a chance to improve their own speaking and listening skills.

Increasing Self-Regulated Improvement

Early in my teaching career, most of the feedback my students received came from me, and as I circulated around the classroom, all they had to do was get my attention in order to receive invaluable feedback on whatever in-class writing assignment was the *task du jour*. I was the go-to guy, the man with the answers, and I dispensed feedback with the rapidity of an overworked espresso machine trying to keep up with the orders after work on Friday night. I knew nothing of rubrics or checklists to which students could refer to check their own progress; working myself into exhaustion was part of why I got paid the big bucks. I was Rubric Man . . . and I was also exhausted at the end of a day that did not end until late in the evening on many occasions.

I did not understand that useful feedback can come from many legitimate and—today more than ever—easily accessible sources, including the student sitting right next to Norm. Because I thought a compliant and quiet classroom is a productive classroom, I trained my students to raise their hands when they had questions or needed a bit of feedback on something they had written. It did not occur to me that if two hands were in the air, I could help only one of those students at a time. This brought progress for the other student to a halt while I spent my time with the student nearest to me. I was concerned about the order of things, while the student who did not get chosen was simply concerned with moving forward on the task or assignment.

If students have a plethora of sources for feedback, and if they are not afraid to avail themselves of those sources at the time they are needed, the teacher doesn't have to be part of the solution at that moment. An example would be the elementary student earlier in this chapter who turned to his neighbor to help with the meaning of a word in the story he was reading. The teacher encouraged such interactions; the student who received the help was satisfied, and the student who provided the assistance felt good about that. The key is for students to know which strategy fits at that time. The ninth grader writing an essay in an English class where the teacher has employed the "three before me" system of editing can simply exchange drafts with a classmate, and both of them can provide and sign off on a bit of written feedback.

I once met a teacher who lamented the fact that she was up until the wee hours many nights grading papers. I asked if she had students provide formative feedback prior to turning in the drafts, and she admitted that was not part of her practice. She was, after all, the CIO, and that included giving all the feedback for her students' papers. As we saw earlier, students who have a chance to read and provide feedback for peers learn a great deal in the process. They are also exposed to different perspectives and new ideas as they peruse and analyze the work of peers. Providing feedback becomes *part* of the learning process for students. If students are part of the feedback loop up front, the teacher has less to do later on, and the students who gave and received the peer feedback both benefited from the experience.

Knowing What to Do When They Don't Know What to Do

Getting boxed in during the 3200-meter run his junior year was in itself feedback for Curt and his coach. The kinds of questions the coach asked on the bus after that meet were intended to help Curt "monitor and self-regulate" his learning in a way that would serve him well down the road, on or off the track. This kind of feedback, "can guide the learner on 'when,' 'where,' and 'why' in selecting or employing task and process-level knowledge and strategies" (Hattie, 2012, pp. 134–135). The way his coach handled the mistake Curt made in allowing himself to get and stay boxed in for so long made it possible for them to have a reflective conversation, without Curt having to worry about having made the mistake.

We want students to get to the point where they know what to do when they don't know what to do. In my early classrooms, they were trained to come directly to me, when there may have been other sources readily available had I encouraged their use. The student who does not know where to turn or what to do next while engaged in a task or assignment may simply disengage out of frustration. This is particularly true for students who are struggling anyway. "These students can become cognitively overwhelmed during learning due to high performance demands and thus may benefit from supportive feedback designed to decrease the cognitive load" (Shute, 2008, p.157). Students who know exactly where to turn for feedback are much less likely to give up and punch out.

One way for students to increase their self-sufficiency is for teachers to provide checklists (essentially a roadmap guiding students through a process) and rubrics (steps to improving the quality of the work) (Burke, 2010). Questions students might ordinarily ask the CIO can be answered using these two easily accessible tools. They can be made available in print or on the teacher's website, or both.

A checklist may not dispose of all the questions students might have, but it is a tool that will go a long way toward making students more self-sufficient. Burke (2010) has given an example of what might be included in a checklist used in the production of a persuasive essay. To illustrate, I have adapted this and given only a portion of the entire checklist. Under the heading *Does my writing engage the reader?* might be three related questions:

1. Is my purpose in writing clear? (to persuade)

2. Do I create a "speaker's voice"?

3. Do I use one of the following strategies to develop reader interest? (such as a question, startling fact, scenario, dazzling description, anecdote, or quotation)

Under the heading "Do I state a clear position or perspective in support of my *proposition* or *proposal?*" might be the following:

1. Is the problem clear to the reader?

2. Is my opinion clear to the reader?

3. Do I have a clearly developed thesis statement? (p. 76)

Students who are encouraged to seek feedback from peers could easily have a classmate read the essay and help determine whether those components are present. If the teacher adopts a "three before me" process during the writing of the essays, by the time the essay gets to the teacher many questions will have been answered. Also, the feedback included from other students will give the teacher insights into what they know or understand. The system created by the language arts teacher who includes a checklist like this one is meant to assist students who learn to take advantage of whatever forms of feedback are available—including the checklist itself and the peer editing that has become standard in that classroom.

Feedback Is a Two-Way Street

In my early years as a teacher, my students and I raced from test to test at breakneck speed. Those tests were all summative, of course, as were the quizzes that were supposed to check for understanding along the way. Time was of the essence, though, and the quizzes did little more than provide me with more points for the grade book. The only feedback I actually sought *from* my students came at the end of the year, when I asked them to evaluate my teaching. By then the proverbial horses were out of the barn and out of the state. It was a pretty good evaluation form, but it did those students no good at all, falling as it did on the last day of school.

Teachers looking into a sea of faces often want to know where students are when it comes to something they have just seen, heard, or read. I often hear teachers say, as I did many times, "Does everyone understand?" The result is a veritable sea of nodding heads, something approximating bobblehead night at the ballpark. Of *course* they understand. Or a teacher may say, "If you understand this concept, raise your hand." The problem here is that there are students who have no clue and would like to ask questions, but would rather die than keep their hands down when hands are going up like so much popcorn all over the room. For Norm, the frustration of not understanding is trumped by not wanting everyone to *know* he is lost or confused. It is far easier to raise his hand, sending the message that he understands, when in fact he isn't close to understanding. The problem here is that these procedures are completely public, and may result in a false reading. Teachers who really want to move on can use all those raised hands as a cue to shift gears and go on to something else.

Here is something I saw in a classroom years ago that provided feedback for the teacher (and was borrowed by "Mr. B" in Chapter 3). The teacher had three small 3 oz. cups stacked on the corner of each student's desk. The bottom of each of the three cups was painted red, yellow, or green. When she wanted to do a brief check for understanding, she had each student pick up a cup and point it directly toward her. Green meant, "I've got this." Yellow meant, "I need more practice or I have just a few questions." Red meant, "I really don't understand this at all." One or two red cups among a sea of green told her to work with those kids later. Cups that were mostly red and yellow indicated she needed to reteach the information and do it differently. Whatever she did the first time did not take. Because she was looking into the cups, no one else in the room could see which cup was being used, and she made sure they were looking at her the whole time, not glancing around the room.

Another variation on this theme is what O'Connell and Vandas (2015) call the traffic light. Students can respond in writing to three prompts at the end of the day or class period:

Green—What I learned or understand: _____

Yellow—What I am unclear on or sort of understand: _____

Red—What I don't understand: _____

Time devoted after school to reading what the students have written will allow the teacher to take action the next day (pp. 103–104).

An exit ticket can accomplish much the same thing. Some teachers will ask students to write comments or questions on an index card at the end of the day, class period, or block. By collecting these and looking them over that evening, teachers can gain valuable feedback as to where students are at the moment. A piece of paper in the form of a circle gives students a chance to tell the teacher what questions are still going 'round in their minds. A square provides students the opportunity to let the teacher know what they have squared away. Students who would never dream of commenting or asking questions in front of their peers may well be willing to raise questions and provide feedback for their teachers in a way that is much more private. The cups, traffic-light prompts, and exit tickets all accomplish that.

One sure way for teachers to receive valuable feedback is to circulate among the pairs in a standing pair share, listening to the students as they talk. Content-laden conversations will either demonstrate that most students seem to understand the concept or topic, or they may indicate that students lack the basic knowledge to talk with any confidence about it. If students who normally have no problem at all discussing something with a partner seem confused or reticent, it may be they simply lack the context for a substantive and successful discussion. It may also be that what the teacher hears as she circulates indicates some deep misconceptions about the subject. Listening closely to several paired conversations can give valuable feedback to a teacher who may have to approach the material in a different way, while making the decision to postpone whatever summative assessment is scheduled for the near future.

These are all ways of checking to see where students are, or where their comfort level is, at the end of a class period, block, or at the end of the day. Reflecting on the information provided by the traffic-light activity or the exit tickets can help teachers make adjustments to their instruction at critical junctures. Observing and listening to students as they discuss a given concept or topic can do the same thing. For teachers willing to pause long enough to invite student feedback on a regular basis, their input can help improve instruction. It also sends the signal to the students that this particular teacher is interested in—and willing to make use of—their feedback.

Final Thoughts

Students who expect to improve in any area or skill set must know where they are, where they are going, and what they need to do in order to get there. They need to know that there are multiple sources of excellent feedback available from peers, teachers, classroom resources, checklists, rubrics, and online. Students also need to know it is safe to ask questions and make mistakes in the presence of teachers and peers. The teacher who makes her classroom an emotionally safe place has removed a barrier to learning.

Teachers can also train students in the art of giving feedback, which should be task-related and not personal. Students who understand the nature and efficacy of good feedback can become an important part of the continuous-improvement process for their classmates. Students can also provide valuable feedback for teachers. They key for students and teachers alike is to *seek* feedback at every turn, not try and avoid it.

In Chapter 9 we'll rejoin our fictional high school teacher, Ed, as he begins the shift from a teacher-centered classroom to one that is more learner-centered. We'll look at ways teachers can get started in their own transition to a more active and interactive classroom experience.

9

Give Them Their 80

On the way to his car in the school parking lot, Ed pulled out his cell phone and called his friend Alex, a middle school physical science teacher. Alex had grown up attending schools in the district just north of the one in which they now taught; it was that neighboring district Ed had just visited. Ed invited Alex and his wife, Brenda, to join him for dinner at Mister Barney's, a local restaurant that had been around since the early 1950s and was run by a couple who were best friends with Ed's parents. They did not take reservations, and it was often crowded, even on a weekday night, but when Ed came in they often brought a small table out from the back, pulled the potted plant out of the corner, and set Ed up within a couple of minutes. It turned out that Brenda was at her book-club meeting, but Alex was free and told Ed he would meet him at the restaurant. It was not busy, and Ed found a booth along the far wall. Members of the wait staff waved and said hello, and not for the first time Ed felt like Norm in *Cheers*, the old TV sitcom.

Ed hardly needed a menu, and no one gave him one, but Stacey, his regular waitperson, brought him a diet soda as soon as he sat down. Alex joined him within a couple of minutes, and they ordered burgers and fries as counterweights to the diet sodas. Alex asked about the team's chances of winning the homecoming game and then noticed that something was bothering his friend.

"What's wrong, Ed? You don't seem your usual ebullient self tonight."

"Basically, Alex, I'm fine, but I've spent the last couple of days doing a lot of thinking. One of our assistant principals asked me to observe the classroom of a U.S. history teacher in the high school in your district. That teacher, Peggy Sandillos, has received a lot of press lately, and our ministration wanted me to visit and find out what she is doing to get such high test scores. I spent a couple of hours with Peggy on Monday, observing a shortened block, and then talking with her over lunch and her prep."

"Interesting," said Alex, "and I have met Peggy. Her sister teaches at my middle school. What did you see that was different in Peggy's classroom?"

Ed smiled and drank some diet soda. "Where do I begin? I got to her classroom during the change of classes, and could hear music playing inside the room. She greeted students as they entered, and had a couple of quiet side conversations with them in the hallway. Students were busy writing in their journals, and one of them greeted me and took me to an empty desk in the back corner of the classroom."

"He knew you were coming?"

"He did, and Peggy had arranged it. She told me later that lots of teachers observe her classes, and she gives the responsibility of greeting visitors to her students. Each of them has a week where he or she greets people. Peggy lets them know in advance who it is, and this ninth grader knew my name and where I taught. It was refreshing, actually. His name was David, and he took a couple of minutes to show me two journals they use in her classroom."

Alex put down his glass. "Two journals?"

"Actually, one was called a learning log and the other a reflective journal. The learning log is more for content, while the reflective journal is a place where she told me later they 'think about their thinking.' She said that after they work in groups or complete a standing pair share, they often sit down and write about how they did during the group work or conversation. They have a checklist of speaking and listening skills— two separate checklists against which they can see how they did when collaborating with the other kids in the class."

They ate quietly for a couple of minutes, and Alex said, "*Two* journals. I have enough trouble getting my students to write in a notebook. I'm impressed."

Stacey brought their meals and topped off their sodas. When she was gone, Alex said, "Did you say there was music playing in the classroom? What kind of music?"

"There were a couple of upbeat, popular songs playing as students entered, one of them from the seventies. I couldn't help but notice the difference between the way the students entered *her* room and the way they come into mine. Some of my ninth graders sort of drag themselves into my room as if they are headed for a last meal before the execution. She also played music when they transitioned from their seats to standing pairs and back again. I swear they sort of 'grooved' to wherever they were going. She used a remote to control the volume and pause it when necessary. It was an MP3 player of some sort with a small set of speakers.

She held the remote behind her back, controlling it without even looking at it."

Alex laughed. "I would love to see what songs she uses and when. I'm curious about something. You said you arrived during the change of classes. Were there any students late to her class? I fight that constantly in middle school."

"That is one of the amazing things, Alex. Not only were there no tardies, she told me she rarely has one, and she credits the music and the change in her teaching methodology. Peggy said she used to have tardies in the days before she—her words now—'looked in the mirror and realized the status quo wasn't working.' The environment in that classroom, Alex, was incredibly energetic, and every bit as upbeat as the music she played when her ninth graders arrived."

Ed took a bite of his burger, and Alex said, "They have block scheduling at that high school. Are you saying the energy was there for ninety minutes?"

Still chewing, Ed nodded his head vigorously. "Well, what I observed was a shortened block, but I get the feeling the energy is there every day, and here's the kicker, Alex. *They* did the work. The *students* did most of the work. There was no teacher's desk in the room, and the student desks were arranged along the walls, so that the center and front of the classroom was opened up. I thought this arrangement odd until she had them pair up in the open space to discuss a short story they had just read on the Underground Railroad. Peggy moved around the room, listening to various conversations, and then stood on a short stool in the front corner of the room as she called the conversations to a halt. Using some upbeat music again, she moved them back to their desks."

Ed gobbled a couple of fries, and Alex jumped in with, "Did the students really talk about what they were *supposed* to be talking about?"

Nodding, Ed said, "Absolutely. When we met after the block, Peggy told me she spends the first five days of school on nothing but process. She uses those days to get them used to talking with a partner while seated, discussing things in standing pairs and trios, and holding group discussions about what they see when they look at a particular graphic or picture displayed on her screen. While in pairs or trios, she has them talk about everything from their favorite vacations to their favorite movies. All those conversations about things they were familiar with led to the content-oriented conversations I saw when I was in her classroom on Monday. She told me she did not even crack the textbook until the last day of the first week of school. I hit the textbook on the first day, figuring I need all the time I can get to present the information."

"I do that, too, in my science classes. Her test scores are high?"

"Not only are her standardized test scores extremely high, she tells me the students simply take those spring tests in stride. She says the difference between how her students *used* to approach those tests and the way they do so now is like night and day. Her pass rate each year is at or close to 100 percent, Alex!"

Alex sat back in his seat. "A hundred percent?"

"Yes, but she says she does not really think much about those state tests during the year. During that first week of school, her goal is to get her students—her words again—'doing 80 percent of the *doing*' in her five classes. She models, they do. She models, they do."

"Amazing," said Alex, finishing the last of his fries. "It's no wonder so many teachers visit her classroom. And someone greeted you at the door, and it was no big deal. Just another visitor, apparently."

"That's what my assistant principal had told me, and Peggy confirmed it. Her students take all this in stride. They are used to having teachers and administrators spend time in there, and I think they are rather proud of it. After the students had these standing conversations in pairs, they took some time to write in their journals, and I walked around and looked at some of them. The student who had met me at the door handed his journal to me and showed me the back section where he charts his own progress in terms of test results. It was in the form of a run chart."

They sat in companionable silence for a few minutes, finishing their meals and pushing the plates to the outer edge of the booth. Finally, Alex said, "It seems that Peggy's classroom really clicks for her and the students. If it is like that in all her classes, I suspect the day passes quickly for all of them. I have to admit that there are times I feel like I am talking to kids who are either elsewhere in their minds or are simply *watching me work*. From what you say, it appears that Peggy has found a way to get her students engaged and doing most of the work—most of 'the doing,' as she told you."

There was a pause as Stacey brought the small serving of home-made vanilla ice cream that was Mister Barney's trademark dessert. She poured them some coffee and left the check.

Alex stirred some cream into his coffee, laying the spoon down. "I hate to admit this, but I think most of the 'doing' in my classroom is done by me. It sounds like you have come to that conclusion as well."

"You're right on the money, Alex. I'm the one doing the lecturing, the explaining, the describing . . . Peggy told me that earlier in this unit on slavery she displayed an image of a slave ship on the screen, the one where the slaves are chained next to each other in rows below decks. Instead of describing to her students what *she* saw, she put them in trios and quartets in the center of the room, and she asked them to discuss with each other what *they saw and felt*. As she walked around the room, she said she heard some really insightful and revealing comments. She asked some of them to share, and by doing this *she introduced the whole unit on slavery*. Peggy said it was like someone flipped a switch; one minute they knew little of slavery in America, and within five minutes they could not wait to learn more. She had them go home and use the

Internet to uncover more about the 'Middle Passage' in the slave trade, *and they did it!*"

Ed was gesticulating wildly now, and Alex laughed so hard he almost spit coffee all over his friend. "They did their homework? What a concept!"

"She didn't even call it homework, Alex. She never *used* the word; she just used the picture of that slave ship to pique their interest and get them engaged. The next day, she put them back in groups of three or four, and had them share with each other what they found out the night before. She was so excited telling me about this that I was tempted to go home and Google 'Middle Passage' . . . I truly was, and I've been teaching the subject for eighteen years!"

"Correct me if I'm wrong, Ed, but I'm guessing you may seek to change the way you do some of the things you do in your classroom. Truth be told, I may not be far behind. I wish I knew of a science teacher who taught that way."

Ed put his credit card next to the check, and said, "I don't think the subject area matters, Alex, I really don't. You could visit Peggy's class-room tomorrow and get a great deal out of it. I was never bored—not for one minute. More important, her ninth graders were not bored either. You want to know the kicker? The same kid who greeted me at the door and showed me his journal thanked me for visiting their classroom when I left."

Stacey brought back Ed's card, and Ed signed the store's copy. "I'm going to make some changes, Alex; it remains to figure out how I want to do that. Peggy told me she always has an eye on the skills in commu-nication and collaboration that these kids are going to need when they enter the workforce, and she has committed to getting them ready. Their learning logs were full of writing; she said they write frequently, and they are used to peer editing using twelve copy-editing marks. Alex, the bottom line is that the students are doing the bulk of the work in class, they are developing skills they can use on the outside, their test scores are extremely high, and they love coming into that classroom every other day for a block that, from what I could see, flies by for everyone in the room—I include myself in that assessment."

Alex and Ed stood and walked among the tables to the front door. Ed stopped briefly to say hello to family friends, and then he and Alex emerged into the parking lot. "Thanks for inviting me to dinner, Ed. I'm sorry Brenda couldn't make it, because she would have enjoyed the con-versation. In her job as a kindergarten teacher assistant, she sees plenty of interaction at that level. It seems that as kids get older, that energy and curiosity disappears somehow. That becomes even clearer to me during our dinner conversations about work."

Alex took out his car keys. "You know, Ed, our principal just sent around a flyer for a one-day Saturday workshop on how the brain learns.

I kept the flyer to show it to Brenda, but I'm wondering if you and I or even the three of us could go? The workshop is in mid-November; it is only an hour from here, and I'm thinking it might just help us jump start something new in *both* our classrooms. What do you think?"

"I would love to go, actually. E-mail me the website when you get home, and I'll check it out. I might even be able to get my principal to pay for it. Thanks again for joining me, Alex, and give my best to Brenda."

"And thanks again for paying for dinner, Ed. You didn't have to do that, but I appreciate it. What do you say we meet at Mister Barney's in December and talk about whatever changes we have made in our classrooms? That meal will be on me. Okay?"

"Sold," said Ed. "Have a great day in school tomorrow, and enjoy your weekend. You do realize that our homecoming game tomorrow night is against your old high school?"

"I know, and I'll see you there. We both went to that high school, and she wouldn't miss this game."

Ed laughed, and they shook hands. As he opened the door to his car, Ed thought about how much he enjoyed this conversation with Alex. It had given him a chance to talk with someone and think out loud; he was able to process a great deal of information and perhaps come to some preliminary conclusions.

The next day, Friday, Ed had already planned to have his students read a section of the textbook and answer the questions at the end. He also intended to lecture for about fifteen minutes on the origins of slavery in the colonies. Instead, he gave those who had not yet completed the worksheet he had given them earlier in the week some time to finish it. With these two classroom assignments underway, Ed decided he would closely observe his students as they worked their way through the twin tasks. What they were doing was very similar to what he had himself done in the old school building for Mr. Porter, his former U.S. history teacher.

While the students worked, rather than sit behind his desk as he used to do, Ed walked around the room, watching his students carefully. What he noticed was that many of them seemed to "hunker down" when he was near and then ease up when he was on the other side of the classroom. He also noticed how many of them had not finished, or even started, the worksheet he had given them on Monday. It was due after the weekend, but most of them had left it all until when . . . Sunday? Except for Mary, of course. Mary was almost done with everything, and Ed wondered what was going through her mind. Bored out of her skull? Not challenged? Then there was Fred, who sat where Ed ("Eddie" in those days) used to sit in most of his classes as a student—in the last seat in the center of his five rows of desks. Fred, Ed calculated, had maybe three minutes of worksheet in him. Ed remembered that in his own freshman year, he probably had maybe five minutes of worksheet in him before he went to a better place in his mind. If Mr. Porter looked back at him, however, "Eddie" would smile and seemingly redouble his efforts on the task—but not really. Ed had been good at posturing and playing the game called school.

So how many of these ninth graders in this classroom, and those from previous years, for that matter, had gone elsewhere mentally as they gazed out of windows or opened the windows of their own minds to possibilities beyond U.S. history? What was he accomplishing here? More important, perhaps, what were his *students* accomplishing here? From year to year, he realized, his test scores—both his own and those administered by the state—stayed about the same. These kids normally completed their assigned tasks; why, exactly? Because they liked him and did not want to disappoint him? Because it was part of surviving ninth grade? Inertia?

Peggy, the teacher whom he had observed on Monday, had told him that she stopped having her students do worksheets in her history class because they did not seem to be accomplishing anything, and it was too much like busywork. Is that what Ed had them doing? Busywork? Two or three students now had their heads on their desks, the assignment completed or, in the case of Fred, not. Bits and pieces of what he had seen and heard in Peggy's class kept surfacing in his mind, and by the end of the class period, he knew he would be making some changes on Monday. The rest of the day was spent continuing to observe his students in class after class, and he went to homecoming that night convinced that whatever years he had left teaching history would be substantially different from the first twenty-seven. If Peggy could do this with ninth graders just a few miles away, Ed could do this with his students.

At the homecoming game that night, Ed sat in the stands with Alex and Brenda, and he and Alex agreed to work together on this. Alex, too, had been doing some thinking, and together they decided to make some similar changes in the status quo in their classrooms. They looked into the brain-based learning workshop in November, and their respective principals had agreed to pay for registration, if Ed and Alex would pay any additional travel- or food-related expenses.

Something else happened just prior to Thanksgiving. Ed and several other teachers on his hallway received brand new electronic Smart Boards. Ed, digital immigrant that he was, had heard about their purchase a few weeks ago and then dismissed it from his mind. While learning how to use this new piece of technology might not be easy, his new attitude toward his own teaching methodology now had him in the right place to successfully incorporate the Smart Board into his classroom system. Aside from the technical training on its use, Ed found out that a neighboring district was going to allow teachers from his school to sit in on some high school classes where teachers had developed ways to use the technology and engage students in the process. This was welcome news, and Ed remembered how successful and enjoyable his visit to Peggy's classroom had been.

The bottom line to Ed and his students was that he was now committed to changing his classroom environment to his and their benefit. He understood that not all the changes he contemplated would be instituted immediately. Peggy had spent a good deal of time during the first week of school helping her students develop the listening skills necessary to make pairing and sharing a success. She told Ed she had practiced getting them from their seats to standing pairs over and over again until the time was reduced to just a few seconds. She wanted no wasted time, and she knew that transitions could be deadly. Ed decided to talk with his students about the changes he intended to make, and get their input. He also committed to surfacing with them six or seven listening skills that would make paired conversations easier and more productive. This would mean putting some content on hold, but Ed was determined to rattle the status quo in his classroom to benefit his students . . . and himself. It was a start.

Getting Started With Ed

This book is built around getting kids off the bench and into the game. It is not just about having them move for movement's sake, although there is real value in that; it is about getting them into seated or standing pairs, trios, or quartets to process information or reflect on what they might have just seen, heard, or read. It is about letting them deal with open-ended questions that challenge their thinking and raise even *more* questions. It is about reducing the amount of teacher talk and increasing the amount of student-to-student dialogue. Yair (2000, as cited in Hattie, 2012) found, in a study of 865 students from Grades 6 through 12, that students were engaged only half the time, and the lowest engagement levels came when teachers did most of the talking. Hattie (2012) reports that teachers "talk between 70 and 80 percent of class time, on average" (p. 80). When Ed observed Peggy, she spoke of giving the kids their 80. She realized she used to do most of the work in her classroom, and it was she who did most of the talking. She managed to turn that around, increasing engagement on the part of her ninth graders; she did less talking while they did more. She tossed the worksheets in favor of collaborative work. For Ed, it was watching Peggy teach, along with observing his own students struggling through a good deal of individual seatwork on that Friday, that provided the stark and undeniable contrast between Peggy's instructional practices and his own.

Teachers who want to join Ed and take the on-ramp to the continuous-improvement highway can begin to ask some serious, reflective questions related to how involved and engaged students are in their classrooms.

Teachers can reflect on the *how* of what they do and consider to what extent they may be doing most of the work in their classrooms. What follows are some steps teachers can take to shift that work load, get their students into the game, and create an environment more conducive to learning.

Open the Door and Look Around

At every turn in my professional career as a writer and workshop facilitator, I recommend that teachers take the time to find out which teachers inside or outside the district are having a great deal of success engaging students in classroom environments conducive to learning. By this I mean that those teachers have succeeded in shifting the work load from themselves to their students; those teachers have created an environment where students feel safe to express themselves in pairs, quartets, or in front of the entire class; those teachers have replaced teacher talk with student-to-student discussions; those teachers have high test scores and a high level of confidence on the part of their students; those teachers waste not a minute in the classroom and have processes in place that effectively facilitate learning. Teachers should go watch these people teach and then take the time to meet with them and discuss with them how they do what they do.

Many of the highly successful teachers I know were not always so. Many of them, like Ed, perhaps earlier in their careers, took the time at some point to reflect on exactly what was going on in their classrooms. Some teachers make the transition from a traditional classroom (teacher talk, worksheets, videos) to a much more active and engaging classroom in one summer, or in a couple of weeks during the course of the school year. Still others incorporate change more gradually, replacing ineffective strategies with those that prove more successful one by one, over time. It is great to hear teachers who have transformed their classrooms talk about the changes they made, along with the changes they *saw* in their

> Growth may be at times slow or rapid, but it is relentless.

students. In many cases, it all began when those teachers took the time to go see other teachers teach. Yet, Goodlad (2004) found, after more than twenty data collectors returned from observing in thirty-eight schools and more than a thousand classrooms, that the teachers in those schools collaborated with colleagues on committees or projects only rarely. "Nor did they visit other schools or receive visitors from them very often." In fact, as Goodlad and his team discovered, "Teachers rarely worked together on schoolwide problems" (p. 187).

Administrators can assist by arranging classroom visits and providing covers and substitutes so teachers can take the time to observe and, if time permits, have a follow-up conversation with the teacher or teachers in whose classrooms they spent some time. One substitute teacher could be in one classroom in the morning and another in the afternoon, allowing two teachers to spend up to three hours each in classrooms where they can sit and observe, take notes and reflect, and write down some questions they might ask the observed teacher later on—all safe in the knowledge that there is a good substitute teacher minding the store at home.

If we go through our careers in isolation, closing our classroom doors each day and doing what we always do, we are missing out on the kinds of multiple perspectives that others bring to the profession. Those peers whom teachers observe don't even have to teach the same subject; it is *process* on which we can concentrate when in those classrooms—the *how* more than the what. The social studies teacher who sees students working together successfully in a science class can learn just as much about process as if he were in a social studies classroom. The important thing is to *take* the time to *make* the visit.

In districts all over the country, teachers are finding unique ways to incorporate interactive whiteboards, laptops, and the power of blogging into the pedagogical fabric. Students may find it far more interesting to write that paragraph or essay and then post it for all their classmates to see, and blogging sites can be set up so that only a select group of students has access. Students can peer edit and otherwise comment on the writings of classmates, and the feedback is immediate, fitting right in with the immediacy today's kids want in terms of their own social networks. While sitting at the computer screen at home, students can make a quick visit to the teacher's website for last-minute directions before proceeding with a writing assignment—all without moving away from the keyboard. Building administrators and central office instructional specialists can take the time to locate classrooms where teachers have successfully embraced the technology, after which they can provide the encouragement and the time necessary to get teachers out of their own traditional classrooms and into classrooms where creative and innovative teachers have moved into a much more highly interactive and technologically advanced reality.

Open the Door and Let Someone In

There are two ways teachers can gain interesting insights as to what is actually happening in their own classrooms. One is to have a lesson or two videotaped, and the other is to invite a colleague into the classroom to play the part of an objective observer of process. Many who read this may recoil from either one, but I can say from experience that both have their uses. I had two of my seventh-grade social studies classes videotaped, and I was able to make a great many adjustments in terms of my presentation skills. For example, I found I was using the nonword *um* a great deal, and I was able to get a handle on that by pausing instead . . . silence really *is* golden. Also, I gestured entirely too much, in a way that I realized had to distract my students. I would have fit right in on any cheerleading squad. I also noticed my voice dropped off at the end of my sentences, so that I could not hear the last two or three words. If *I* couldn't hear myself on the tape, neither could my students.

After I began doing a good deal of training for the school district for which I worked, I had a colleague critique my presentation, and he was, as I recall, particularly honest in his assessment. I cringed at the time, but I benefitted (as did my workshop participants) from the feedback because—and this is the important point—it was not personal. It was simply feedback. Viewing the videotape of my classroom with the sound off told me much about my body language and facial expressions; listening with the picture off told me a great deal about voice modulation, timing, volume, and pitch. Anyone who is willing to see feedback as feedback—and not as personal criticism—can benefit from opening the door and letting a colleague (or a camera) in.

There are other things that someone who is in a teacher's classroom can look for during as little as thirty minutes. For example, *Are the kids engaged?* Someone not caught up in teaching the class is in a unique position to watch the students—not the teacher! Other questions an observer can pose include, *Are the students sitting at their desks for too long a time? Does the teacher provide enough wait time after asking a question, so that students have a chance to process and get ready to come up with a response? Do students have an opportunity in the course of thirty minutes to stand, pair up, and process information concerning what they have just heard, seen, or read? Are transitions accomplished in a short period of time, with little or no confusion on the part of students?* Teachers who invite colleagues into their classrooms might have them answer only one, or at the most two, of these questions. A follow-up session during planning time or even briefly after school would provide both teachers with a chance to debrief, and the upshot here is that *both teachers can benefit.* The observer may recognize in that thirty minutes some things she needs to change, and she may also pick up a few pointers concerning particularly effective strategies or processes she can then incorporate into her own instruction.

Anyone who wants to get better at what she does must receive feedback of some kind. As we saw in Chapter 8, feedback is the lifeblood of improvement. Any teacher or administrator who wants to travel down the continuous-improvement highway must make up his mind to seek input from colleagues, administrators, and, perhaps most important, the students who enter the classroom every day. The best teachers I have met over the years don't really care who comes into their classrooms to visit;

they do what they need to do in the best interests of the kids they serve; feedback is just feedback, and feedback should be welcome.

Awareness Leads to Choice

Each of us wants our doctor to read trade journals, talk with other doctors about what constitutes best practice in the field of medicine, and attend every single professional development seminar in sight. We hope our automobile mechanic has more tools than a hammer and screwdriver, and we all want our dentists

> The synergy created when several teachers get together around an instructional area of common interest can be powerful.

and dental hygienists to be up to date on the latest techniques. By the same token, parents and students have a right to expect that teachers are not dependent on their four years of college many years ago to provide them with every-thing they need to know about how modern teachers teach and today's kids learn. Teachers, professionals all, need to read, reflect, and ramp up their own professional-development journeys.

Administrators can help here by making sure every single school media center has a comprehensive professional-development library, complete with journal subscriptions (paper or electronic, or both), the latest books on how the brain learns, and classroom management materials of every sort. A subscription to ProQuest will give teachers access to articles and dissertations about every subject with any relevance in the field of education. The room where all this information is accessible should be a place where teachers can go at any time to spend some time thinking and collaborating with colleagues. Administrators must then see to it that these valuable resources help accelerate the professional-development process in the building.

Blankstein (2004) recommends the formation of professional study groups composed of teachers who research best practices and share the information gained from articles and books with colleagues. Blankstein also supports the creation of short-lived professional interest teams, where "staff members who are interested in a specific approach or inno-vation (e.g., cooperative learning) form groups to research the approach; receive training; develop implementation strategies; and provide recip-rocal observation, review, and evaluation" (p. 132). The synergy created when several teachers get together around an instructional area of com-mon interest can be powerful, especially when they are wide open to receiving the training and working out ways to implement the approach in the building or district.

Teacher leaders and administrators can also arrange for book talks and vertical discussions that will connect teachers *across* grade levels, not just horizontally. The fifth-grade teachers in a school need to meet with the fourth-grade faculty in regular meetings. The topic of dialogue on those occasions ought to be what the teachers in the fourth grade can do to make certain that incoming students are ready for fifth grade in the areas of reading, writing, oral language development, and math. To the extent that students are not ready, teachers in the higher grade level learn what is known on the assembly line as *rework.* If students are not ready, the fifth-grade teachers not only have to teach what is expected at their level but also have to make up for what has not happened on the way to fifth grade. This is true of any grade level, and the only thing keeping things on an even keel here is a concerted effort to collaborate vertically, and *not* simply play the blame game. There is a tendency for teachers at every grade level to blame those below them, and it solves nothing. It fixes nothing. It gets to the root cause of nothing.

Quality control in education should be in the hands of teachers and students, not just the Department of Testing and Accountability for the district. Groups of teachers can work at developing checklists and rubrics, along with common assessments, that will help them benchmark progress over time in a formative way. Getting better at something may involve a journey of small steps, but the progress is relentless for each student, and it allows for individual differences and rates of growth among students. The same is true of teachers; their own professional growth may be a result of small but significant changes that are planned, tried out in the classroom, evaluated for effectiveness, and adjusted before being put into play again. Once again, growth may be at times slow or rapid, but it is relentless.

My advice to teachers and administrators alike is to concentrate on finding what works in the classroom. When a teacher works with another teacher toward this end, there are two perspectives rather than one. When grade-level teachers collaborate, there are many different but mutually supportive perspectives and experience levels in play. When groups work across grade levels, teachers can learn some interesting things about what their colleagues need and expect. When teachers at these meetings can share what they read about what the research shows or what teachers around the country or around the world have found effective, this shared knowledge can translate into game changers that improve instruction and learning. Administrators can't simply hope that these exchanges take place, or that teachers happen to stop by the professional-development library on occasion. School leadership teams, whatever their makeup, must commit to the powerful and positive synergy that comes from collaboration at and across all levels.

Building-Level Systemic Improvement

Unfortunately, professional-development budgets may be the first on the chopping block in times of recession or a reduction in tax revenues, but this should not be an excuse for avoiding a vibrant program of improvement in the building. Most of the costs associated with getting better at something are not monetary, but what economists would call *opportunity costs*. It does take time to read what needs to be read, but much of that can be found online free of charge. Administrators can create time in the schedules of teachers for groups to meet together and plan common assessments, checklists, rubrics, or authentic assessment pieces—all of which provide valuable feedback to teachers and students alike. The human resources in the building are the most valuable when it comes to making forward progress; it is necessary to stop making excuses and tap those resources in a way that capitalizes on the relative strengths, ideas, experiences, and successes that teachers and administrators bring to the table every day.

The perfect place for collaboration at the building level is in the development and execution of the school improvement plan (SIP). If one of the goals of the plan is to have all students at an elementary school reading on grade level by the end of second grade, the improvement team (selected administrative and instructional leaders in the building) can work to put the following in place in support of reading improvement:

- Task the improvement team with developing a training plan.
- Investigate available professional development that provides training on reading comprehension strategies.
- Locate funding to support implementing the training and paying for substitutes if needed.
- Purchase the relevant materials.
- Implement the first training sessions.
- Plan staff time to reflect on the training sessions, and commit to classroom-based applications related to the training.
- Plan staff time to share successes and challenges related to implementation. (Nash & Hwang, 2013, p. 136.)

The key here is in following through at every stage of this process, from the plan itself, through the funding, training sessions, classroom application, and evaluation. The continuous-improvement process will break down if the plan is simply a binder on the shelf in the principal's office. The plan must be a living document, and teachers must be part of its implementation every step of the way. Part of this involves using research-based instructional strategies that expand on a regular basis the tools teachers need to succeed.

When I was about twelve years old, my Uncle Griff stood with me in his garage and invited me to look around. There were no cars in his two-stall garage; it was a giant woodworking shop full of wood, paint cans, woodworking machinery . . . and tools. Tons of tools. He stood there and gave me the following piece of advice: "Ronnie, you can never have enough tools." Because the most elaborate thing I ever made using woodworking tools was a cutting board, that advice was pretty well lost on me, but I now realize that to do the miraculous things he was able to do in his garage/woodworking shop, his never-ending search for more modern and effective tools made a great deal of sense.

I believe the same is true of teaching. The great teachers have a toolbox full of engagement and process-management tools that allow them to do great things in their classrooms. Teachers who are limited to lecture, videos, worksheets, having students read out loud in round-robin fashion, and various forms of teacher talk will get limited results—this is a time in our history as a nation when we need to give students their own toolbox full of twenty-first-century strategies. These are the strategies that will allow them to think critically, solve problems, communicate effectively, and become productive and intelligent citizens. Finding those tools does not cost much money; it does require teachers to step outside their own classrooms and communicate and collaborate with colleagues in a search for every tool that will get the job done for today's students.

Final Thoughts

Teachers who are willing to break the hold of isolationism that is the status quo in schools all across the country can take four steps to get started—steps that cost little or nothing in monetary terms but that, if pursued with an eye toward improvement, can have great consequences:

1. Take the time to evaluate the *how* of what you do in your own classroom. Are the various processes you are using on a daily basis effective in connecting with and engaging today's students? Are they really engaged in their own learning?

2. Check in with your students regularly to find out how they are doing, along with how they think *you* are doing. A simple time-out every couple of weeks would allow you to solicit feedback from those most able to give it to you, and for whom whatever adjustments you make mean the most.

3. Open the classroom door to colleagues who are willing and able to give valuable and objective feedback as a way of helping you on your continuous-improvement journey. Give them specific things to look for when they are in your classroom, and take time to debrief with them after the observation.

4. Visit the classrooms of teachers inside or outside your district to observe firsthand how those who seem to be highly successful year after year accomplish that. Spend as much time as you can in

reflective conversations with those teachers, and borrow as many tools as you can for your own toolbox.

5. Develop, implement, and evaluate school-based continuous-improvement plans that will improve teaching and enhance learning in every classroom. Teachers should be actively involved every step of the way in this process.

Even veteran teachers with many years under their belts can, as Ed did, come to the conclusion that the status quo might have to be shown the door. Getting students up and moving in pairs, trios, and quartets, processing information and asking questions, is something every teacher can do. Every teacher can identify areas of strength and interest in their students and help them to accelerate growth in those areas, building strong and lasting relationships in the process. All teachers can immerse students in problem-solving activities that sharpen their critical-thinking skills. Teachers can also sharpen the oral language skills of students as a way to reinforce reading and writing skills. Finally, teachers today need to be thinking of ways to capitalize on myriad technological advances that can be incorporated into the classroom environment. The familiarity of students with such technology demands that we change how classrooms are run.

Most important, teachers need to make certain that the students are doing 80 percent of the work in the classroom. I tell teachers to keep the 20, but give the kids their 80. The teacher's 20 involves extensive modeling, small amounts of direct instruction, clear directions, effective processes, powerful relationships, a sense of humor, flexibility, high standards, and a willingness to take risks on behalf of kids. Keep the 20, and give the rest to them. Give them their 80.

Doing this may mean teachers have to confront the status quo, wrestle with the proverbial alligator, and make some serious changes. Showing the status quo the door is the topic of our final chapter.

10

Show the Status Quo the Door

The status quo is a powerful drug; our natural tendency as educators is to introduce a new group of students to the wonders of our status quo each August or September. As a teacher, I wanted to fold them into "the way things are" within the four walls of my classroom. The way things were in my classroom was probably pretty much the same as the way things were in most classrooms in the junior/senior high school in which I began my teaching career in the 1970s. The bell rang to tell students to hurry on to class; the bell rang to tell them they were late if they were still in the hallway; the bell rang to tell all of us it was time to go somewhere else; the students and their desks were in straight rows; we asked them to sit straight and "pay attention"—this was the status quo four decades ago, and in most middle and high schools today, it is still a comfortable setup for many. A student's day consists of a series of classes that follow one another as part of the overall schedule; the student goes from math to English to science to social studies to whatever else the schedule calls for on that particular day.

To those among us who hail from the industrial age, this was pretty much like it was in the factories and on the assembly lines in the boom period following World War II. Each shift was the approximate length of the school day, and breaks and lunch at regular intervals broke up the workday in the workplaces of that era. In this postindustrial era, things have changed, at least on the workplace side of things. Millions of people now work out of their homes and on their own schedules; the commute may be a few feet down the hall, with a detour to the kitchen on the way to the desktop or laptop. Breaks and lunch can be taken when convenient, or ignored altogether. In other modern workplaces today, employees work in teams, or temporary teams of temporary workers may be hired for a specific project. Employees go from job to job and from company to company far more frequently than in the past; it is rare to have someone stay at a company for his entire career. The workplace is evolving rapidly, and the skills required to succeed in the global economy are increasingly those of communication, collaboration, problem solving, creativity, and innovation.

The educational system is slowly changing to meet this challenge, even as the status quo creates a serious drag on that change. In the economy, jobs go unfilled not because there are not enough *people* among the vast ranks of the unemployed to fill them, but because the skill sets required by the employers of the twenty-first century do not match the skill sets of those who may be desperate for work. The work has changed; indeed, the *world* has changed, but our educational system lags behind as we continue to push all our students through on the same basic college track. Having four years of college, or even a two-year college degree, increases the chances of today's students finding tomorrow's jobs, to be sure, but there are trade-related jobs that require commitment and training, and not everyone wants to go to college; I grew up with a neighbor who wanted to be a truck driver. That is all he wanted to be, and he is still at it five decades later. He loves it, and he is making a good living at it.

We think that is setting one's sights too low, and so we drag students kicking and screaming (or sleeping and daydreaming) through four years of a traditional educational system that may not try to find out what students really want to do, or what they might be suited for in the world of work. All the while, a high percentage of our students don't stay in high school because it may not be meeting their needs. Writing "Johnny could do the work if he just applied himself!" on a report card is no substitute for finding out what makes Johnny tick or discovering what needs to be done to make him a functioning, satisfied contributor to our society and to his own future.

Beginning *before* students drop out of school in frustration, we need to work with middle school students to identify where their talents lie. If we can catch them in middle grades and convince them we have something meaningful for them when they get to the high school, we can use those three years between Grades 6 and 8 to develop the skills that will help them succeed not just in high school but in the workplace and in life as well. We need our citizens to be well informed and capable of solving problems, making critical decisions, sorting fact from fiction, identifying propaganda, acting in an ethical manner, and thinking critically and with a healthy degree of skepticism when communicating with someone who might want to sell them the proverbial bill of goods. It may mean that we need to abandon the chronological teaching of history in favor of a more conceptual framework; the Internet allows students to travel back and forth through more than three centuries of U.S. history as they ponder the role of religion, slavery, government, immigration, industry, labor, conflict, and civil rights in shaping our nation. Yet the status quo is a powerful force: it is perhaps easier to follow a textbook divided into chapters in a school divided into classrooms, class periods, and discrete subject areas.

When teaching U.S. history at the secondary level, I used to say to myself in the spring, "Can I get to the Vietnam War by June?" Trying to cover decade after decade, week after week left little time to delve deeply into the primary sources that comprise the stuff of history. In *Teaching U.S. History Beyond the Textbook*, Yohuru Rashied Williams (2010) shares investigative strategies that allow students to go deeply into the history of our country. By using mock trials and other engaging and thought-provoking strategies, Williams shows that history can be more than a series of dates, facts, and historical figures. Getting students deeply involved in this way requires time, and it may mean that a strictly chronological approach to "covering the material" has to be curtailed or abandoned altogether, in favor of a more conceptual approach.

At a time when our students need to become deep thinkers and problem solvers, we as a nation are caught up in a testing frenzy, and success on those ubiquitous state exams drives everything we do. It is a classic case of the tail wagging the dog. Yet I have observed in classrooms at every grade level where teachers are taking students deep into the content by giving them the tools to navigate a plethora of information and think for themselves while acting interdependently with peers. In those classrooms, teachers facilitate process and students do the work; no one—students or teachers—perseverates or frets over the upcoming tests.

Great teachers pose questions and turn students loose in a classroom where it is safe for them to ask their own questions, make their own mistakes, and come to their own conclusions. In those classrooms, I have observed students who have come off the bench and into the game, *and the tests take care of themselves.* I have interviewed students who told me they don't worry about the state tests, and they often look forward to taking them for the simple reason that they are confident in their own ability to deal with whatever comes their way—including standards-based testing.

From Attendees to Willing and Eager Participants

I believe we will eventually wean ourselves away from classrooms where teachers hold forth in an effort to pass information to their students; instead, we will identify the relative strengths of teachers and students alike and match them accordingly as students work with peers on projects and problems that mirror what they will encounter in adulthood. Teachers will facilitate process and serve as advisers and learning partners, and teachers and students alike will make remarkable progress. When educators take this realistic approach to their futures, I believe we will find willing and even eager participants. I believe students want to be meaningfully engaged in something of value and substance; preparing for a test simply does not generate much enthusiasm, and the battle cry "Pay attention, now, because this will be on the exam" gets old after a few years. My observation is that when students are treated as if they have something to offer, rather than something to memorize, they respond well. When students understand that teachers have something to offer by engaging them directly in their own continuous-improvement process, they take notice and get themselves into the game.

When I was working in central office, we had to substitute in classrooms five days per year, and I had occasion to work with twenty-four high school seniors on their last day of school in June. I was with them for a ninety-minute block, and I had these students in groups of six as they rotated from chart to chart, answering very open-ended questions at each chart. As they rotated, the marker each group was using passed from one group member to another; when they were done, they chose someone to report out from each group. This reporting led to a wider discussion of the topic at hand, and when we were finished, I had time to talk with them and ask them why they liked what they had done. Most of their heads nodded as one student articulated that they liked it because I treated them like adults. They got to brainstorm and express their opinions, and they enjoyed that. They thanked me, a total stranger, for giving them something meaningful to do and for providing them with an opportunity to share what they knew and thought about the topic displayed on the charts, then processed in groups, and subsequently shared with their peers. I set it all up and then gave them their 80.

The Pause That Refreshes . . . and Leads to Deeper Understanding

I used to subscribe to several print publications that contained long articles and opinion pieces. In fact, I could sit for much of a winter weekend afternoon reading article after article with some classical music playing softly in the background. I would occasionally stop and reflect a bit, in no real hurry and with few, if any, distractions. Reading a novel or a journal article or book review was a quiet, reflective exercise, and this accommodated the side of me that wanted to relax and get lost in the printed word. I read virtually without interruption.

The Internet has changed all this. What was once a calm pursuit with plenty of time for reflection and processing is now being transferred to a medium that is *by design* distracting. It is set up to provide both information *and* interruptions. Reading an article online today means being constantly distracted by hyperlinks, video links, someone flapping his arms in an attempt to get the reader's attention (and her money), and by ads that suddenly fill the entire screen and require the reader's intervention to do away with them. I now have to stop to get rid of something on the screen I did not ask for in the first place. Transferring from the printed page to the digital universe has changed everything. "The linearity of the printed book is shattered," says Carr (2010), "along with the calm attentiveness it encourages in the reader" (p. 104). The deep thinking that once accompanied reading a book or print article on those weekend afternoons tends to disappear because it is hard for the mind to concentrate in the face of the hypermedia that is pervasive and ever expanding.

Carr (2010) reports the result of an experiment that attempted to gauge the effects of hypertext on comprehension. The researcher gave groups of people the same online article, the only difference being the number of hyperlinks built into each one. After they had read the material, she asked them to summarize what they had read and answer a few multiple-choice questions. The researcher's conclusion was that more links led to lower comprehension:

> Readers were forced to devote more and more of their attention and brain power to evaluating the links and deciding whether to click on them. That left less attention and fewer cognitive resources to devote to understanding what they were reading. (p. 128)

Every time I read an online article, I find my concentration broken by links and advertising, and if it is distracting for digital natives, it can be doubly disconcerting for digital immigrants.

If we want students to truly understand and remember whatever it is we bring to the table in the way of content, we must provide multiple opportunities to wrestle with it *in ways that allow them to concentrate and focus*. When I worked with those high school seniors on their last day of school, they worked collaboratively using a simple set of cooperative norms (listen attentively, let others finish, don't make disagreement personal) and they moved from chart to chart and from one open-ended question to another in a way that all of us appreciated. Had I been their regular teacher, we would have spent a good deal of time in the first week of school on collaboration techniques that would have included defending a point of view without trashing someone else's opinion. In this case, we were working at the first level of brainstorming and did not go much more deeply than that given the limited amount of time we had to work together. This was a pleasant change for them, as they informed me when we were done, and they would have liked to have done more of it in their high school careers.

When students move from an electronic world built for distractions, it is the classroom teacher's job to provide moments of focus and concentration where students can move up the cognitive ladder by brainstorming, explaining, summarizing, asking questions, examining, inferring, drawing conclusions, and learning to defend those conclusions in a respectful way. Students need to learn to cooperate and collaborate in ways that will increase their understanding. Teachers can provide sufficient wait time after asking questions so that those who do not process quickly can do so. Brooks and Brooks (1999) encourage teachers to pose a question and then let small groups of students deliberate for a bit before opening a general discussion. "This format allows the teacher to call on students to deliver the group's initial responses without putting anyone on the spot" (p. 115). I have found that this also gives teachers the opportunity to listen to each group while circulating around the classroom, asking one or two students if they would mind sharing with the whole group what the teacher just heard them say. In these instances, students who don't normally share can be given a chance to do so, *but only after they have worked it all out in the smaller group.*

Access to any number of electronic platforms makes it possible for students to explore and collect far more information about any imaginable topic than was possible when most Boomers or Gen X teachers were kids. But there comes a time when all that information needs to be sifted, sorted, examined, authenticated, talked about, considered, questioned, and otherwise grappled with . . . and this can be done in the classroom by teachers who understand that the classroom can be a convenient and powerful laboratory for collaborating in a safe environment. Students can work together to make sense of what they have seen, heard, or found in the way of information related to the topic at hand.

The important thing here is that this phase of learning does not have to include anything other than the students, the teacher, some effective operational norms, and a whiteboard or chart pad. An effective hybrid system of learning can and should include whatever technological advances can accelerate learning, but the key is the partnership between teachers who are willing to challenge the status quo and students who are willing to partner with peers and teachers alike in an effort to prepare themselves for a future that involves skills related to communication, collaboration, critical thinking, problem solving, and decision making. Teachers and administrators need to work together in an attempt to acknowledge the strengths and interests of the students in their care, and then accelerate the continuous-improvement journey of those children, adolescents, and young adults. The same cooperation and collaboration that increasingly need to be part of classrooms at every grade level also must be part of the way adults approach continuous improvement for themselves and their students. The status quo can best be challenged by a coordinated and concerted effort to improve processes and systems in classrooms, buildings, and districts.

Moving Deliberately Along the Change Continuum

In Chapter 9, Ed, a teacher with twenty-seven years under his belt, believed that he needed to make a few changes in the way he taught his high school students. With maybe three years to go before retirement, Ed could have ridden the metaphorical bus for the last three years or so. Instead, and after observing a very effective teacher in a way that made him sit up and take notice, Ed made the decision to make some changes. These changes would almost certainly benefit his students and—after observing and talking with Peggy, the teacher whom he observed— would no doubt raise Ed's energy level as well. Digital immigrant that he is, Ed's progress from seatwork to feetwork might be relatively modest, but he became convinced that his last three years in the classroom might well be an improvement for everyone in his social studies classrooms, including himself.

Teachers like Ed who have become comfortable with a status quo that has them doing too much of the work don't necessarily have to become *experts* in the use of the latest technology, and they need not be frightened by it. Teachers *do* need to make an effort to understand where their students are when it comes to the Internet, and it is possible to harness that electronic skill set, for example, when a brand new Smart Board shows up in front of the old blackboard (or whiteboard) in the classroom. The reality of this new technology, combined with

> The status quo, like any barrier to progress, needs to be sent packing before any real and meaningful change can occur.

students who can benefit from its advantages, ought to tell teachers they need to become—if not experts—at least attuned to what the new technology can contribute to the continuous-improvement journeys of their students. The job of administrators who put that Smart Board into the classrooms is to help teachers maximize the potential of that piece of technology.

But technology by itself is not the panacea to success for students who show up in August or September. The role of the teacher is *still* to provide a classroom climate where students can move up and down the cognitive ladder with ease as they learn to ask more questions, question more answers, construct meaning, work collaboratively with peers, make inferences, draw conclusions, defend their points of view, acknowledge the perspectives of others, and learn to do all this under the skillful hand of a teacher who has learned to move students from seatwork to feetwork—shifting the workload to them and creating a more learner-centered environment.

The Role of the Organization

Ed's assistant principal made it possible for him to visit Peggy's classroom. The assistant principal had heard about Peggy and wanted Ed to find out what she was doing that caused the district and the local press to sit up and take notice. We don't know what Ed was thinking before he went to the other high school, but we know what he thought once he returned. He made an individual decision to stand at the mirror and look at his own classroom and the existing status quo. The problem, of course, is that what Ed and his close friend Alex were willing to do was limited to their two classrooms. None of this was part of any systematic effort to change the status quo of either Ed's high school or Alex's middle school. It was two teachers coming to the realization that they needed to do something different.

For individual teachers, schools, and districts, there is often a gap that exists between what everyone thinks or even knows what needs to be done. Pfeffer and Sutton (2000) call this the *knowing–doing gap.* Managers in organizations read great books, bring in powerful trainers, and agree that something needs to be done in the name of continuous improvement. On occasion, the training offered a while ago is repeated. "Regardless of the quality of the content, the delivery, or the frequency of repetition, management education is often ineffective in changing organizational practices" (p. 2). The same is true in education: Administrators at every level read the great books, bring in superb trainers, brainstorm for improvement, create tab-indexed binders, and send the word out far and wide that there's a new program in town—and yet the changes do not take place at scale; the status quo swamps the drive for change on many occasions at the building or district level.

Effective change happens at the classroom level, and administrators at every level in the district need to go beyond *telling* teachers about "the new thing" coming toward them soon. Building administrators working closely with teachers, and providing lots of formative support and making frequent classroom visitations, can accomplish much more than any program or binder ever could. Ed will probably wind up changing one or two things at a time *over time.* If the school's continuous-improvement plan—developed by a school-leadership team that may well include Ed—supports change and improvement in certain areas (as we saw in Chapter 9), those changes can come slowly and over time as well. Teachers are often frightened by whole-scale improvement efforts that drop like a rock from the top; the cooperation and collaboration we want teachers to display in their classrooms can and should be tapped at the organizational level as well. The administrator who wants to see collaboration in the classroom would do well to model collaboration at the building level. The teacher asked to confront and maybe alter his status quo needs to know that administrators at all levels, but especially at the building level, are willing to walk the walk.

Final Thoughts

It has been my observation that teachers who are willing to show the status quo the door in their own continuous-improvement journeys are much happier human beings once they no longer have to do most of the work in their classrooms. I have also observed that the truly engaged students display more energy, and that energy transfers to teachers who have learned to facilitate process rather than do all the work themselves. The changes required to shift students to the role of active participants can be small at first, but the status quo, like any barrier to progress, needs to be sent packing before any real and meaningful change can occur. As for the students, my experience is that kids who have warmed the bench for a long time really do enjoy getting into the game for good.

Veteran teachers have, over the years, no doubt found much that works well for the students in their care, but excellent teachers are never satisfied with the status quo, whatever it is. The key is to keep looking for strategies that engage students and get them climbing the cognitive ladder in ways that will benefit them in the workplace and in life in general. Good teaching, when all is said and done, is about the choices teachers make. Good teachers are not afraid to look in the mirror and confront what may have become a comfortable status quo. They are ever in search of new ideas and new and novel ways to facilitate process and progress in the classroom. In the name of continuous improvement, those teachers are willing to discard what does not work in favor of what the research, along with their own eyes and experience, tell them works best for kids, and everyone wins.

There is a joy in learning and a joy in teaching that takes place at the happy convergence of curiosity on the part of kids and understanding on the part of teachers. The internet has allowed us to tap into a limitless electronic universe full of information of every sort, but the *classroom* continues to be the laboratory where students can sift through fact and opinion, pause and focus, ask questions, question answers, analyze in pairs and groups, and regularly present evidence in support of conclusions and opinions. It is a place where students can learn to write, speak, and *listen* effectively. Classrooms are safe places where sarcasm and humiliation are not welcome, and where creativity and innovation are valued friends. In those classrooms, students are *participants* rather than *attendees.* They can laugh and learn, discover and dance, share and sing, and enjoy being in that room with a teacher who made it all possible by her willingness to seek new ways to challenge herself and her students in the name of continuous improvement.

Appendix A
Providing Support for Speakers and Listeners

When working in pairs, trios, quartets, whole-class conversations, or when a student is making a formal presentation, there is a great deal students can do to support each other. At any given time, one of the partners in a standing pair is either in listening or speaking mode, and *each* of those roles is active, not passive. When I am observing students involved in paired discussions, I often note that the listener is not really listening. His body language may betray in turn boredom, impatience, or an unwillingness to engage in any meaningful—or helpful—way with his partner. He may believe that the only important role is that of speaker, and it isn't *his* turn yet. When it's his turn to speak, he'll shift out of neutral and into drive.

One problem may be that students have become accustomed to a passive role most of the time, especially in the upper grades. Teachers have traditionally been the main speakers in their classrooms, with less than 5 percent of class time devoted to any kind of group discussion (Hattie, 2012). When those discussions do occur, they involve only a few students and the teacher. In courses and classrooms driven by standardized testing and a curriculum-driven pacing guide, listening is what we imagine—and hope—students are doing as teachers practice the verbal skills they learned in college and honed through many years in the front of the room. In classrooms dominated by teacher talk, listening is a passive exercise relegated to a captive audience.

Take the kid who thinks listening amounts to sitting quietly and not interrupting while the teacher is talking and put her in front of a classmate in a standing pair share; she can perhaps be excused for continuing her passive listening role while her partner does the talking. It is what she knows; it is what she does, and she may have developed this habit over many years. The implicit message of all this teacher talk in class-rooms may well be that the most important role is speaking (the trans-mission of information), while listening amounts to waiting off stage while someone else performs.

But listeners and speakers alike benefit from active participation on the part of both partners in the pair share. The speaker may not be confident or entirely sure what she is saying has merit; she may not completely understand the topic or concept she is attempting to explain. It is the role of the listener to help lead both of them to a deeper under-standing by nodding if he understands, asking questions when he does not, and paraphrasing to help both of them bring what they are discuss-ing into sharper focus. The listener is an active partner, not simply an observer, in the conversation. Listening is not a subordinate function; it is critically important in the thinking—and learning—process.

If, then, listening is as important as speaking, then teachers need to begin by modeling excellent listening skills in the classroom. New teach-ers just spent at least four years in college, preceded by four years in high school, where teacher talk predominated, and listening may have been relegated to a minor—and unassertive—role. Teachers, new and experienced, "struggle with learning to listen, yet listening is one of the powerful ways we show respect for and interest in our people's think-ing" (Ritchart, 2015, p. 82). Listening begins when one person taking part in a standing pair really *attends to* and *shows an interest in* what his or her partner has to say.

In classrooms where teachers do most of the talking and consistently use the language of compliance (*Sit quietly! Pay attention! Sit up straight! See if you know the answer to this question!*), students can be forgiven for slipping into a largely passive role. In classrooms where teachers use the language of thinking (*What do you see that makes you say that? What do you think happens next in the story? What might we conclude from this?*), students are brought off the bench and into the game as participants, not as attendees or mere observers. Teachers can have students share their thinking on any of those three questions with each other in pairs or small groups. This gives them many opportunities to use and improve their listening and speaking skills. If there are thirty students in the classroom at any given time, there are fifteen conversations going on, and everyone has an active role in those discussions.

One of the things I like about putting students in pairs (rather than in trios or quartets) is that *no one can hide in a pair*. This is not true of larger groups. At any given time during a seated or standing pair share, the speaker and the listener ought to be engaged in the activity. The student doing the speaking is talking directly to the listener, and part of the lis-tener's job is to support and encourage the speaker. Students who meet with diverse partners frequently in standing pairs over the course of the first few days and weeks of school can develop skills related to speaking and listening that will serve them well as they shift from pairs to trios or quartets. The listening skills developed with one partner after another will serve kids well in whole-class discussions as well. Twenty-plus students who know how to attend to and support one of their classmates as he serves in the role of speaker will give that person a great deal of confidence.

Again, both roles are supportive in nature. Let's begin with some things the listener—or listeners—can do to assist the speaker.

How the Listener(s) Can Support the Speaker

Make appropriate eye contact.

It isn't a staring contest, and the listener can actually look away briefly while her partner is speaking. The listener should avoid making eye contact with someone else in a way that is distracting for his partner (or, if eye contact is made with another student, someone *else's* partner). With a class full of listeners, the same holds; most speakers don't want twenty-four pairs of eyes trying to make unblinking eye contact. It may be that the listeners in a class-size audience need to take some notes, and that's fine, of course. They may also want to jot down a question or two when something needs clarification later on.

Nod occasionally in acknowledgment.

This positive bit of body language will encourage the speaker, as long as it is not overdone. This isn't bobblehead night at the ballpark. It is best done as an authentic and natural reaction to what the speaker has just said, or a point he has made. It can be accompanied by, "I see" or "I understand."

Stay focused.

Nothing is more discouraging for the speaker than having the listener break contact altogether by acknowledging someone in the room, doodling absentmindedly if partners are seated, or glancing at the wall clock repeatedly. Some teachers who are about to have students share with a partner while seated will have them clear off their desks of everything not directly related to the discussion. Out of sight, out of mind may apply here.

Ignore distractions.

If someone from the buildings and grounds department for the school district is mowing the lawn outside the window, the listener(s) in the room can support the speaker by ignoring it. If Norm waves at his uncle on the riding mower, this is not going to help the speaker. It may also be distracting to his uncle.

Ask a question by way of clarification.

Without interrupting in mid-syllable, the listener can pause and then ask a question at an appropriate time. The listener honors the speaker by asking a question that will further the conversation or make something clear.

Paraphrase to clarify.

After his standing-pair-share partner finishes a thought or a series of them, the listener can pause, turn his head to the side for a few seconds, and turn back to his partner, saying, "So, you're suggesting. . . ." This stem tells the speaker that a paraphrase is on the way. Other stems might include the following:

You're proposing . . .

So, you are thinking . . .

What you're wondering . . .

So, your hunch is . . . (Costa, 2008, p. 135)

When students serve in the role of speakers in a whole-class setting, what they say may need a bit of clarification, and the teacher can invite a bit of paraphrasing by using the following prompts:

How might you say that with fewer sentences?

How can we condense what you said?

Can you paraphrase that for us? (Zwiers, 2014, p. 68)

Keep the conversation focused on content, not personality.

Showing impatience or getting personal with comments will not serve any collaborative effort. "Do you really believe that nonsense?" is not likely to facilitate the continuous improvement process. In an age when everything on Facebook *is* personal, there may be a steep learning curve here for students.

Teachers who do less speaking and more listening as part of their classroom routine are in a position to model supportive actions. To help students with this, one teacher on an inclusion team can model pair shares with the special education teacher on the team, or with a teacher assistant.

Just as there are things the listener can do to assist the speaker, there are conversation and presentation norms available to speakers as well.

How the Speaker Can Support the Listener(s)

Make eye contact.

For someone speaking in front of the entire class, making brief eye contact with as many classmates as possible is a good idea. It shows confidence, and in my experience, the speaker who makes it a point to look at members of the audience will find those people will return the compliment throughout the presentation. In pairs, the same rule applies as with the listener. No staring, but frequent eye contact is helpful.

Use positive body language.

While it is important that speakers—in pairs, small groups, or whole-class settings—display energy, they should avoid gestures that quickly pass useful on the way to frenetic. Using fingers to highlight points one, two, and three is fine. Gesturing wildly with one's arms tends to be distracting. Generally speaking, positive body language will have a positive effect on the audience or one's partner. Frowning or rolling one's eyes with hand on hip is sure to send a negative message.

Adjust voice volume appropriately.

A good speaker will raise the volume a bit and then, abruptly, lower it to a whisper. Students are used to hearing voices at a steady volume, not too loud and not too soft. Any change from this makes listeners focus, if only briefly. A particularly important message or fact can be delivered in a whisper, to great effect. The key here is to avoid a monotone or voice volume so loud it annoys the listener.

Avoid verbal distractors.

In one conference session many years ago, the speaker used the non-word *um* so many times I began to count them. From that moment on, I was concerned only with the tally, not with the message. Other distractors include *uh, you see,* and the ever popular *you know?* These verbal distractors are an attempt to buy time while we think of what we want to say next. The best speakers I know simply pause, looking to the side, perhaps, but not saying anything. Silence is a powerful tool for a speaker; *um* and *you know* are just distracting.

Keep movement to a minimum.

Pacing back and forth constantly may have the effect of hypnotizing one's audience. However, moving to a stool to relay a story provides a nice change of state for the speaker and the listener. In standing pairs or trios, speakers should stay in one place.

Avoid talking while moving to a new location.

When teachers are in the role of speaker, it pays to think about when moving to a different part of the classroom will help students refocus. When moving to the front of the room from the side, or to a stool or captain's chair to tell a story, it is best to stay silent until one is in the new location and facing the audience. Otherwise, the visual competes with the auditory, and the movement can distract listeners. If the teacher as speaker has just made a point or delivered an important message, the move will provide time for the students as listeners to process the information—but not if the teacher is talking the whole time she is moving.

Slow down.

Many students (and teachers) tend to speak at a rapid pace. Without periodic pauses and a bit of reflective time, students may be lost when information comes at them with the force of water leaving a fire hose. The person who said, "Too much, too fast, won't last!" had it exactly right.

Invite questions.

Speakers can help listeners by inviting questions at appropriate intervals. This may require an extended pause, but it is worth it if it will help clear up any misunderstanding listeners may have. My experience is that once the first question is asked, others follow, and many of them piggyback on previous queries. This is the way the brain works; it makes connections. Listeners need time to process information.

Pause for visuals.

Speakers will often reveal a slide on the screen, only to read it in its entirety to the audience. The brain is capable of doing one thing at a time, and the listener has to make a choice: read it, listen to the speaker read it, or simply go to a better place in one's mind. The rule of thumb here is this: the audience can read, so let them do it. I also recommend that the speaker face the screen and read the sentence, paragraph, or passage silently. Most likely, when the speaker is done reading at a medium rate of speed, the audience is done as well. Speakers using a graphic should once again give listeners time to look it over before explaining it. Otherwise, my experience from observing presentations over the years is that listeners will give their attention to the graphic, not the speaker.

Teachers as Speakers and Listeners

All this begins with the classroom teacher. If teachers want students in their role as speakers to support their classmates as listeners, then teachers need to model and work with students on those skills. If teachers want students to be good listeners, then students need to know what good listening entails, and how what they do can support their peers in the role of speakers. One way for a teacher to find out where she is when it comes to speaking and listening skills is to get someone to tape her in action. In suggesting this to individual teachers, I have observed a great deal of eye rolling and responses that amount to, "I don't think I could do that." I thought that way, too, but went ahead and had our librarian tape a couple of my seventh-grade social studies classes.

Here is what I discovered when I looked at myself (with the sound off) and listened to myself (with the video off):

- I spoke too quickly and I tended to be too loud. I rarely paused long enough for anyone, including myself, to reflect or process anything.
- Some of my words were indistinct.
- My gestures were overpowering.
- I used *um* regularly.
- My voice dropped off at the end of sentences (something my twelfth-grade English teacher told me in 1966; I'm a slow learner).
- I tended to talk to students in one side of the room, while ignoring the others. (This also surfaced in my end-of-year evaluation from the students. Too bad I saved the evaluation until the end of the year!)
- My tie was crooked.

Years later, when I began presenting for our school district, I had myself taped again. While there were still problems (some of the same problems as before), I had improved in a number of areas. Again, my recommendation is to view the tape (okay, the digital recording) without sound the first time, and without the video later. I found this allowed me to focus on the visual and the auditory without distractions.

It is important for listeners to support speakers in pairs, groups, or in whole-classroom situations. Students can begin by practicing speaking and listening skills in the relatively benign structure of seated or standing pairs. Once students are confident in both roles, teachers can introduce trios or larger groups into the mix. Teachers who simply throw students together and tell them to cooperate and behave are asking for trouble; students who don't have the foggiest idea what listening or speaking really entail may flounder, act up, or simply disengage altogether. The previous suggestions can help keep conversations flowing smoothly, and ultimately enhance and accelerate the continuous-improvement process for students of all ages.

Appendix B

Maximizing the Use of Time in Classrooms

If there is one constant theme running through the chatter in faculty lounges all over the United States, it is that there is not enough time to do what needs to be done in classrooms—whatever the grade level or subject area. This has probably always been the case and forever will be so. To make matters worse, standardized testing days and testing-prep days reduce the amount of time even further. Once the district calendars are set, there is a finite amount of class time devoted to instruction.

Thankfully, students who have access to the Internet can accomplish much more outside the classroom than when I was in school. After hours, students have access to teacher blogs, online learning platforms, teacher websites, and more resources than any Boomer ever thought possible. Teachers not concerned about being the CIO can turn their attention away from lecture and toward more meaningful engagement on the part of students who may not be all that interested in watching teachers work.

As teachers shift students from passive observers to active participants in their own learning during school hours, student-to-student interaction will increase as the time devoted to teacher talk and worksheets declines. When seatwork gives way to feetwork in classrooms, it makes perfect sense to use time wisely, avoiding when possible those things that are not productive or simply waste those precious minutes.

A few years ago, I was observing in an elementary classroom, and students were told they had five minutes to complete the task before them. The teacher asked if there were questions, got them started, and went to her desk to do some paperwork. Five minutes passed, then turned into ten. After twenty or so minutes, the teacher stood and got the attention of her students. The task they had been given should have taken no more than five minutes, had they believed they had only that amount of time. My sense, as I looked at the students while they worked, was that they knew they had all the time in the world; there was no reason to hurry. Worse, the teacher sitting behind her desk sent the message that what *she* was doing was more important than what *they* were doing.

One middle school teacher gave her students a set of perhaps six or seven verbal instructions all at once, put them to work, and spent the next several minutes answering questions and clearing up misunderstandings. As soon as she told them to get started, hands popped up all over the room in popcorn fashion. The two minutes giving one direction after another in rapid-fire fashion was wasted time; students heard part, but not all, of what she said. For many of them, everything came to a halt as they waited for her to arrive to clear things up and sort things out. She looked harried as she scurried from desk to desk, taking time she would rather have spent on course content to deal with entirely process-related issues.

If the time allotted by the district is a sort of zero-sum game, at least in the classrooms, then teachers who want to optimize the time they have can begin by making sure it is not wasted. There are ways to ensure that things run smoothly and efficiently in classrooms at every level, and observing and coaching in hundreds of classrooms has brought me to some conclusions regarding these powerful timesavers. I have seen them all used effectively over the years.

Prepare Students to Work in Pairs and Groups

I long ago lost count of the number of teachers frustrated when they put students in collaborative situations, only to find out students have absolutely no idea how to actually interact and otherwise work together without confusion, chaos, and conflict. They don't know what it really means to attend to a partner or partners in conversations and more complicated group work. I covered this in more detail in Chapter 7, but it bears repeating. Much time is lost when students are placed in pairs, trios, or quartets without being properly trained in the use of good listening skills. In Chapter 5 we looked at the importance of perspective and empathy in collaborative work; students who run into perspectives alien to them may react in ways that quickly and completely derail the whole process. These concepts and related skills should be frontloaded in the first two weeks of school. It is not enough to say, "Remember, as you work on this project, treat your partners with respect and good will!" That means nothing if the partners have no idea what those things mean, and posters on the wall exhorting students to "Respect Others!" may not help.

After having a brainstorming session on what makes a good collaborative effort, some teachers have students develop a list of specific actions necessary to keep things going and actually accomplish something worthwhile. In one classroom, the list was short (six items or so) and was composed of questions like the following:

Did we all contribute in a positive way today?

Did we ask questions when necessary?

Did we avoid interrupting someone who was talking?

What can we do to improve our interaction next time?

Students wrote in their reflective journals before responding, and shared the answers with their teammates during a reflective session. The teacher walked around listening to the conversations, asking someone on occasion to elaborate or give further particulars. When we plan lessons, we prepare the work for the students, but the job is only half done if we have not prepared the students for the work. Students who have no earthly idea what is going on when they are thrown together are going to waste everyone's time and the resulting confusion will serve as a barrier to progress every time.

Give One Direction at a Time

The teacher who wants to deal with content, not process, as she circulates while students begin their work can save time by giving directions one at a time. If students are about to pair up to share while standing, using their journals, it might go something like this:

Direction 1: "Open your journal to the page on which you wrote this morning." (Wait.)

Direction 2: "Take your journal in your left hand and stand behind your desk." (Wait.)

Direction 3: "With your journal in your left hand, raise your right hand and go shake hands with someone with whom you have not met today, someone other than your shoulder partner." (Play some upbeat music and wait.)

Direction 4: "Stand next to your partner and face me." (Wait.)

With every student in the room facing the teacher (with their journals and next to a partner), she is ready to put them to work. There is no need for them to know exactly what is going to happen *until they are where they need to be*. Get the process-related directions out of the way first; then deal with content.

Stay With Stated Time Limits

Students who learn that time limits are like traffic lights in Rome (just suggestions) will draw things out, knowing there are no consequences. The same goes for the start of the class period in middle school or the high school block. Teachers who chat with colleagues three minutes into the high school class period should not be surprised when students arrive late. "He'll still be in the hall talking when I get there. No hurry." Time limits should be well thought out to begin with, and then followed. Teachers who demonstrate they are serious about getting things done on time in class are more likely to find homework completed on time as well.

The amount of time devoted to a single standing pair share will need to be adjusted, and some teachers give way too much time for these discussions and wind up with students standing around looking at the clock on the wall after they are done. The teacher who says, "Take about five minutes to talk about this" is going to find this is much too much time. To drive this home, look at the clock right now and count off a minute. That sixty seconds is an eternity for an eighth grader, and talking for five minutes on some content-related topic may be a proverbial bridge too far. Sixty seconds is probably plenty of time for students who just saw a short video to reflect together on what they saw and heard, even with prompts. It is better to have two short conversations with two separate prompts; this lets them concentrate on one thing at a time, and it means the teacher who is walking around the room listening and observing is tuned in to the same basic conversation.

Keep Transitions Short

Getting students from their seats to a standing pair, or from a standing activity back to their desks, should happen in no more than thirty seconds. Teachers using iTunes can come up with an upbeat song that has been cut to that half-minute, and students can practice those transitions until they get them down. For elementary teachers who have their students clean up and then line up before leaving the classroom for lunch or PE, one upbeat song can be used for the cleanup phase, while another upbeat piece of music can signal the lineup. Again, whatever time is allotted for these transitions can be practiced until there is virtually no wasted time.

Use One Proven Way of Getting Everyone's Attention

Teachers often try to get the attention of students using a variety of methods. In one classroom a middle school teacher tried four or five verbal cues, with no results. The most successful teachers I have met over the years, regardless of grade level, use only one tried and true cue, and they practice this with students during the first week of school until students have it down. My recommendation to teachers is to use something that combines the visual with the auditory. Using a command tone of voice (not a singsong or approachable voice), one teacher simply raises her palms up and out toward her students, saying, "Pause. Look this way please." It works every time because it has been ingrained in the daily routine. Also, she practices it until students can finish their thoughts, and then turn toward her. If they are not recovering fast enough, she does it until they do. If it needs practice later in the school year, she does it then too. The teacher cannot simply wait forever for students to recover from their conversations while looking at her watch and rolling her eyes. Make it clear and make it routine.

Cut Down on the Time Students Are Effectively Disengaged

When one student is answering a question posed by the teacher, the rest of the students are not hanging on every word. They may know how to play the game by smiling, holding a pencil at the ready, and nodding occasionally during the teacher-to-student exchange, but they may not be psychologically present. If the conversation between the teacher and Samantha takes a minute or more, that time is lost for the others. As we saw in Chapter 4, that teacher could pose that same question to the group, and ask them to turn to a partner and discuss possible answers. This leaves the teacher free to wander from pair to pair, listening and observing. It may be that the teacher eventually asks two or three students to share what they talked about, but the initial paired conversations involves all the students.

Occasionally, I'll see a kindergarten teacher have a student retell part of a story she has just read to her. This means only one among two-dozen kids is doing the retelling, while the others are encouraged to "pay attention." In a Virginia kindergarten classroom a number of years ago, I watched as the teacher moved her kids to the rug. I noticed they had moved into pairs without being asked, and I found out later that they had permanent partners they sat with unless told to find someone else. One partner in each pair was the "badger," while the other was the "bear." After reading part of a story, the teacher asked the badgers to retell the story to the bears. If there were twenty-four kindergartners in the room, there were twelve retellings going on. She read the rest of the story, and had the bears retell that part of the story to the badgers. Everyone was involved, and she was free to listen and observe. She told me she learned a great deal about her students and their communication skills by doing this.

In another elementary classroom, the teacher worked at the interactive whiteboard in the front of the room with a second grader on a math problem. The idea was that the other students would do the same in their minds while their classmate worked with the teacher in the front of the room. What I observed was that the other students seemed to be in another place in their minds; they would engage when it was their turn up front. Only a couple of students were working out the problems on scratch paper. This represents wasted time.

One elementary teacher has her students use their individual whiteboards several times a day. They sit on the floor and work on the same math problem, comparing answers with each other and explaining their work. They are all involved, and the teacher and teacher assistant are free, once again, to observe and intervene if necessary. My sense was that the students were heavily engaged from start to finish. The student furniture in that classroom was arranged around the outside, leaving the middle of the room open for this kind of work, and for standing pair shares. The transitions were smooth at the beginning of this activity and at the end, and there was no wasted time. The fact that they were empowered to help each other was another plus.

Make Materials Easily Accessible and Students Responsible

The search for materials in many classrooms may resemble a treasure hunt, with students who did not hear the directions or who have no earthly idea where the items they need for the upcoming task are located. In one science classroom, everything the students needed for the lab was clearly labeled and within reach of every student. A picture appeared on the screen, showing students exactly what they needed and where it should be placed on the lab tables. As one lab partner obtained what was needed, the other arranged things as shown in the photo on the screen. There was little room for ambiguity, and the teacher did not have to say a thing. She simply pointed to the picture, played some music while students pulled it all together, and then moved on. It was totally visual, *and it was effective.* At the end of the lab, students set up the table exactly the way it will need to be during the next class period, unless returning all the materials to the cupboards and shelves makes more sense.

A fifth-grade teacher (who teaches social studies and language arts) has a jar full of sharpened pencils students may use if they don't have one. Before students leave the room to go across the hall to the classroom presided over by her teammate (who teaches math and science), she plays a song that she plays only when all the materials used during the day are returned to wherever students found them. One student picks up the pencils, another cleans off the desktops, and everyone has a job that—in a short time—leaves the classroom in exactly the state the students found it when the day began.

A middle school teacher has a hard plastic bag attached to the side of the students' desks. The bag holds markers, tape, scissors, and anything else students may need during the course of the class period. Again, while music plays at the end of the period, everything goes back in the bag for the students who will follow at the change of classes.

In each preceding case, students are responsible for securing the materials and returning them. Teachers should not spend the time between classes or after school running around cleaning, straightening, returning things . . . and mumbling about going into real estate rather than teaching.

Save Time With Online Learning Platforms

When my yearbook staff members peer edited copy, which was constantly, it was done in my classroom after school, which was the only time available for us to meet. Today, of course, this editing could be done online. More and more teachers are using online learning platforms like Edmodo to save classroom time by allowing students to read, edit, and provide feedback online and after hours. Students can check in with teachers electronically as questions arise; students or teachers with something important to communicate don't have to wait until the next day. Teacher websites can contain project information that can be accessed by students and parents alike. Work can be done and feedback provided virtually 24/7.

Use Individual Conferences and Lots of Sticky Notes

Students often have questions about projects on which they are working, and no teacher wants to discourage these questions. However, if Steve asks a question in class that directly relates to his own project, it may take precious time from an already jammed class to provide the answers or necessary feedback. I suggest teachers put a permanent chart on the wall or bulletin board, encouraging students to post questions on sticky notes, with the message on the sticky side. The message and the student's name is not visible, and the teacher can take the sticky notes down and deal with them in mini-conferences the next day, or on her website or online learning platform. If face-to-face time is needed, the mini-conference will suffice. This also gives students practice with listening and speaking skills.

One Virginia sixth-grade social studies teacher has her students post questions and comments on a huge piece of chart paper at the end of each class period, and this provides valuable feedback for her, along with questions they may have. She trains her students to provide feedback that will help with her own continuous-improvement process. Comments like "I really liked the way we . . ." or "That activity this morning helped me understand . . ." Or "I'm still not sure about . . ." gave her valuable feedback. She told me several notes expressing confusion about the same topic told her she needed to revisit it, approaching it differently this time. Individual questions that came up on the stickies allowed her to follow up individually with a particular student in a conference setting or just at the student's desk, rather than answer them in front of the whole class. For her these sticky notes provided feedback and saved time.

Teachers often put a great deal of thought into *what* they are going to cover in a particular class period or in a block of time in an elementary setting. They may even plan *how* they will cover it. Lesson plans can be beautiful things until the train leaves the station at the beginning of the lesson. It is advisable to think about what I call derailment opportunities. A classroom train moving along smoothly can be derailed when a teacher gives too many directions at once, followed immediately and predictably by a great deal of confusion. Another derailment point comes when a long conversation between one student and the teacher results in disengagement for many of the others. The classroom train can derail when transitions take too long or are badly managed. On these occasions, the train can slow down or even stop, requiring a great deal of unanticipated and costly repair work on the part of the teacher.

Turn Procedures Into Routines Early

"Classroom procedures," affirm Wong and Wong (2009), "increase on-task time and greatly reduce classroom disruptions" (p. 170). I have observed elementary classrooms, for instance, where getting into line at the side of the room preparatory to heading to lunch is accomplished quickly and efficiently. By contrast, I have seen students coming down a hallway behaving in a way that made teachers slam their classroom doors in frustration. It is not enough for a teacher to state her procedures at the beginning of the year. "Behaviors must be taught, modeled, practiced, monitored, and retaught" (Wong & Wong, 2009, p. 176). In classrooms where teachers simply post their procedures and "go over them" on day one, the price will be paid in lost time and disciplinary problems later in the school year—and not too far down the road. Procedures must become routine, and this is a frontloaded process that will pay off immediately.

While necessary, this should not be confused with student engagement. Students are not engaged because they are quiet, have the required materials, and behave in the hallway. Students who are interested in the content and engaged even after the official school day is over will be more likely to bring whatever materials are required. Students who learn to respect the teacher and their classmates are less likely to waste time during class. In the classrooms of the best teachers I have observed and coached over the years, the routines are well established, they contribute to the smooth running of the classroom environment, and they save time.

While adding time to the actual school day may not be possible, precious time can be optimized by putting in place efficient processes that keep things running smoothly.

References

Allen, R. (2008). *Green light classrooms: Teaching techniques that accelerate learning.* Thousand Oaks, CA: Corwin.

Allen, R., & Currie, J. (2012). *U-Turn teaching: Strategies to accelerate learning and transform middle school achievement.* Thousand Oaks, CA: Corwin.

Allen, R., & Rickert, C. (2010). *High-five teaching K–5: Using green light strategies to create dynamic, student-focused classrooms.* Thousand Oaks, CA: Corwin.

Allen, R., & Wood, W.W. (2013). *The rock 'n' roll classroom: Using music to manage mood, energy, and learning.* Thousand Oaks, CA: Corwin.

Allyn, P. (2013). *Be core ready: Powerful, effective steps to implementing and achieving the Common Core State Standards.* Boston: Pearson.

Almarode, J., & Miller, A. (2013). *Captivate, activate, and invigorate the student brain in science and math, grades 6–12.* Thousand Oaks, CA: Corwin.

American Management Association (AMA). (2010, April 15). *AMA 2010 critical skills survey.* Retrieved January 20, 2011, from http://www.amanet.org/news/AMA-2010-critcal-skills-survey.aspx

Baloche, L. (1998). *The cooperative classroom: Empowering learning.* Upper Saddle River, NJ: Prentice Hall.

Blankstein, A. (2004). *Failure is not an option: Six principles that guide student achievement in high-performing schools.* Thousand Oaks, CA: Corwin.

Bluestein, J. (2001). *Creating emotionally safe schools: A guide for educators and parents.* Deerfield Beach, FL: Health Communications.

Bluestein, J. (2008). *The win-win classroom: A fresh and positive look at classroom management.* Thousand Oaks, CA: Corwin.

Brooks, J., & Brooks, M. (1999). *In search of understanding: The case for constructivist classrooms.* Alexandria, VA: ASCD.

Burke, K. (2009). *How to assess authentic learning* (5th ed.). Thousand Oaks, CA: Corwin.

Burke, K. (2010). *Balanced assessment: From formative to summative.* Bloomington, IN: Solution Tree.

Carr, N. (2010). *The shallows: What the Internet is doing to our brains.* New York: W. W. Norton.

Chaffee, J. (2012). *Thinking critically* (10th ed.). Boston: Wadsworth.

Chappuis, S., Stiggins, R. J., Arter, J., & Chappuis, J. (2005). *Assessment for learning: An action guide for school leaders: Vision + competence + action = student success.* Portland, OR: Educational Testing Service.

Costa, A. (2008). *The school as a home for the mind: Creating mindful curriculum, instruction, and dialogue.* Thousand Oaks, CA: Corwin.

Darling-Hammond, L. (1997). *The right to learn: A blueprint for creating schools that work.* San Francisco: Jossey-Bass.

Dede, C. (2010). Comparing frameworks for 21st century skills. In J. Bellanca & R. Brandt (Eds.), *21st century skills: Rethinking how students learn* (pp. 51–75). Bloomington, IN: Solution Tree.

Drapeau, P. (2009). *Differentiating with graphic organizers: Tools to foster critical and creative thinking.* Thousand Oaks, CA: Corwin.

Dweck, C. (2007). The perils and promises of praise. *Ed Leadership, 65*(2), 34–39.

Erlauer, L. (2003). *The brain-compatible classroom: Using what we know about learning to improve teaching.* Alexandria, VA: ASCD.

Gardner, H. (2010). Five minds for the future. In J. Bellanca and R. Brandt (Eds.), *21st century skills: Rethinking how students learn,* pp. 9–31. Bloomington, IN: Solution Tree.

Girard, B. (2009). *The Google way: How one company is revolutionizing management as we know it.* San Francisco: No Starch Press, Inc.

Goodlad, J. (2004). *A place called school* (20th anniversary ed.). New York: McGraw-Hill.

Goran, M. I., Nagy, T. R., Gower, B. A., Mazariegos, M., Solomons, N., Hood, V., et al. (1998). Influence of sex, seasonality, ethnicity, and geographic location on the components of total energy expenditure in young children: Implications for energy requirements. *American Journal of Clinical Nutrition, 68,* 675–682.

Gordon, G. (2006). *Building engaged schools: Getting the most out of America's classrooms.* New York: Gallup.

Graham, C., & Misanchuk, M. (2004). Computer-mediated learning groups: Benefits and challenges to using groupwork in online learning environments. In T. Roberts (Ed.), *Online collaborative learning: Theory and practice* (pp. 181–202). Hershey, PA: Information Science Publishing.

Gunter, H., Estes, T., & Schwab, J. (1999). *Instruction: A models approach* (3rd ed.). Needham Heights, MA: Allyn & Bacon.

Hannaford, C. (2005). *Smart moves: Why learning is not all in your head.* Salt Lake City: Great River Books.

Hattie, J. (2009). *Visible learning: A synthesis of over 800 meta-analyses relating to achievement.* New York: Routledge.

Hattie, J. (2012). *Visible learning for teachers: Maximizing impact on learning.* New York: Routledge.

Hattie, J., Biggs, J. & Purdie, N. (1996). Effects of learning skills interventions on student learning: A meta-analysis. *Review of Educational Research, 66*(2), 99–136.

Hattie, J. & Yates, G. (2014). *Visible learning and the science of how we learn.* New York: Routledge.

Heritage, M. (2010). *Formative assessment: Making it happen in the classroom.* Thousand Oaks, CA: Corwin.

Hoff, R. (1992). *"I can see you naked."* Kansas City, MO: Andrews and McMeel.

Howard, P. (2006). *The owner's manual for the brain: Everyday applications from mind-brain research.* Austin, TX: Bard Press.

James, A. (2007). *Teaching the male brain: How boys think, feel, and learn in school.* Thousand Oaks, CA: Corwin.

James, A., Allison, S., & McKenzie, C. (2011). *Active lessons for active brains: Teaching boys and other experiential learners, grades 3–10.* Thousand Oaks, CA: Corwin.

Jensen, E. (2005). *Teaching with the brain in mind.* Alexandria, VA: ASCD.

Jensen, E. (2008). *Brain-based learning: The new paradigm of teaching* (2nd ed.). Thousand Oaks, CA: Corwin.

Johnson, D., Johnson, R., & Holubec, E. (1990). *Circles of learning: Cooperation in the classroom* (3rd ed.). Edina, MN: Interaction Book Company.

Jones, F. (2007). *Tools for teaching: Discipline, instruction, motivation.* Santa Cruz, CA: Fredric H. Jones & Associates, Inc.

Kagan, S. (1994). *Cooperative learning.* San Clemente, CA: Kagan Cooperative Learning.

Karoly, L., & Panis, C. (2004). *The 21st century at work: Forces shaping the future workforce and workplace in the United States.* Santa Monica, CA: Rand Corporation.

Keene, E. O. (2012). *Talk about understanding: Rethinking classroom talk to enhance comprehension.* Portsmouth, NH: Heinemann.

Keene, E. O., & Zimmermann, S. (2007). *Mosaic of thought: The power of comprehension strategy instruction* (2nd ed.). Portsmouth, NH: Heinemann.

Kendrick, M. (2010). Using student collaboration to foster progressive discourse. *English Journal, 99*(5), 85–91.

Kitsis, S. (2010). The virtual circle. *Educational Leadership, 68*(1), 50–54.

Kohn, A. (1999). *Punished by rewards: The trouble with gold stars, incentive plans, A's, praise, and other bribes.* New York: Houghton Mifflin.

Lengel, T. & Kuczala, M. (2010). *The kinesthetic classroom: Teaching and learning through movement.* Thousand Oaks, CA: Corwin.

Levin, B. (2010, February). What did you do in school today? *Phi Delta Kappan, 91*(5), 89–90.

Lipton, L., & Wellman, B. (2000). *Pathways to understanding: Patterns and practices in the learning-focused classroom* (3rd ed.). Guilford, VT: Pathways.

McInnerney, J., & Roberts, T. (2004). Collaborative or cooperative learning? In T. Roberts (Ed.), *Online collaborative learning: Theory and practice* (pp. 203–214). Hershey, PA: Information Science Publishing.

Maccoby, E. E. (1998). *The psychology of sex differences.* Stanford, CA: Stanford University Press.

Marzano, R. (2003). *Classroom management that works: Research-based strategies for every teacher.* Alexandria, VA: ASCD.

Marzano, R., Pickering, D., & Pollock, J. (2001). *Classroom instruction that works: Research-based strategies for increasing student achievement.* Alexandria, VA: ASCD.

Marzano, R., Yanoski, D., Hoegh, J. & Simms, J. (2013). *Using common core standards to enhance classroom instruction & assessment.* Bloomington, IN: Marzano Research Laboratory.

Medina, J. (2008). *Brain rules: 12 principles for surviving and thriving at work, home, and school.* Seattle, WA: Pear Press.

Nagel, D. (2015). *Effective grading practices for secondary teachers: Practical strategies to prevent failure, recover credits, and increase standards-based/referenced grading.* Thousand Oaks, CA: Corwin.

Nash, R. (2011). *Harness the power of reflection: Continuous school improvement from the front office to the classroom.* Thousand Oaks, CA: Corwin.

Nash, R. & Hwang, K. (2013). *Collaborative school leadership: Practical strategies for principals.* Lanham, MD: Rowman & Littlefield.

National Governors Association Center for Best Practices, Council of Chief State School Officers (2010). *Common Core State Standards.* Washington, DC: Author.

O'Connell, M. J., & Vandas, K. (2015). *Partnering with students: Building ownership of learning.* Thousand Oaks, CA: Corwin.

Pfeffer, J., & Sutton, R. (2000). *The knowing–doing gap: How smart companies turn knowledge into action.* Boston: Harvard Business School Press.

Pink, D. (2006). *A whole new mind: Why right-brainers will rule the future.* New York: Riverhead Books.

Prensky, M. (2006). *Don't bother me mom—I'm learning!* St. Paul, MN: Paragon House.

Prensky, M. (2010). *Teaching digital natives: Partnering for real learning.* Thousand Oaks, CA: Corwin.

Ratey, J. (2008). *Spark: The revolutionary new science of exercise and the brain.* New York: Little, Brown.

Ratey, J., & Manning, R. (2014). *Go wild: Free your body and mind from the afflictions of civilization.* New York: Little, Brown.

Ritchart, R. (2002). *Intellectual character: What it is, why it matters, and how to get it.* San Francisco: Jossey-Bass.

Ritchart, R. (2015). *Creating cultures of thinking: The 8 forces we must master to truly transform our schools.* San Francisco: Jossey-Bass.

Schmoker, M. (2011). *Focus: Elevating the essentials to radically improve student learning.* Alexandria, VA: ASCD.

Shute, V. (2008). Focus on formative feedback. *Review of Educational Research, 78*(1), 153–189.

Smilkstein, R. (2003). *We're born to learn: Using the brain's natural learning process to create today's curriculum.* Thousand Oaks, CA: Corwin.

Smith, J. R., & Smith, R. L. (2015). *Evaluating instructional leadership: Recognized practices for success.* Thousand Oaks, CA: Corwin.

Smith, L. (2008). *Schools that change: Evidence-based improvement and effective change leadership.* Thousand Oaks, CA: Corwin.

Sousa, D. (2011). *How the brain learns* (4th ed.). Thousand Oaks, CA: Corwin.

Sprenger, M. (2009). Focusing the digital brain. *Educational Leadership, 67*(1), 34–39.

Tapscott, D. (2009). *Grown up digital: How the Net Generation is changing your world.* New York: McGraw-Hill.

Tate, M. (2010). *Worksheets don't grow dendrites: 20 instructional strategies that engage the brain.* Thousand Oaks, CA: Corwin.

Trilling, B., & Fadel, C. (2009). *21st century skills: Learning for life in our times.* San Francisco: Jossey-Bass.

Vatterott, C. (2009). *Rethinking homework: Best practices that support diverse needs.* Alexandria, VA: ASCD.

Wagner, T. (2008). *The global achievement gap: Why even our best schools don't teach the new survival skills our children need—and what we can do about it.* New York: Basic Books.

Wagner, T. (2012). *Creating innovators: The making of young people who will change the world.* New York: Scribner.

Wicks, C., Peregoy, J., & Wheeler, J. (2001). *Plugged in! A teacher's handbook for using total quality tools to help kids conquer the curriculum.* New Bern, NC: ClassAction.

Williams, R. B., & Dunn, S. E. (2008). *Brain-compatible learning for the block.* Thousand Oaks, CA: Corwin.

Williams, Y. R. (2010). *Teaching U.S. history beyond the textbook: Investigative strategies, grades 5–12.* Thousand Oaks, CA: Corwin.

Solutions you want. Experts you trust. Results you need.

AUTHOR CONSULTING

Author Consulting

On-site professional learning with sustainable results! Let us help you design a professional learning plan to meet the unique needs of your school or district. www.corwin.com/pd

INSTITUTES

Institutes

Corwin Institutes provide collaborative learning experiences that equip your team with tools and action plans ready for immediate implementation. www.corwin.com/institutes

ECOURSES

eCourses

Practical, flexible online professional learning designed to let you go at your own pace. www.corwin.com/ecourses

READ2EARN

Read2Earn

Did you know you can earn graduate credit for reading this book? Find out how: www.corwin.com/read2earn

Contact an account manager at (800) 831-6640 or visit **www.corwin.com** for more information.

A SAGE Company

Helping educators make the greatest impact

CORWIN HAS ONE MISSION: to enhance education through intentional professional learning.

We build long-term relationships with our authors, educators, clients, and associations who partner with us to develop and continuously improve the best evidence-based practices that establish and support lifelong learning.

Index

Wolk, R. (2010). Education: The case for making it personal. *Educational Leadership, 67*(7), 16–21.

Wolk, R. (2011). The high stakes of standards-based accountability. *Education Week, 30*(23), 32, 24.

Wong, H., & Wong, R. (2009). *How to be an effective teacher: The first days of school.* Mountain View, CA: Harry K. Wong Publications.

Yair, G. (2000). Educational battlefields in America: The tug-of-war over students' engagement with instruction. *Sociology of Education, 73*(4), 247–69.

Zacarian, D. (2013). *Mastering academic language: A framework for supporting student achievement.* Thousand Oaks, CA: Corwin.

Zwiers, J. (2014). *Building academic language: Meeting common core standards across disciplines* (2nd ed.). San Francisco: Jossey-Bass.

Zwiers, J. & Crawford, M. (2011). *Academic conversations: Classroom talk that fosters critical thinking and content understandings.* Portland, ME: Stenhouse.